ARISTOTLE

RHETORIC
TRANSLATED BY W. RHYS ROBERTS

POETICS
TRANSLATED BY INGRAM BYWATER

INTRODUCTION BY EDWARD P. J. CORBETT

The Ohio State University, Columbus

THE MODERN LIBRARY

NEW YORK

DISTRIBUTED BY McGRAW-HILL, INC.

ADVISOR

Donald McQuade

Queens College
The City University of New York

This translation by W. Rhys Roberts and Ingram Bywater is reprinted
from the Oxford Translation of Aristotle by permission of the Jowett
Trustees and the Clarendon Press, Oxford.

The selection from the notes to the Roberts and Bywater edition has
been made by Professor Solmsen, who has also made the emendations
enclosed by brackets.

The translations from the Greek shown in the footnotes on pages
254–263 are taken from Professor Lane Cooper's *Aristotle on the Art of
Poetry,* by the kind permission of the publishers, The Cornell University
Press.

First Edition

24 25 26 27 28 29 30 BAN/BAN 0 9

Copyright © 1954, 1984 by Random House, Inc.

LIBRARY OF CONGRESS CATALOGING IN PUBLICATION DATA

Aristotle.
  Rhetoric.

  Bibliography: p.
  Includes index.
  1. Rhetoric, Ancient. 2. Poetry—Early works to 1800.
3. Aesthetics—Early works to 1800. I. Roberts, W. Rhys
(William Rhys), 1858–1929. II. Bywater, Ingram, 1840–
1914. III. Aristotle. Poetics. English. 1984.
IV. Title. V. Title: Poetics.
PN173.A7R6   1984   808.5   84–3466
  ISBN-13: 978-0-07-554602-3
  ISBN-10: 0-07-554602-7
Manufactured in the United States of America

INTRODUCTION

The *Rhetoric* and the *Poetics* are two of Aristotle's contributions to the arts of language. His third contribution is the collection of treatises on logic known as the *Organon*.[1] One might say that the *Rhetoric*, the *Poetics*, and the *Organon* constitute the Aristotelian trivium. The third member of the medieval trivium, of course, was grammar, but in the Greco-Roman schools and even in the medieval schools, one of the areas of study under the heading of grammar was the sort of thing that Aristotle considers in the *Poetics*.

The Separate Provinces of Rhetoric and Poetics

Although all three texts occasionally discuss common topics, each of them has its distinctive province. The treatises in the *Organon*, for instance, treat such subjects as the meaning of individual words, the formulation of propositions by putting individual words into subject-predicate relationships, strict logical reasoning in the form of the syllogism, and the art of dialectical discussion. The main province of the *Rhetoric* is the art of persuasive oratory. The *Poetics* deals primarily with the art of fiction—more particularly with the art of storytelling in the form of the drama and the epic. But in each of these treatises, there are implicit and explicit cross references to the other two, thus confirming the interrelationship of these arts of language.

There have been times, however, when the lines of demarcation between these allied but distinctive provinces have become blurred. The distinctions between the provinces of rhetoric and poetics have been especially liable to being confused. Starting with the Italian Renaissance in the sixteenth century, it was frequently difficult to tell whether a particular creative writer or literary critic was operating in the realm of rhetoric or the realm of poetics.

[1] The English titles often assigned to the six documents in this collection of logical treatises are the *Categories*, *On Interpretation*, the *Prior Analytics*, the *Posterior Analytics*, the *Topics*, and *On Sophistical Refutation*.

Wilbur Samuel Howell's collected essays, entitled *Poetics, Rhetoric, and Logic: Studies in the Basic Disciplines of Criticism* (1975),[2] try to correct the misconceptions that had developed about these three disciplines and to protest the exclusion of rhetoric and logic from modern literary theory. Howell may seem to want to have it both ways: to keep the distinctions between the three disciplines clear and yet to give rhetoric and logic as much of a place in literary theory as poetics has. But Howell is concerned that critics have not kept in mind the differences between mimetic or imitative discourse and nonmimetic discourse. Mimetic discourse, on the one hand, is a "literature of symbol"; nonmimetic discourse, on the other hand, is a "literature of statement." "The simplest way to describe this difference," Howell maintains, "is to say that the words which make up the rhetorical utterance lead the reader to states of reality, whereas the words making up the poetical utterance lead the reader to things which stand by deputy for states of reality."[3] Howell's main point is that the failure of critics to recognize the distinction between mimetic discourse and nonmimetic discourse and to give a place to logic and rhetoric along with poetics has prevented them from developing a literary theory comprehensive enough to deal with texts as different as Milton's *Paradise Lost*, an epic poem, and his *Areopagitica*, an essay in which he argues against censorship.

But if some critics have not been concerned about the differences between the provinces of poetics, rhetoric, and logic, Aristotle, with his lifelong passion for taxonomies, recognized and preserved the distinctions. The mere fact that he wrote treatises in all three areas suggests that he was aware of the distinctions. But philosophically too, he was committed to recognizing the differences. He classified the various arts and sciences into the theoretical, the practical, and the productive. Another way to put this classification is to say that he viewed the arts and sciences as being devoted to *knowing* (the theoretical) or to *doing* (the practical) or to *making* (the productive). What characterized theoretical sciences such as physics, mathematics, and

---

[2] Wilbur Samuel Howell, *Poetics, Rhetoric, and Logic: Studies in the Basic Disciplines of Criticism* (Ithaca, N.Y.: Cornell University Press, 1975).

[3] Ibid., pp. 223–224.

metaphysics was that they dealt with things that could not be other than they were; they dealt with the necessary, not the contingent.

The difference between the necessary and the contingent was also the basis for the difference that Aristotle saw between science (*epistemē*) and art (*technē*). The sciences dealt with the necessary, with the invariable, with what *had* to be; the arts dealt with the contingent, with the probable, with those areas where there were *choices* to be made. So those disciplines in the *Organon* dealing with strict demonstration or proof—that is, with reasoning or inference based on absolute premises leading to a necessary conclusion—were closer to being sciences than arts. But dialectical reasoning, which operated in the area of the contingent or the probable, was an art. If it was indulged in primarily for the sake of *knowing*, it was a theoretical art; if, on the other hand, it was indulged in for the sake of improved *doing* or *acting*, it was a practical art.

As Aristotle says in the very first sentence of his text on the subject, rhetoric is the counterpart of dialectic. As a way of *doing* or *acting*—specifically, as a way of arguing persuasively about contingent human affairs on the basis of mere probabilities—it is a practical art, like two other practical arts that Aristotle wrote treatises on, ethics and politics. Although a product usually results from rhetorical activity—namely, a speech—rhetoric is primarily an art of process. The art and the practice of rhetoric is even more prevalent today than it was in Aristotle's time. One can hardly get through a single day without being exposed dozens of times to some form of persuasive discourse, the main concern of the art of rhetoric. It is not too much to claim that rhetoric is the art that governs those human relationships that are conducted in the medium of spoken and written words.

Poetics, however, was primarily an art of product. It was indeed a productive art. The Greek words *poēsis* and *poiētikē* are derived from the verb *poiein*, "to make." Aristotle distinguishes *useful* arts, such as pottery, from *fine* arts, such as sculpturing. Poetics was a fine art, an art of composing imaginative literature—lyrics, plays, stories. The two kinds of imaginative literature that Aristotle ultimately focuses on in the *Poetics* are epic and tragedy. There is an indication, right in the text of the *Poetics*,[4] that Aristotle devoted a section of this treatise to a discussion of comedy, but that section is lost.[5] What has survived of the *Poetics*, however, has become the most influential—though not always the most revered—text in literary criticism.

Aristotle: The Man and His Works

What little is known about the life of Aristotle and about the circumstances surrounding the composition of his works has been gained (1) from remarks that Aristotle himself makes in his extant works, (2) from references to him and his works in the surviving texts of his contemporaries and of later classical authors (e.g., Cicero and Quintilian), and (3) from inferences and conjectures made on the basis of other surviving documentary evidence. Before we go on to consider the principal concepts and some of the key terminology of the *Rhetoric* and *Poetics*, we might review the generally accepted historical information about the man and his works.[6]

Aristotle was born in 384 B.C. in the little town of Stagira, in Macedonia, on the peninsula of Chalcidice, which juts into the Aegean Sea. His father, Nicomachus, was the court physician for Amyntas II, king of Macedonia and the father of Philip the Great. Aristotle's interest in the natural sciences and his penchant for classification may have been due to the early medical training he received from his father. In 367 B.C., at the age of seventeen, Aristotle went to Athens and enrolled as a student in Plato's Academy, remaining there for the next twenty years, as a student and a teacher, until Plato's death in 347 B.C.. He left

---

[4] See the beginning of Chapter 6 of the *Poetics*: "Reserving hexameter poetry and Comedy for consideration hereafter, let us proceed now to the discussion of Tragedy." The promised treatment of hexameter poetry—that is, the treatment of epic poetry—is provided in Chapters 23 and 24, but we do not find the promised treatment of comedy in the extant text.

[5] Lane Cooper has provided a hypothetical reconstruction of the lost section about comedy with his translation of the *Tractatus Coislinianus*, an anonymous Greek fragment, in his *An Aristotelian Theory of Comedy* (New York: Harcourt, Brace, 1922).

[6] For a brief account of Aristotle's life and works, see W. D. Ross, *Aristotle: A Complete Exposition of His Works and Thought*, 5th ed. (New York: Meridian Books, 1959), Chapter 1.

Athens at that time, largely because of the anti-Macedonian feeling that had sprung up there as a result of Philip's military victories, which weakened the Greek confederacy. He spent the next five years in Assos in Asia Minor and in Mitylene on the island of Lesbos, studying and teaching biology and zoology. In 342, Philip appointed Aristotle as tutor to his son Alexander, who was then only thirteen years old. It would be interesting to know what Aristotle taught this future military conqueror of the Middle East during the two years that he served as his teacher. In 335, on the death of Philip, Aristotle returned to Athens, where he entered on the most fruitful period of his life. He founded the famous Peripatetic School of philosophy at the Lyceum, where he lectured on a wide variety of subjects and wrote or revised most of his surviving works. With the death of Alexander the Great in 323, anti-Macedonian feeling again broke out in Athens, and Aristotle, after turning over his school to his pupil Theophrastus, retired to his native land, where he died a year later, in 322.

If the facts about Aristotle's life are meager and somewhat vague, the facts about the composition and publication of his works are even more scarce and uncertain. In Aristotle's time, there was no such thing as publication in the modern sense of that term. A manuscript culture prevailed at the time, and it was more likely that a literate slave enscribed the copy of a text than that the author laboriously wrote out the words. Very often, the students themselves made copies of the lectures delivered in the schools.

We do not know for certain when the text of the *Rhetoric* was written or "published," but classical scholars have made some educated guesses.[7] Because of a number of topical references in the text itself to Athenian events and concerns, one can feel quite secure in deducing that the *Rhetoric* was addressed to an Athenian audience. That inference in turn suggests that the *Rhetoric* was written either during Aristotle's first residence in Athens (367–347) or during his second residence (335–322). To

---

[7] A good account of the publishing history of Aristotle's text is to be found in Keith V. Erickson, "A Brief History of Aristotle's *Rhetoric*," pp. 1–18, which serves as an introduction to his bibliographic volume, *Aristotle's Rhetoric: Five Centuries of Philological Research* (Metuchen, N.J.: Scarecrow Press, 1975).

determine which of these periods is the likelier one, one has to consider other textual and historical evidence. For instance, because of the many references in Book III of the *Rhetoric* to other Aristotelian works—the *Poetics* for one—about whose dates there is a fair degree of certainty, it seems safe to conjecture that Book III was written not only much later than Books I and II but also as late as the second period of residency. The latest historical reference in the *Rhetoric* occurs in Book II, Chapter 23, 1398a, where there is an allusion to the embassy that Philip sent to Thebes before the battle of Chaeronea, which it is known took place in 338 B.C. Ultimately, internal evidence of this kind supports the contention of E. M. Cope, perhaps the most learned of the nineteenth-century commentators on Aristotle's text, that although parts of the *Rhetoric* may have been conceived and even written quite early during Aristotle's first residency in Athens, the text that we have today was not finished and certainly not "published" until after 335, the beginning of his second and final residency in that Greek city.[8]

On the other hand, the available evidence confirms that all the lost rhetorical works of Aristotle were composed rather early in the period of the first residency. There is evidence that soon after he enrolled in Plato's Academy, Aristotle began to deliver afternoon lectures in rhetoric and that his earliest written composition was the dialogue *Gryllus*, which dealt with the nature of rhetoric.[9] Since the extant text of the *Rhetoric* creates the impression of being a tentative, unfinished set of lecture notes, it seems likely that Aristotle has incorporated some, if not most, of the notes he used in the elementary lectures that he was delivering in the years 360–353. Another of the lost rhetoric texts—part of which must have figured in those early lectures—was a text that bore the Greek title of *Synagōgē Technōn*, which can be translated as *A Collection of Rhetorical*

[8] E. M. Cope, *An Introduction to Aristotle's Rhetoric* (London: Macmillan, 1867), p. 47.
[9] See Anton-Hermann Chroust, "Aristotle's Earliest 'Course of Lectures on Rhetoric,'" *L'Antiquité classique* 33 (1964): 58–72, and by the same author, "Aristotle's First Literary Effort: The *Gryllus*, a Lost Dialogue on the Nature of Rhetoric," *Revue des Etudes Grecques* 78 (1965): 576–591. Both of these essays are reprinted in *Aristotle: The Classical Heritage of Rhetoric*, ed. Keith V. Erickson (Metuchen, N.J.: Scarecrow Press, 1974).

Handbooks. According to the testimony of his contemporaries who mentioned this text in their own works, this collection of excerpts from rhetoric textbooks past and present constituted a quick history of rhetoric from its origin, right up to the time when the anthology was compiled. Another text, which was questionably attributed to Aristotle, was entitled *Theodectea,* reputedly in honor of his friend and former pupil Theodectes. The *Rhetorica ad Alexandrum,* long thought to have been written by Aristotle, partly because he once tutored the young Alexander, was eventually rejected by classical scholars as being part of the Aristotelian canon and was attributed by some of them to a contemporary of Aristotle's, Anaximenes. What all of this history of the Aristotelian rhetorical texts indicates is that Aristotle became interested in rhetoric very early in his academic career and maintained an active interest in it throughout most of his life.

Most students of Aristotle's works regard the *Poetics* as being one of his later works. They assign it to the period of second residency in Athens and fix the completion date as falling somewhere in the range of 334–330 B.C. But throughout his voluminous commentary on the text, Gerald F. Else has presented suggestive, if not conclusive, evidence that "the basic stock of the *Poetics* text is early rather than late, i.e., belongs to the Assos-Mytilene period (347–342) or even to the time before Plato's death (347), rather than to Aristotle's last period in Athens (after 335)."[10] We may never be able to settle definitively the date of this influential text because, as John Gassner has pointed out, the oldest surviving Greek manuscript of the *Poetics* is dated about 1000 A.D..[11]

In any case, Aristotle's interest in the poetic branch of the language arts seems not to have developed until later in his professional career. In fact, one can no more read the *Poetics* in iso-

---

[10] Gerald F. Else, *Aristotle's Poetics: The Argument* (Cambridge, Mass.: Harvard University Press, 1967), p. xi. See also p. 667 for the list of the additions that Else maintains Aristotle himself made to his own text.

[11] See John Gassner, "Aristotelian Literary Criticism," Gassner's prefatory essay to the first American edition of S. H. Butcher *Aristotle's Theory of Poetry and Fine Art with a Critical Text and Translation of the Poetics,* 4th ed. (New York: Dover Publications, 1951), p. xlvi.

lation from Aristotle's other works than one can read and adequately understand the *Rhetoric* apart from his other philosophic works. Richard McKeon has conveniently summarized
how considerations of various aspects of the poetic art are inter-
woven through the fabric of some of the other famous texts of
Aristotle:

> Poetry is treated as such in the *Poetics;* its educational function is
> taken up in the *Politics;* the statements and arguments of poets
> and of characters in poetry are analyzed in the *Rhetoric*; the moral
> situations and moral aphorisms of poets are used in the *Nicoma-
> chean Ethics;* and poetry and mythology are quoted as evidence in
> the *Metaphysics*.[12]

Considering his honorific treatment of both rhetoric and
poetics, Aristotle may well have developed very early in his student days in the Academy an interest in these two subjects and
have resolved that some day he would counteract the deroga-
tory treatment they had received from his mentor Plato. It is
easy to find statements in the *Rhetoric* and the *Poetics* that
seem to be direct contradictions of statements about rhetoric
and poetics preserved in such Platonic dialogues as the
Phaedrus, the *Gorgias*, the *Ion*, and the *Republic*.

Both the *Rhetoric* and the *Poetics* have been subjected to extensive and intensive analysis and interpretation. The very per-
sistence of the commentary indicates the importance that
scholars have attached to these two texts in the history of ideas.
The very fact that learned scholars still argue with one another
about many of the pregnant passages is evidence that these me-
ticulously scrutinized texts do not readily yield their meaning.
Part of the continuing difficulty with the texts is that one is
dealing with translations from an ancient language. But even
when the texts are read in their original language, it is difficult
to get a secure grasp on the meaning because of the vagueness
or ambiguity of many of the Greek words. Problems with the
words are compounded by the fact that the texts that have
come down to us represent sets of incomplete, unrefined lecture
notes. Many of the statements in both texts that are now puzzling were undoubtedly elaborated on and illustrated in the

[12] Richard McKeon, "Aristotle's Conception of Language and the
Arts of Language, Part II," *Classical Philology* 42 (1947): 37.

classroom. Those oral glosses would be invaluable now if they could be recovered. Lacking them, one has to depend on one's own skill in reading, on the help to be had from astute classical scholars, and on the illumination offered by pertinent passages of other extant works by Aristotle.

The Rhetoric

The Aristotelian text known as the *Rhetoric* is concerned with the art of persuasive oratory. Partly in response to the negative views of rhetoric expressed by Plato in his dialogues called the *Gorgias* and the *Phaedrus*, Aristotle wanted to give this art a more systematic, a more philosophical, treatment than it had received in previous handbooks (*technai*) of rhetoric. Although Aristotle was not as popular a teacher of rhetoric as his contemporary Isocrates, he did produce a seminal and, in many ways, an original treatise. Not everything that is included in the following exposition of the Aristotelian rhetorical system represents an original contribution to the Greek tradition of rhetoric;[13] but even when he is repeating the commonplace concepts of rhetoric, Aristotle manages somehow to give them the stamp of his distinctive authority.

There were three kinds of persuasive oratory: (1) deliberative or political oratory—the oratory of the public forum; (2) judicial or forensic oratory—the oratory of the law courts; and (3) epideictic or demonstrative oratory—the oratory of ceremonial occasions. With his great penchant for symmetrical classifications, Aristotle worked out this neat scheme for the three types of oratory (see Chapter 2 of Book 1):

Forensic

1. Time province—the past
2. End or objective—the establishment of justice and injustice
3. Procedural means—accusation and defense

---

[13] A convenient summary of Aristotle's original contributions to rhetoric can be found in Friedrich Solmsen's article "The Aristotelian Tradition in Ancient Rhetoric," *American Journal of Philology* 62 (1941): 35-50, 169-190. This article is reprinted in *Aristotle: The Classical Heritage of Rhetoric*, ed. Keith V. Erickson (Metuchen, N.J.: Scarecrow Press, 1974), pp. 278-309.

Epideictic
1. Time province—the present
2. End or objective—the establishment of honor and dishonor
3. Procedural means—praise and blame

Deliberative
1. Time province—the future
2. End or objective—the establishment of the expediency or the harmfulness of a proposed course of action
3. Procedural means—exhortation and dehortation

As in most classifications, the categories here occasionally "leak," but it is surprising how often they remain firm.

Before we look in some detail at Aristotle's advice about how to manage the arguments in these three types of oratory, we would do well to get an overview of the whole of the *Rhetoric*. One way to get this overview is to look at the contents pages of this edition, where W. Rhys Roberts provides detailed annotations of each of the chapters. But these annotations may be too detailed to give the reader an easily comprehensible overview of the complete text. The following brief outline of the main divisions of the three books of the *Rhetoric* may be easier to grasp:

Book I
1. General introduction to the art of rhetoric (Chapters 1–3)
2. The special topics (*eidē*) for each of the three types of oratory (Chapters 4–15)
3. The "non-artistic" (*atechnoi*) means of persuasion (Chapter 15)

Book II
1. The ethical appeal (*ethos*) (Chapter 1)
2. Analysis of contrasting pairs of emotions for the emotional appeal (*pathos*) (Chapters 2–11)
3. Analysis of types of human character according to age and fortune (Chapters 12–17)

A chapter of recapitulation and transition (Chapter 18)
4. The common topics (*koinoi topoi*) for inventing and refuting arguments (Chapters 19–26)

Book III
1. The style of persuasive speeches (Chapters 1–12)
2. The arrangement or organization of persuasive speeches (Chapters 13–19)

Introduction *xv*

There are some questionable parts in this line-up of chapters.
One wonders, for instance, why the common topics were not
treated immediately after the special topics. Such mysteries
lead one to conclude that Aristotle never finally edited his lecture notes before they were published. Overlooking questionable features of this sort, W. Rhys Roberts, the translator of the
text of the *Rhetoric* used in this book, gives us this rather tidy
outline of the text:

> If we consider the work as a whole, the first Book may perhaps be
> described as mainly logical and political, the second as mainly
> ethical or psychological, the third as mainly literary or stylistic
> The speaker perhaps counts most in Book I, the audience in Book
> II, and the speech itself in Book III. To the man who aspires to
> oratorical success, Book I seems to say: "Be logical. Think clearly.
> Reason cogently. Remember that *argument* is the life and soul of
> persuasion." Book II: "Study human nature. Observe the charac-
> ters and emotions of your audience, as well as your own character
> and emotions." Book III: "Attend to delivery. Use language right-
> ly. Arrange your material well. End crisply." And the whole
> treatise presupposes good wits and a fine general education.[14]

At the beginning of Chapter 2 of Book I, Aristotle gives his
unique definition of rhetoric: "Rhetoric may be defined as the
faculty (*dynamis*) of observing in any given case the available
means of persuasion." There are a number of things to be noted
about this definition. First of all, although the generic term that
Aristotle uses here to define rhetoric is *dynamis* ("faculty" or
"power" or "ability"), in most other places in the text, he
speaks of rhetoric as being an *art* (*technē*). We can reconcile
these two terms by taking the position that if one has mastered
the *art* of rhetoric, one has the *faculty* or *ability* to discover the
available means of persuasion. Aristotle does not designate persuasion as the end or function of rhetoric; rather, the function of
rhetoric is to observe or discover the potentially persuasive arguments (*pisteis*) in a particular case. With this emphasis, Aristotle relieves rhetoric of the onus of having to achieve persuasion at any cost. He implies here and elsewhere that if one
acquires the ability to discover the available arguments, one
will be guided in making a choice of the most effective and legiti-

[14] W. Rhys Roberts, *Greek Rhetoric and Literary Criticism* (New
York: Longmans, Green, 1928), p. 50.

mate arguments by one's intellectual and moral disposition. One final feature to note about the definition is that there is no mention that the act of persuasion is a verbal art. There is no such phrase as occurs in the definitions proposed by Cicero and Quintilian: "by means of speaking" (*in dicendo* or *scientia bene dicendi*). Aristotle probably felt that the verbal nature of rhetoric was so obvious that he did not need to be explicit about it in his famous definition.

Aristotle touches on virtually all of the key concepts and key terms of his system of rhetoric in the first three chapters of Book I. For that reason, these three chapters should be read very carefully, sentence by sentence. The remainder of the *Rhetoric* spells out in detail, and occasionally with illustrations, the general outline of Aristotle's rhetoric as it is laid out in these introductory chapters. Here we will review the main terms and concepts that figure in the *Rhetoric*.

One of Aristotle's innovative contributions to the art of rhetoric is his concept of the "available means of persuasion." The first division that he makes of these means is the dichotomy of "artistic proofs" (*entechnoi pisteis*) and "non-artistic proofs" or "non-technical proofs" (*atechnoi pisteis*). Basically, the distinction is made between those proofs that are produced in the art (*entechnoi*, literally, "in the art") of rhetoric and those proofs that are available from outside the art (*atechnoi*, literally, "not part of the art"). The non-artistic proofs are such substantiating data as laws, contracts, oaths, testimony of witnesses, and evidence given under torture (see Book I, Chapters 2 and 15). Speakers do not have to "invent" these proofs; they merely have to seek them out. These external proofs (except the last one perhaps) play a more prominent role in modern persuasive situations than they did in Aristotle's time.

But "the true constituents of the art—by which Rhys Roberts in Chapter 1 means the essence of rhetoric—are the artistic proofs: the appeals to reason (*logos*), the appeals to the emotions of the audience (*pathos*), the appeals exerted by the character of the speaker (*ethos*). This tripartite division of the artistic proofs probably represents Aristotle's most original and most influential contribution to the art of rhetoric. These three species of proofs were picked up by virtually all subsequent rhetoricians and elaborated on and refined. Although all three of these kinds of proofs play a part in all three kinds of oratory, the logical proof is perhaps most prominent in judicial discourse, the ethical proof most prominent in deliberative discourse, and the emotional proof most prominent in epideictic discourse. And although the three proofs overlap somewhat, the ethical proof is most concerned with the speaker, the emotional proof with the audience, and the logical proof with the speech itself.

Aristotle observes in Chapter 2 of Book I that far from being the weakest of the means of persuasion, as some rhetoricians believed, the ethical appeal is probably the "most effective." He is astute enough to recognize that if an audience does not admire or trust the speaker, all the skill in the world in managing the logical and emotional appeals will go for naught. He treats very briefly this most potent means of persuasion in the first chapter of Book II, telling the reader there that his previous analysis of virtue in Chapter 9 of Book I and his subsequent treatment of good will and friendliness under the emotions are pertinent to the ethical appeal. The most significant thing he says about *ethos* at the beginning of Book II is that a speaker will inspire the audience's confidence if he can create an image of himself as a person of good sense (*phronēsis*), goodwill (*eunoia*), and good moral character (*aretē*). Since Aristotle does not elaborate on these qualities in the *Rhetoric*, one has to consult some of his other philosophical works—especially the *Ethics*—in order to understand adequately everything that is encompassed in these three constituents of the speaker's ethical appeal.

Aristotle devotes ten chapters of Book II to a discussion of how to manipulate the emotions of the audience in argumentative situations, even though in the first chapter of the *Rhetoric*, he seems to deplore the use of emotional appeals. But what he really deplores in the first chapter is the stirring of emotions in inappropriate situations and the concentrating on emotional appeals to the utter exclusion of appeals to the rational faculties of the audience. Like Plato, Aristotle would prefer that people always made their choices and decisions on rational grounds; but realist that he is, he knows that people are creatures of passion and emotion as well as of reason. Far from believing that the stirring of human emotions is inherently immoral, Aristotle recognizes that if speakers do not responsibly arouse emotions, they will frequently not be able to persuade people to change their minds or be able to move them into action, even though the audience has been won over logically. Although subsequent rhetoricians acknowledged the importance of arousing or allaying the emotions of the audience, none of them devoted as much attention as Aristotle does in this book to an analysis of the basic emotions and of the way to stir them or calm them. Long before the development of a science of psychology, he gave us a remarkable analysis of the emotional mechanism of the human psyche.

Aristotle devotes considerable attention in the *Rhetoric* to the third mode of persuasion, the appeal to reason; but he expects his students to be familiar with what he has said about logical argument in the six treatises that constitute his *Organon*. He says in the very first sentence of the *Rhetoric* that "rhetoric is the counterpart of dialectic." One of the notions implicit in that pregnant first sentence is that there are some ways in which rhetoric and dialectic are similar. One similarity is that they both appeal to human reason but in a less formal and strict fashion than prevails in scientific demonstrations. The two basic ways in which the human mind reasons are induction (*epagōgē*) and deduction (*sullogismos*, "syllogism"). The rhetorical equivalent of induction is the example (*paradeigma*); the rhetorical equivalent of deduction is the enthymeme (*enthumēma*). As he says in Chapter 2, "When we base the proof of a proposition on a number of similar cases, this is induction in dialectic, example in rhetoric; when it is shown that, certain propositions being true, a further and quite distinct proposition must also be true in consequence, whether invariably or usually, this is called syllogism in dialectic, enthymeme in rhetoric."

The principles and rules and the fallacies of inductive and deductive reasoning are covered in the traditional logic course, but this is not the place to go into all the intricacies of that formalized system of reasoning. Suffice it to say here that whereas the enthymeme today denotes for many people a syllogism in which one of the premises is missing but clearly understood, it was for Aristotle a much more complex mode of reasoning. The differences might be summed up in this way: the Aristotelian enthymeme (1) often involved premises that were merely probable, thus leading to conclusions that were only generally or usually true; (2) allowed for the ethical and emotional dimensions of argument as well as for the logical; and (3) depended for its success in persuasion on the consensus that existed or was generated between the speaker and the audience.[15]

The topics (*topoi*) represented the system devised by the classical rhetoricians to aid the speaker in finding the available arguments in a particular case. Aristotle divides the topics into two kinds: the common topics (*koinoi topoi*) and the particular topics (*idia* or *eidē*). The particular topics are associated with the special subject or discipline that the discourse is considering. If, for instance, one was arguing a case at law, the particular topics resorted to would yield arguments or proofs pertinent to that legal case. Those same lines of argument would not be relevant, and therefore not effective, in a case of physics. In commenting in Chapter 2 on the particular topics, Aristotle observes that "most enthymemes are in fact based on these particular or special Lines of Argument" but that "the better the selection one makes of propositions suitable for special Lines of Argument, the nearer one comes, unconsciously, to setting up a science that is distinct from dialectic and rhetoric." As we saw in the outline on page xiv, Aristotle deals in Chapter 4–15 of Book I with the particular topics as they relate to the three types of oratory.

He first mentions the common topics in Chapter 2 of Book I and then treats them extensively in Chapters 19–26 of Book II. Because the common topics are not tied to any particular subject matter or to any specific type of oratory, they have wide applicability. For instance, the common topic of More or Less (or what might be called the topic of Degree) is equally applicable to discussions in the area of ethics or law or politics or the natural sciences—virtually to any and all subjects.

[15] For a full and enlightened treatment of the Aristotelian enthymeme, consult the following sources: James H. Burney, "The Place of the Enthymeme in Rhetorical Theory," *Speech Monographs* 3 (1936): 49–74; Lloyd F. Bitzer, "Aristotle's Enthymeme Revisited," *Quarterly Journal of Speech* 45 (1959): 399–408; and William M. A. Grimaldi, "The Sources of Rhetorical Argumentation by Enthymeme," *Studies in the Philosophy of Aristotle's Rhetoric* (Wiesbaden, Germany: Franz Steiner Verlag, 1972); Chapter 4: pp. 115–135. The first two articles are reprinted in *Aristotle: The Classical Heritage of Rhetoric*, ed. Keith V. Erickson (Metuchen, N.J.: Scarecrow Press, 1974), pp. 117–140 and 141–155, respectively.

The four common topics that he mentions and discusses in Chapter 19 of Book II are (1) The Possible and the Impossible; (2) Past Fact; (3) Future Fact; and (4) Size (Big and Small; More and Less). But in Chapter 23 of Book II, he lays out twenty-eight general Lines of Argument. William M. A. Grimaldi demonstrates that these twenty-eight topics can be reduced to three inferential or logical patterns: (1) Antecedent-Consequent or Cause-Effect; (2) More-Less; and (3) some form of Relationship.[16] Interested readers can consult Grimaldi's article to find out to which of the three categories he assigns each of the twenty-eight topics. He has further argued that the particular topics (*eidē*) are *material topics* because they yield content or factual information on the subject being discussed and that the common topics (*koinoi topoi*) are *formal topics* because they are modes or forms of inference and are therefore more universal than the particular topics.[17]

There are some other technical terms in the *Rhetoric*, but readers can be left to discover and interpret those terms for themselves. The terms discussed here are the crucial ones for understanding Aristotle's system of rhetoric.

The Poetics

The *Poetics* considers the art of what might be called imaginative literature or, more specifically, the art of fiction—that is, made-up or invented narratives. But it is not a complete or a completed art of fiction. For one thing, it analyzes only one kind of fiction—imitative narratives—and only two species of those—tragedy and epic (the section on comedy was lost). For another thing, the *Poetics*, like the *Rhetoric*, is a fragmentary, unfinished treatise—probably a set of lecture notes. Yet despite its incompleteness, the *Poetics* has been unquestionably the most influential and the most discussed document of literary criticism in the Western world.

[16] William M. A. Grimaldi, "The Aristotelian *Topics*," *Traditio*, 14 (1958): 1–16. This article has been reprinted in the above-mentioned Erickson anthology, *Aristotle: The Classical Heritage of Rhetoric*, pp. 176–193. See also the chapter of the Grimaldi monograph mentioned in the previous note.

[17] Grimaldi, "The Aristotelian *Topics*," in *Aristotle: The Classical Heritage of Rhetoric*, p. 186.

Because of the missing parts and the sometimes seemingly misplaced parts, scholars have studied the twenty-six chapters that constitute the extant text of the *Poetics* to see whether they could discern any tenable rationale for the organization of the book. On the contents pages preceding his translation of the *Poetics* in this book, Ingram Bywater has done some grouping of the twenty-six extant chapters into five larger categories, which he marks off with letters of the alphabet from A to E and with headings of his own devising. His designation of the major parts of this treatise has been generally accepted by later commentators on the text. Various critics, of course, might differ slightly about the number of the major parts and about the phrasing of the headings for the parts. For instance, it is defensible to combine Bywater's D and E and to end up with a four-part structure for the *Poetics* that would look like the following:

1. A general discussion of the art of imitative poetry (Chapters 1–5)
2. A discussion of the art of tragedy and its parts (Chapters 6–22)
3. A discussion of the art of epic poetry (Chapters 23–24)
4. A discussion of the problems of evaluating poetry, especially tragedy and epic (Chapters 25–26)

This structure is forecast in the very first sentence of the *Poetics*: "Our subject being Poetry, I propose to speak not only of the art in general but also of its species and their respective capacities; of the structure of the plot required for a good poem; and likewise of any other matters in the same line of inquiry." The discussion moves from the broad perspective of the imitative arts in general to a progressively narrowing focus on the species of imitative poetry (primarily tragedy). As we have seen, the discussion in the *Rhetoric* also moved in that broad-to-narrow way: from the general treatment of the art of rhetoric in the first three chapters to a discussion in the subsequent chapters of the specific means of achieving persuasion.

Elder Olson, one of the noted contemporary commentators on the *Poetics,* has pointed out that the way in which Aristotle has organized the *Poetics* is consonant with the rationale of any productive art,[18] When one is trying to figure out the principles governing any productive art, he says, one starts out by looking at a completed product of that art. One determines inductively or empirically what the governing principles of that completed whole is. This exploratory examination enables one to establish a formula for producing the whole. In the *Poetics*, the inductively derived formula is the definition, given at the beginning of Chapter 6, of one species of imitative poetry, tragedy. Using this definition or formula, one then proceeds deductively to determine what the constituent parts of such a whole must be, what the nature and the quality of those parts must be, and how those parts must be put together.

The *Poetics* starts out with a consideration of the imitative arts, such as music, dancing, painting, sculpture, and poetry. Aristotle seeks to determine inductively what the common and the differentiating principles of these arts are by looking at the objects they imitate, the means or medium they use in imitating, and the manner of their imitation. Even the brief history of poetry that Aristotle presents in Chapter 4 and carries over into Chapter 5 is part of his inductive quest for the formula of the kind of imitative poetry he will concentrate on. Once he has presented this formula in Chapter 6, he proceeds deductively from that point to the end, examining the nature and the structure of the six qualitative parts of a tragedy—plot, character, thought, diction, melody, and spectacle.

One might use this formula or definition as an entrée into a discussion of some of the key concepts and terms that figure in the *Poetics*. At the beginning of Chapter 6 of the *Poetics*, Ingram Bywater translates Aristotle's definition of tragedy into these words:

> A tragedy, then, is the imitation of an action that is serious and also, as having magnitude, complete in itself; in language with pleasurable accessories, each kind brought in separately in the parts of the work; in a dramatic, not in a narrative form; with incidents arousing pity and fear, wherewith to accomplish its catharsis of such emotions.

[18] Elder Olson, "The Poetic Method of Aristotle: Its Powers and Limitations," in *Aristotle's Poetics and English Literature: A Collection of Critical Essays,* ed. Elder Olson (Chicago: University of Chicago Press, Gemini Books, 1965), p. 181.

As the classical scholar Gerald Else has pointed out,[19] all the concepts and terminology in this definition up to the final clause, which mentions the catharsis of pity and fear, were touched on in one of the first five chapters of the *Poetics*. Most of the commentary written about this treatise has centered on this definition, and most of it has been concerned with the meaning of the final clause.

At the beginning of Chapter 1, Aristotle observes that the various species of the imitative arts are characterized by the differences in the means, the manner, and the object of the imitation. In defining the imitative art that he is going to discuss for the next sixteen chapters, Aristotle assigns tragedy to the genus of imitation (*mimēsis*). In the subsequent parts of the definition, then, he differentiates tragedy from other kinds of imitative arts. For instance, he differentiates tragedy from comedy by pointing out that tragedy dramatizes a serious (*spoudaias*) action (its distinctive *object* of imitation). He differentiates tragedy from epic by saying that the action is dramatized rather than narrated (its distinctive *manner* of imitation). He distinguishes tragedy from some of the musical arts such as flute-playing and dancing by pointing out that tragedy is delivered in language (*logos*) embellished with rhythm and harmony (its distinctive *medium* or *means*).

Another way in which to view this definition is to see it as designating the four causes of a tragedy. According to Aristotle, the four causes of anything coming into existence are the *material* cause, the *formal* cause, the *efficient* cause, and the *final* cause. The four causes of a kitchen table, for instance, would be the carpenter (the efficient cause, the maker), who took wood (the material cause, the substance from which it is made) and shaped it in such a way (the formal cause, its form or structure) that it would be a suitable piece of furniture at which to sit and eat breakfast (its final cause, its purpose or use). Applying this formula to tragedy, we could say that the material cause would be what Aristotle calls the *object* of imitation (human actions); the formal cause would be a combination of the *means* (embellished language) and the *manner* (a dramatized presentation); the final cause, which is the one cause not discussed in the previous five chapters, would be the catharsis of the tragic

[19] Else, *Aristotle's Poetics*, p. 224.

emotions of pity and fear; the efficient cause, which is not explicitly mentioned in the definition but is implied, would be, immediately, the poet and, ultimately, the poetic art (the *poiētikē*).

The most troublesome term in the definition is *catharsis*. Curiously enough, the word *catharsis* in the sense that it has in the definition never appears again in the *Poetics*. In his *Politics* (Book VIII, Chapter 7, 1341b), where he is talking about the capacity of music to purge religious frenzy (*enthusiasmos*), Aristotle promises that he will speak more precisely about the term *katharsis* when he comes to talk about poetry (presumably in the *Poetics*); but he never does explain the term, and his failure to do so has encouraged countless critics and commentators to offer their interpretation of the term.

This is not the place to review the complex discussion of this puzzling term.[20] Suffice it to say that most interpreters have translated the Greek word *katharsis* in the medical sense of "purgation" or "purification." Most of them agree that a *change* of some kind takes place in the spectators or the readers of the tragic play. What critics quarrel about is such questions as "Is it the audience that is purged of pity and fear, or is it the pity and fear themselves that are purged?" "Are the emotions of pity and fear in the audience for the play, or are they qualities of the incidents in the play itself?" "Are the tragic emotions of pity and fear removed (purged) altogether by the play, or are they merely refined (purified) by the experience of the play and rendered pleasurable?"

The definition leads into the long discussion, carried on over the next sixteen chapters, of tragic drama. This discussion is organized according to the six constituent parts of a tragedy: plot (*mythos*), character (*ethos*), thought (*dianoia*), diction (*lexis*), song (*melos*), and spectacle (*opsis*). Plot, character, and thought are related to the *matter* of the play; diction and song are related to the *medium*; and spectacle is related to the *manner* of the presentation. In Chapter 6, Aristotle establishes a hierarchy for these parts, putting them in this order of decreasing importance: plot, character, thought, diction, song, and spectacle.

One of the ways in which Aristotle differs from later theorists

[20] Else has listed the seven points that are implied in most interpretations of *katharsis*. See his *Aristotle's Poetics*, p. 226

of the narrative art is in arguing that plot, the structure of the action or the incidents, is for him the most important element in storytelling. Most modern theorists would rate character as the chief element. Aristotle argues for his position in this way (Chapter 6):

> Tragedy is essentially an imitation not of persons but of action and life, of happiness and misery. All human happiness or misery takes the form of action; the end for which we live is a certain kind of activity, not a quality. Character gives us qualities, but it is in our actions—what we do—that we are happy or the reverse. In a play, accordingly, they do not act in order to portray the Characters; they include the Characters for the sake of the action. So that it is the action in it, i.e., its Fable or Plot, that is the end and purpose of the tragedy; and the end is everywhere the chief thing. Besides this, a tragedy is impossible without action, but there may be one without Characters.

In a creative-writing class or in a seminar on literary criticism, almost every sentence in that passage is liable to be challenged by someone in the class. Some people will contest even a basic philosophical principle such as the one in which Aristotle declares that "the end for which we live is a certain kind of activity, not a quality." It is partly because the *Poetics* provokes spirited assent or dissent that it has remained, to this day, one of the vital documents of literary aesthetics.

The *Poetics* has been the informing document for whole schools of literary criticism, such as the "Chicago school"—so called because many of its practitioners taught at the University of Chicago. The *Poetics* made it possible for critics to ask certain kinds of questions about the structure of a literary text that other methods of criticism did not allow. They did not deny, however, that other critical approaches are legitimate and useful if one has other sets of questions that one wants to ask of a literary text.

Furthermore, Aristotle laid down some principles about how to construct a story that are as sound today as they were in his day. He is talking in this document about one kind of storytelling—a tale of tragedy rendered in the dramatic form—and he is talking about the only kind of tragic drama that he is familiar with—the plays of such contemporary playwrights as Aeschylus, Euripides, and Sophocles. If he were alive today, he would be the first to admit that his *Poetics* is not broad enough to cover some of the tragic dramas that have been written since his time—Shakespeare's, for instance. But he probably would still maintain, and many modern critics and playwrights would agree with him, that a contemporary tragedy constructed according to his principles could be a powerful play, capable of stirring and ultimately purging emotions of pity and fear in a twentieth-century audience. For instance, plots in which the sequence of events is linked together in some kind of cause-and-effect way are more likely to be aesthetically satisfying than episodic plots, where the relationship between the successive incidents is simply arbitrary or at best merely temporal. And do we not still find those stories more lastingly satisfying in which the sequence of event has been made to seem not just possible but probable or, best of all, necessary?

Several other viable principles of this sort can be found in the *Poetics*, principles governing not just the construction of plots but the creation of characters, the establishment of the verbal style, and the management of the staging of the play. Those who are new to the *Poetics* are likely to meet with a number of surprising discoveries about the soundness and timelessness of the discussion and of the advice offered in this text. It is a treatise for all seasons.

SELECTIVE BIBLIOGRAPHY

General

The Basic Works of Aristotle. Edited by Richard McKeon. New York: Random House, 1941.
> A handy collection of English translations, by various hands, of twenty-one of Aristotle's philosophical works, most of them complete, for those who want to read the *Rhetoric* and the *Poetics* in the context of the author's other works.

Corbett, Edward P. J. *Classical Rhetoric for the Modern Student*, 2nd ed. New York: Oxford University Press, 1971.
> This text presents a coherent and comprehensive adaptation of the precepts of classical rhetoric to the teaching of writing.

Howell, Wilbur Samuel. *Poetics, Rhetoric, and Logic: Studies in the Basic Disciplines of Criticism*. Ithaca, N.Y.: Cornell University Press, 1975.
> A collection of eight of Professor Howell's essays, written over a thirty-year period, all of them dealing with one or more of the three language arts named in the title.

Marrou, H. I. *A History of Education in Antiquity*. Translated by George Lamb. New York: Sheed and Ward, 1956.
> A fascinating account of how grammar, logic, poetics, and rhetoric were taught in the ancient schools of Greece and Rome.

McKeon, Richard. "Aristotle's Conception of Language and the Arts of Language, Part I." *Classical Philology* 41 (October 1946): 193–206; "Part II." ibid. 42 (January 1947): 21–50.
> In this two-part article, Richard McKeon deals in a very basic but thoroughgoing way with Aristotle's views, as expressed in his various works, on the nature and function of language and the arts of language. Both installments of this article are more readily available in the anthology *Critics and Criticism: Ancient and Modern*, edited with an introduction by Ronald S. Crane, pp. 176–231. Chicago: University of Chicago Press, 1952.

McKeon, Richard. "Rhetoric and Poetic in Aristotle." In *Aristotle's Poetics and English Literature*, edited by Elder Olson, pp. 201–236. Chicago: University of Chicago Press, 1965.

Roberts, W. Rhys. *Greek Rhetoric and Literary Criticism*. New York: Longmans, Green, 1928.
> The translator of the text of the *Rhetoric* used in this book reviews the development, relationship, and influence of Greek theories of rhetoric and poetics.

Ross, W. D. *Aristotle: A Complete Exposition of His Works and Thought.* 5th ed. New York: Meridian Books, 1959.
This text provides the general reader with a quick but reliable introduction to Aristotle's life, times, and philosophical works.

Weiss, Steven M. "Rhetoric and Poetics: A Re-evaluation of the Aristotelian Distinction." *Rhetoric Society Quarterly* 12 (Winter 1982): 21–29.
This article reviews the most important published work dealing with the distinction; analyzes and assesses the bases on which the distinction was made; and suggests another way of making the distinction.

The Rhetoric

Cope, E. M. *An Introduction to Aristotle's Rhetoric, with Analysis, Notes, and Appendices.* London and Cambridge: Macmillan, 1867.
These chapter-by-chapter, at times line-by-line, notes on the text were published ten years before Cope published his three-volume translation of, and commentary on, Aristotle's *Rhetoric*.

Cope, E. M. *The Rhetoric of Aristotle.* 3 vols. Revised and edited by John E. Sandys. Cambridge: Cambridge University Press, 1877.
A translation and interlinear commentary on the *Rhetoric*, posthumously edited by Sandys. In 1966, the Wm. C. Brown Co. of Dubuque, Iowa, published a facsimile edition of this three-volume text and of the *Introduction* listed in the previous entry.

Erickson, Keith V., comp. *Aristotle's Rhetoric: Five Centuries of Philological Research.* Metuchen, N.J.: Scarecrow Press, 1975.
This well-nigh exhaustive bibliography lists 1,600 primary and secondary works (but not medieval manuscripts) published between 1475 and 1974.

Erickson, Keith V., comp. "A Decade of Research on Aristotle's *Rhetoric*: 1970–1980." *Rhetoric Society Quarterly* 12 (Winter 1982): 62–66.
This compilation, of international scope, picks up where the previous bibliography left off.

Erickson, Keith V., comp. "A Bibliography for the Study of Aristotle's *Rhetoric*." *Rhetoric Society Quarterly* 12 (Winter 1982): 55–61.
This bibliography "comprises entries that the compiler considers essential for a proper reading and understanding of Aristotle's *Rhetoric*." The 243 entries in this basic bibliography include books and articles written in German, French, and Italian, as well as in English.

Erickson, Keith V., ed. *Aristotle: The Classical Heritage of Rhetoric.*
Metuchen, N.J.: Scarecrow Press, 1974.
A collection of seventeen "classic" articles by twentieth-century
scholars that deal with virtually all of the important aspects of
Aristotle's rhetorical system.

Grimaldi, William M. A., S. J. *Studies in the Philosophy of Aristotle's
Rhetoric.* Wiesbaden, Germany: Franz Steiner Verlag, 1972.
A closely reasoned interpretation of such fundamental concepts in
Aristotle's *Rhetoric* as the rhetorical proofs (*pisteis*), the topics
(*topoi*), and the enthymeme (*enthumēma*) and example
(*paradeigma*).

Grimaldi, William M. A. *Aristotle, Rhetoric I: A Commentary.* New
York: Fordham University Press, 1980.
An even more thoroughgoing commentary than the one published
by E. M. Cope a century earlier. Grimaldi intends to publish comparable commentaries on Book II and Book III of the *Rhetoric.*

Kennedy, George. *The Art of Persuasion in Greece*, Chapter 3, "The
Development of Aristotle's Rhetoric," pp. 82–114. Princeton, N.J.:
Princeton University Press, 1963.
This chapter in Kennedy's history of Greek rhetoric gives a good
summary of Aristotle's *Rhetoric* and puts it in a historical context.

The Poetics

Butcher, S. H. *Aristotle's Theory of Poetry and Fine Art, with a
Critical Text and Translation of the Poetics.* 4th ed. London: Mac-
millan, 1907, and New York: Dover Publications, 1951.
This classic edition features the Greek text of the *Poetics* and Butcher's
English translation on facing pages, and eleven chapters of com-
mentary on such topics as " 'Imitation' as an Aesthetic Term,"
"The Dramatic Unities," "The Ideal Tragic Hero," and "Plot and
Character in Tragedy." For the first American edition of this text
published in 1951 by Dover Publications, John Gassner wrote a
special essay, "Aristotelian Literary Criticism," pp. xxxvii–lxxi.

Cooper, Lane, and Alfred Gudeman. *A Bibliography of the Poetics of
Aristotle.* New Haven: Yale University Press, 1928.
This 193-page bibliography is supplemented by the bibliographies
published by Marvin T. Herrick, *American Journal of Philology* 52
(1931): 168–174, and by Gerald Else, *Classical World* 48
(1954–1955): 73–82.

Cooper, Lane. *An Aristotelian Theory of Comedy, with an Adaptation
of the Poetics and a Translation of the "Tractatus Coislianus."* New
York: Harcourt, Brace, 1922.

Because the *Tractatus Coislianus,* a fragmentary document presumably dating somewhere between the fourth and the second centuries B.C., contains a number of parallels, even in wording, with the *Poetics,* some scholars, including Lane Cooper, have attempted to use that document to reconstruct the lost Second Book of the *Poetics,* which supposedly dealt with comedy.

Crane, Ronald S. *The Languages of Criticism and the Structure of Poetry.* Toronto: University of Toronto Press, 1953.
In these Alexander Lectures, originally delivered in March 1952 at the University of Toronto, Ronald Crane, the spokesman for the so-called Chicago school of criticism, compares the Aristotelian type of criticism of his group with other modern systems of literary criticism; and in the second lecture, entitled "Poetic Structure in the Language of Aristotle," he delivers a 40-page analysis of the *Poetics.*

Else, Gerald F. *Aristotle's Poetics: The Argument.* Cambridge, Mass.: Harvard University Press, 1967.
Much like William Grimaldi in his close analysis of Book I of the *Rhetoric,* Else goes through the twenty-six chapters of the *Poetics* paragraph by paragraph, giving his translation of the Greek passage and then analyzing and interpreting the passage. Butcher's text and Else's text are the indispensable handbooks for anyone seriously interested in the study of the *Poetics.*

Olson, Elder, ed. *Aristotle's Poetics and English Literature: A Collection of Critical Essays.* Chicago: University of Chicago, 1965.
Comparable to Keith Erickson's collection of essays on the *Rhetoric,* this collection of fourteen essays, beginning with three essays written in the eighteenth century and ending with three essays by members of the "Chicago school," illuminates several aspects of the *Poetics.*

Wimsatt, William K., Jr., and Cleanth Brooks. *Literary Criticism: A Short History,* Chapter 2: "Aristotle's Answer: Poetry as Structure," pp. 21–34, New York: Random House, 1967, and Chapter 3: "Aristotle: Tragedy and Comedy," pp. 35–56.
A good starting point for the student who wants to get a historical fix and a quick overview before settling down to a serious reading of the *Poetics.*

A NOTE ON THE TEXTS

The first edition of *The Rhetoric and the Poetics of Aristotle*, which was published in 1954, carried W. Rhys Roberts's translation (1924) of the *Rhetoric* and Ingram Bywater's translation (1909) of the *Poetics*, with an introduction and notes by the renowned classical scholar Friedrich Solmsen of Cornell University. This edition retains the two Oxford translations and the notes but adds a completely new introduction and a selective, annotated bibliography.

The four-digit numbers in the outer margins—for example 1364^b—refer to pages in Immanuel Bekker's edition (1837) of the Greek text of Aristotle. The one- and two-digit numbers in the outer margins are the line numbers on a particular page of the Bekker edition. The customary way to refer to a particular passage in any edition or translation of Aristotle's works is to use a notation such as this: 1364^b 17. If you look for that number in this edition, you will find it attached to a passage in Book I, Chapter 7, of the *Rhetoric*, beginning with the words "Here the principle is applied to judgments of goodness..." The numbers in the inner margins refer to the chapters of the *Rhetoric* or the *Poetics*.

From the Oxford edition of the *Rhetoric* by Roberts and of the *Poetics* by Bywater, Professor Solmsen selected the notes that occur in footnotes throughout this edition. The notes enclosed in square brackets are Solmsen's own, except for the translations of the Greek in the footnotes on pages 254–263 of the *Poetics*, which are taken from Lane Cooper's *Aristotle on the Art of Poetry* (1947), by permission of the publishers, the Cornell University Press.

Professor Solmsen's introduction was written for the initiate, for the reader who is already well acquainted with both the *Rhetoric* and the *Poetics*. In writing my introduction, however, I had in mind the reader who is interested in the two famous texts by Aristotle but who either has not yet read the texts or not yet studied them carefully. With such an audience in mind, I decided not to include a lengthy bibliography that would just overwhelm the reader but instead to present a brief, annotated bibliography—one that would list the kind of essential books and articles that teachers of a course in rhetoric or literary criticism would be likely to put on reserve in the college library.

I have frequently in the text of my introduction put in parentheses a transliteration of the pertinent Greek word or phrase. Seeing the equivalent Greek work may illuminate the text for those who have studied classical Greek. (The mark [-] over the *o* and the *e* in these transliterations distinguishes the long Greek *o* [*omega*] from the short *o* [*omicron*], and the long *e* [*ēta*] from the short *e* [epsilon].) I hope that the short outlines I have provided for the *Rhetoric* and the *Poetics* will serve as a helpful overview for readers who are not yet familiar with these texts.

I am grateful to the Jowett Trustees and the Clarendon Press, Oxford, for permission to use the two Oxford translations of Aristotle and to the Cornell University Press for permission to use the translations by Lane Cooper. For their helpful suggestions about the contents and the style of this introduction, I am indebted to Frederick Crews of the University of California at Berkeley; Frank J. D'Angelo of Arizona State University; Richard L. Larson of Herbert Lehman College, CUNY; Donald McQuade of Queens College, CUNY; and Charles Schuster of the University of Washington.

RHETORIC

TRANSLATED BY W. RHYS ROBERTS

CONTENTS

dialectic; (*b*) the enthymeme, corresponding to the syllogism; (*c*) the apparent enthymeme, corresponding to the apparent syllogism. The enthymeme is a rhetorical syllogism, and the example a rhetorical induction. Rhetoric has regard to classes of men, not to individual men; its subjects, and the premisses from which it argues, are in the main such as present alternative possibilities in the sphere of human action; and it must adapt itself to an audience of untrained thinkers who cannot follow a long train of reasoning. The premisses from which enthymemes are formed are 'probabilities' and 'signs'; and signs are either fallible or infallible, in which latter case they are termed τεκμήρια. The lines of argument, or topics, which enthymemes follow may be distinguished as common (or, general) and special (i.e. special to a single study, such as natural science or ethics). The special lines should be used discreetly, if the rhetorician is not to find himself deserting his own field for another.

Chapter 3   31

There are three kinds of rhetoric: A. political (deliberative), B. forensic (legal), and C. epideictic (the ceremonial oratory of display). Their (*a*) divisions, (β) times, and (γ) ends are as follows: A. Political (*a*) exhortation and dehortation, (β) future, (γ) expediency and inexpediency; B. Forensic (*a*) accusation and defence, (β) past, (γ) justice and injustice; C. Epideictic (*a*) praise and censure, (β) present, (γ) honour and dishonour.

Chapter 4   34

(A) The subjects of Political Oratory fall under five main heads: (1) ways and means, (2) war and peace, (3) national defence, (4) imports and exports, (5) legislation. The scope of each of these divisions.

Chapter 5

In urging his hearers to take or to avoid a course of action, the political orator must show that he has an eye to their happiness. Four definitions (of a popular kind: as usual in the *Rhetoric*), and some fourteen constituents, of happiness.

Chapter 6

The political speaker will also appeal to the interest of his hearers, and this involves a knowledge of what is good. Definition and analysis of things 'good.'

Chapter 7

Comparison of 'good' things. Of two 'good' things, which is the better? This entails a consideration of degree—the lore of 'less or more.'

Chapter 8

The political speaker will find his powers of persuasion most of all enhanced by a knowledge of the four sorts of government—democracy, oligarchy, aristocracy, monarchy, and their characteristic customs, institutions, and interests. Definition of the four sorts severally. Ends of each.

Chapter 9

(C) The Epideictic speaker is concerned with virtue and vice, praising the one and censuring the other. The forms of virtue. Which are the greatest virtues?—Some rhetorical devices used by the epideictic speaker: 'amplification,' especially. Amplification is particularly appropriate to epideictic oratory; examples. to political; enthymemes, to forensic.

Chapter 10   63

(B) The Forensic speaker should have studied wrong-
doing—its motives, its perpetrators, and its victims.
Definition of wrongdoing as injury voluntarily inflicted
contrary to law. Law is either (a) special, viz. that
written law which regulates the life of a particular community, or (b) general, viz. all those unwritten principles which are supposed to be acknowledged everywhere. Enumeration and elucidation of the seven causes
of human action, viz. three involuntary, (1) chance,
(2) nature, (3) compulsion; and four voluntary, viz.
(4) habit, (5) reasoning, (6) anger, (7) appetite. All
voluntary actions are good or apparently good, pleasant
or apparently pleasant. The good (or expedient) has
been discussed under political oratory. The pleasant
has yet to be considered.

Chapter 11   67

Definition of pleasure, and analysis of things pleasant.—
The motives for wrongdoing, viz. advantage and pleasure, have thus been discussed in chapters 6, 7, 11.

Chapter 12   73

The characters and circumstances which lead men to
commit wrong, or make them the victims of wrong.

Chapter 13   77

Actions just and unjust may be classified in relation to
(1) the law, (2) the persons affected. The law may be
(a) special, i.e. the law of a particular State, or (b)
universal, i.e. the law of Nature. The persons affected
may be (a) the entire community, (b) individual members of it. A wrongdoer must either understand and
intend the action, or not understand and intend it. In
the former case, he must be acting either from deliberate choice or from passion. It is deliberate purpose that

constitutes wickedness and criminal guilt. Unwritten
law (1) includes in its purview the conduct that springs
from exceptional goodness or badness, e.g. our behaviour towards benefactors and friends; (2) makes up for
the defects in a community's written code of law. This
second kind is equity. Its existence partly is, and partly
is not, intended by legislators; not intended, where they
have noticed no defect in the law; intended, where they
find themselves unable to define things exactly, and are
obliged to legislate as if that held good always which in
fact only holds good usually.—Further remarks on the
nature and scope of equity.

Chapter 14

The worse of two acts of wrong done to others is that
which is prompted by the worse disposition. Other ways
of computing the comparative badness of actions.

Chapter 15

The 'non-technical' (extrinsic) means of persuasion—
those which do not strictly belong to the art (τέχνη)
of rhetoric. They are five in number, and pertain especially to forensic oratory: (1) laws, (2) witnesses, (3)
contracts, (4) tortures, (5) oaths. How laws may be dis-
credited or upheld, according as it suits the litigant.
Witnesses may be either ancient (viz. poets and other
notable persons; soothsayers; proverbs); or recent (viz.
well-known contemporaries who have expressed their
opinions about some disputed matter, and witnesses who
give their evidence in court). Ancient witnesses are
more trustworthy than contemporary. How contracts,
and evidence given under torture, may be belittled or
represented as important. In regard to oaths, a fourfold
division exists: a man may either both offer and accept
an oath, or neither, or one without the other—that is,
he may offer an oath but not accept one, or accept an
oath but not offer one.

BOOK II

Chapter 1

Since rhetoric—political and forensic rhetoric, at any rate—exists to affect the giving of decisions, the orator must not only try to make the argument of his speech demonstrative and worthy of belief; he must also (1) make his own character look right and (2) put his hearers, who are to decide, into the right frame of mind. As to his own character: he should make his audience feel that he possesses prudence, virtue, and goodwill. This is especially important in a deliberative assembly. In the law courts it is especially important that he should be able to influence the emotions, or moral affections, of the jury who try the case. Definition of the several emotions. In regard to each emotion we must consider (*a*) the states of mind in which it is felt; (*b*) the people towards whom it is felt; (*c*) the grounds on which it is felt.

Chapter 2

In cc. 2-11 the various emotions are defined, and are also discussed (with incidental observations) from the three points of view just indicated. In c. 2, Anger is the subject. The orator must so speak as to make his hearers angry with his opponents.

Chapter 3

Calmness (as the opposite of Anger).

Chapter 4

Friendship and Enmity.

Chapter 5

Fear and Confidence.

prime from thirty to five-and-thirty; the mind about forty-nine.

Use of maxims. A maxim is a general statement about
questions of practical conduct. It is an incomplete enthymeme. Four kinds of maxims. Maxims should be used
(a) by elderly men, and (b) to controvert popular sayings. Advantages of maxims: (a) they enable a speaker
to gratify his commonplace hearers by expressing as a
universal truth the opinions which they themselves hold
about particular cases; (b) they invest a speech with
moral character.

Enthymemes. In enthymemes we must not carry our
reasoning too far back, nor must we put in all the steps
that lead to our conclusion. There are two kinds of
enthymemes: (a) the demonstrative, formed by the
conjunction of compatible propositions; (b) the refutative, formed by the conjunction of incompatible propositions.

Enumeration of twenty-eight topics (lines of argument)
on which enthymemes, demonstrative and refutative, can
be based [*see* Index, under 'argument, lines of']. Two
general remarks are added: (a) the refutative enthymeme has a greater reputation than the demonstrative,
because within a small space it works out two opposing
arguments, and arguments put side by side are clearer
to the audience; (b) of all syllogisms, whether refutative
or demonstrative, those are most applauded of which we
foresee the conclusions from the beginning, so long as
they are not obvious at first sight—for part of the pleasure we feel is at our own intelligent anticipation; or
those which we follow well enough to see the point of
them as soon as the last word has been uttered.

Chapter 24   155

Nine topics of apparent, or sham, enthymemes [*see*
Index, under 'fallacious arguments'].

Chapter 25   160

Refutation. An argument may be refuted either by a
counter-syllogism or by bringing an objection. Objections may be raised in four ways: (a) by directly attacking your opponent's own statement; (β) by putting
forward another statement like it; (γ) by putting forward a statement contrary to it; (δ) by quoting
previous decisions.

Chapter 26   163

Correction of two errors, possible or actual: (1) Amplification and Depreciation do not constitute an element of enthymeme, in the sense of 'a line of enthymematic argument'; (2) refutative enthymemes are not
a different species from constructive. This brings to an
end the treatment of the thought-element of rhetoric—
the way to invent and refute persuasive arguments.
There remain the subjects of (A) style and (B) arrangement.

BOOK III

Chapter 1   164

(A) Style. It is not enough to know what to say; we
must also say it in the right way. Upon the subject of
delivery (which presents itself here) no systematic
treatise has been composed, though this art has much
to do with oratory (as with poetry). The matter has,
however, been touched upon by Thrasymachus in his
'Appeals to Pity.' As to the place of style: the right thing
in speaking really is that we should fight our case with
no help beyond the bare facts; and yet the arts of lan-

guage cannot help having a small but real importance, whatever it is we have to expound to others. Through the influence of the poets, the language of oratorical prose at first took a poetical colour, as in the case of Gorgias. But the language of prose is distinct from that of poetry; and, further, the writers of tragic poetry itself have now given up those words, not used in ordinary talk, which adorned the early drama.

Chapter 2   167

Still, in the main, the same definition and methods apply alike to poetical and to prose style. Style, to be good, must be clear; it must also be appropriate, avoiding both meanness and excess of dignity. How these qualities may be attained. Rare, compound, and invented words must be used sparingly in prose; in which, over and above the regular and proper terms for things, metaphorical terms only can be used with advantage, and even these need care. The language of oratorical prose should, in fact, be like that of ordinary conversation. Some discussion of metaphor.

Chapter 3   171

Four faults of prose style, with illustrative examples: (1) misuse of compound words; (2) employment of strange words; (3) long, unseasonable, or frequent epithets; (4) inappropriate metaphors.

Chapter 4   173

The simile is a full-blown metaphor. Similes are useful in prose as well as in verse; but they must not be used often, since they are of the nature of poetry. Instances of simile, from Plato and the orators. Metaphors can easily be turned into similes, and similes into metaphors. The proportional [as defined in the *Poetics*, c. 21] metaphor must always apply reciprocally to either of its co-ordinate terms.

Chapter 5

The foundation of good style is correctness of language, which is discussed under five heads: (1) right use of connecting words; (2) use of special, and not vague general, terms; (3) avoidance of ambiguity; (4) observance of gender; (5) correct indication of grammatical number. A composition should be easy to read and therefore easy to deliver; it should avoid (1) uncertainties as to punctuation, (2) zeugma, (3) parenthesis.

Chapter 6

Impressiveness of style. Six heads: (1) the use of a description instead of a simple name; (2) metaphors and epithets; (3) plural for singular number; (4) repetition of the article; (5) connecting words; (6) description by means of negation.

Chapter 7

Appropriateness. An appropriate style will adapt itself to (1) the emotions of the hearers, (2) the character of the speaker, (3) the nature of the subject. Tact and judgement are needed in all varieties of oratory.

Chapter 8

Prose rhythm. The form of the language should not be metrical, nor, on the other hand, without any rhythm at all. Of the various possible rhythms, the heroic is too grand, the iambic too ordinary, and the trochaic too like a riotous dance. The best rhythm for prose is the paean, since from this alone no definite metre arises. The paean $-\cup\cup\cup$ should be used for the beginning, and he paean $\cup\cup\cup-$ for the end, of a sentence.

Chapter 9

Periodic style. The language of prose must be either

(1) free-running, like that of Herodotus; or (2) compact (i.e. periodic). A period may be defined as a portion of speech that has in itself a beginning and an end,
being at the same time not too big to be taken in at a
glance. It may have one member (clause), or more
than one. A period of more than one member may be
either (*a*) simply divided, or (*b*) antithetical. Antithesis
implies contrast of sense. *Parisosis* makes the two members of a period equal in length. *Paromoeosis* makes the
first or last words of both members like each other.
Homoeoteleuton denotes similarity in terminations only.

Chapter 10

Smart and popular sayings. Three chief features of these
clever, pointed sayings are: (1) antithesis, (2) metaphor, and (3) actuality or vividness (i.e. the power of
'setting the scene before our eyes').

Chapter 11

The graphic power of 'setting things before the eyes'
implies the use of expressions that represent objects
as in a state of activity: Homer often gives metaphorical
life to lifeless things in this fashion. A touch of surprise
also contributes to liveliness. People feel they have learnt
something; hence the pleasure given by apophthegms,
riddles, and puns. Similes, proverbs, and hyperboles also
find a place here, being related to metaphors.

Chapter 12

Each kind of rhetoric has its own appropriate style.
The style of written prose is not that of spoken oratory,
nor are those of political and forensic speaking the same.
The written style is the more finished: the spoken better
admits of dramatic delivery—alike the kind of oratory
that reflects character and the kind that stirs emotion.
The style of oratory addressed to public assemblies resembles scene-painting. In the one and the other, high

finish in detail is superfluous and seems better away.
The forensic style is more highly finished. Ceremonial
oratory is the most literary, for it is meant to be read;
and next to it forensic oratory. To analyse style still further, and add that it must be agreeable or magnificent,
is useless; for why should it have these traits any more
than 'restraint,' 'liberality,' or any other moral excellence?

Chapter 13 199

(B) Arrangement. A speech has two essential parts:
statement and proof. To these may be added introduction and epilogue.

Chapter 14 200

Introduction. The introduction corresponds to the prologue in poetry and the prelude in flute-music. The most
essential function and distinctive property of the introduction is to indicate the aim of the speech. An introduction may (1) excite or allay prejudice; (2) exalt
or depreciate. In a political speech an introduction is
seldom found, for the subject is usually familiar to the
audience.

Chapter 15 205

Prejudice. The various lines of argument suitable for
exciting or allaying prejudice.

Chapter 16 207

Narration. (1) In ceremonial oratory, narration should,
as a rule, not be continuous but intermittent: variety
is pleasant, and the facts in a celebrity's praise are
usually well known. (2) In forensic oratory, the current
rule that the narration should be rapid is wrong: rightness consists neither in rapidity nor in conciseness, but
in the happy mean. The defendant will make less use

of narration than the plaintiff. (3) In political oratory
there is least opening for narration; nobody can narrate
what has not yet happened. If there is narration at all,
it will be of past events, the recollection of which will
help the hearers to make better plans for the future.
Or it may be employed to attack some one's character,
or to eulogize him.

Arguments. The duty of the Arguments is to attempt
conclusive proofs. (1) In forensic oratory, the question
in dispute will fall under one of four heads: (a) the
fact, (b) the existence of injury, (c) the amount of injury, (d) the justification. (2) In ceremonial oratory,
the facts themselves will usually be taken on trust, and
the speaker will maintain, say, the nobility or the utility
of the deeds in question. (3) In political oratory, it will
be urged that a proposal is impracticable; or that,
though practicable, it is unjust, or will do no good, or is
not so important as its proposer thinks. Argument by
'example' is highly suitable for political oratory, argument by 'enthymeme' better suits forensic. Enthymemes
should not be used in unbroken succession; they should
be interspersed with other matter. 'If you have proofs
to bring forward, bring them forward, and your moral
discourse as well; if you have no entnymemes, then fall
back upon moral discourse: after all, it is more fitting
for a good man to display himself as an honest fellow
than as a subtle reasoner.' Hints as to the order in which
arguments should be presented. As to character: you
cannot well say complimentary things about yourself or
abusive things about another, but you can put such remarks into the mouth of some third person.

Interrogation and Jests. The best moment to employ interrogation is when your opponent has so answered one

question that the putting of just one more lands him in absurdity. In replying to questions, you must meet them, if they are ambiguous, by drawing reasonable distinctions, not by a curt answer.—Jests are supposed to be of some service in controversy. Gorgias said that you should kill your opponents' earnestness with jesting and their jesting with earnestness; in which he was right. Jests have been classified in the *Poetics*. 'Some are becoming to a gentleman, others are not; see that you choose such as become *you*. Irony better befits a gentleman than buffoonery; the ironical man jokes to amuse himself. the buffoon to amuse other people.'

Chapter 19   217

Epilogue (Peroration, Conclusion). This has four parts. You must (1) make the audience well disposed towards yourself and ill disposed towards your opponent, (2) magnify or minimize the leading facts, (3) excite the required kind of emotion in your hearers, and (4) refresh their memories by means of a recapitulation.—In your closing words you may dispense with conjunctions, and thereby mark the difference between the oration and the peroration: 'I have done. You have heard me. The facts are before you. I ask for your judgement.'

BOOK I

1 Rhetoric is the counterpart of Dialectic.[1] Both alike are 1354ᵃ
concerned with such things as come, more or less, within
the general ken of all men and belong to no definite
science. Accordingly all men make use, more or less, of
both; for to a certain extent all men attempt to discuss
statements and to maintain them, to defend themselves 5
and to attack others. Ordinary people do this either at
random or through practice and from acquired habit. Both
ways being possible, the subject can plainly be handled
systematically, for it is possible to inquire the reason why
some speakers succeed through practice and others spon- 10
taneously; and every one will at once agree that such an
inquiry is the function of an art.[2]

Now, the framers of the current treatises on rhetoric
have constructed but a small portion of that art. The
modes of persuasion[3] are the only true constituents of the
art: everything else is merely accessory. These writers,

---

[1] 'Rhetoric' and 'Dialectic' may be roughly Englished as 'the
art of public speaking' and 'the art of logical discussion.'
Aristotle's philosophical definition of 'Rhetoric' is given at
the beginning of c. 2.

[2] [Here and in later passages the term 'art' stands for
methodical treatment of a subject.]

[3] Aristotle here means by ['modes of persuasion'] those attempts at *logical argument* on which he would himself
like to see Rhetoric rely. In the next chapter, 1355ᵇ 35-
1356ᵃ4, he gives to the term the wide range it had in
current rhetorical usage, and concludes with a reference
to the argumentative side. . . . A uniform rendering of
the word is hardly possible, but at the outset it is important to stress Aristotle's fundamental view . . . that, from
the nature of its materials, Rhetoric is, in general, *persuasive* rather than fully *demonstrative*. When in later portions of the treatise a single-word rendering is given, 'arguments' will be preferred to 'proofs' . . .

however, say nothing about enthymemes,[1] which are the
15 substance of rhetorical persuasion, but deal mainly with
non-essentials. The arousing of prejudice, pity, anger, and
similar emotions has nothing to do with the essential facts,
but is merely a personal appeal to the man who is judging
the case. Consequently if the rules for trials which are
20 now laid down in some states—especially in well-governed
states—were applied everywhere, such people would have
nothing to say. All men, no doubt, *think* that the laws
should prescribe such rules, but some, as in the court of
Areopagus,[2] give practical effect to their thoughts and
forbid talk about non-essentials. This is sound law and
custom. It is not right to pervert the judge[3] by moving him
25 to anger or envy or pity—one might as well warp a carpenter's rule before using it. Again, a litigant has clearly
nothing to do but to show that the alleged fact is so or
is not so, that it has or has not happened. As to whether
a thing is important or unimportant, just or unjust, the
judge must surely refuse to take his instructions from the
30 litigants: he must decide for himself all such points as
the law-giver has not already defined for him.

Now, it is of great moment that well-drawn laws should
themselves define all the points they possibly can and
leave as few as may be to the decision of the judges; and
this for several reasons. First, to find one man, or a few
1354[b] men, who are sensible persons and capable of legislating
and administering justice is easier than to find a large
number. Next, laws are made after long consideration,
whereas decisions in the courts are given at short notice,
which makes it hard for those who try the case to satisfy
the claims of justice and expediency. The weightiest reason
5 of all is that the decision of the lawgiver is not particular
but prospective and general, whereas members of the
assembly and the jury find it *their* duty to decide on
definite cases brought before them. They will often have

---

[1] Rhetorical arguments.
[2] [Highest criminal court of Athens.]
[3] Here, and in what follows, the . . . reader should understand 'judge' in a broad sense, including 'jurymen' and
others who 'judge.'

allowed themselves to be so much influenced by feelings of friendship or hatred or self-interest that they lose any [10] clear vision of the truth and have their judgement obscured by considerations of personal pleasure or pain. In general, then, the judge should, we say, be allowed to decide as few things as possible. But questions as to whether something has happened or has not happened, will be or will not be, is or is not, must of necessity be left to the judge, since the lawgiver cannot foresee them. If [15] this is so, it is evident that any one who lays down rules about other matters, such as what must be the contents of the 'introduction' or the 'narration' or any of the other divisions of a speech, is theorizing about non-essentials as if they belonged to the art. The only question with which these writers here deal is how to put the judge into a [20] given frame of mind. About the orator's proper modes of persuasion they have nothing to tell us; nothing, that is, about how to gain skill in enthymemes.

Hence it comes that, although the same systematic principles apply to political as to forensic oratory, and although the former is a nobler business, and fitter for a citizen, than that which concerns the relations of private individuals, [25] these authors say nothing about political oratory, but try, one and all, to write treatises on the way to plead in court. The reason for this is that in political oratory there is less inducement to talk about non-essentials. Political oratory is less given to unscrupulous practices than forensic, because it treats of wider issues. In a political debate the [30] man who is forming a judgement is making a decision about his own vital interests. There is no need, therefore, to prove anything except that the facts are what the supporter of a measure maintains they are. In forensic oratory this is not enough; to conciliate the listener is what pays here. It is other people's affairs that are to be decided, so that the judges, intent on their own satisfaction and listening with partiality, surrender themselves to the disputants instead of judging between them. Hence in many places, [1355ᵇ] as we have said already,[1] irrelevant speaking is forbidden in the law-courts: in the public assembly those who have

[1] 1354ᵃ22.

to form a judgement are themselves well able to guard against that.

It is clear, then, that rhetorical study, in its strict sense, is concerned with the modes of persuasion. Persuasion is
5 clearly a sort of demonstration, since we are most fully persuaded when we consider a thing to have been demonstrated. The orator's demonstration is an enthymeme, and this is, in general, the most effective of the modes of persuasion. The enthymeme is a sort of syllogism, and the consideration of syllogisms of all kinds, without distinction, is the business of dialectic, either of dialectic as a whole
10 or of one of its branches. It follows plainly, therefore, that he who is best able to see how and from what elements a syllogism is produced will also be best skilled in the enthymeme, when he has further learnt what its subject-matter is and in what respects it differs from the syllogism of strict logic. The true and the approximately true are appre-
15 hended by the same faculty; it may also be noted that men have a sufficient natural instinct for what is true, and usually do arrive at the truth. Hence the man who makes a good guess at truth is likely to make a good guess at probabilities.

It has now been shown that the ordinary writers on rhetoric treat of non-essentials; it has also been shown why
20 they have inclined more towards the forensic branch of oratory.

Rhetoric is useful (1) because things that are true and things that are just have a natural tendency to prevail over their opposites, so that if the decisions of judges are not what they ought to be, the defeat must be due to the speakers themselves, and they must be blamed accordingly. Moreover, (2) before some audiences not even the
25 possession of the exactest knowledge will make it easy for what we say to produce conviction. For argument based on knowledge implies instruction, and there are people whom one cannot instruct. Here, then, we must use, as our modes of persuasion and argument, notions possessed by everybody, as we observed in the *Topics*[1] when dealing with the way to handle a popular audience. Further, (3)

[1] *Topics*, i. 2, 101ᵃ30-4.

we must be able to employ persuasion, just as strict reasoning can be employed, on opposite sides of a question, 30
not in order that we may in practice employ it in both
ways (for we must not make people believe what is
wrong), but in order that we may see clearly what the
facts are, and that, if another man argues unfairly, we on
our part may be able to confute him. No other of the arts
draws opposite conclusions: dialectic and rhetoric alone 35
do this. Both these arts draw opposite conclusions impar-
tially. Nevertheless, the underlying facts do not lend themselves equally well to the contrary views. No; things that
are true and things that are better are, by their nature,
practically always easier to prove and easier to believe in.
Again, (4) it is absurd to hold that a man ought to be 1355^b
ashamed of being unable to defend himself with his limbs,
but not of being unable to defend himself with speech
and reason,[1] when the use of rational speech is more distinctive of a human being than the use of his limbs. And
if it be objected that one who uses such power of speech
unjustly might do great harm, *that* is a charge which may
be made in common against all good things except virtue,
and above all against the things that are most useful, as 5
strength, health, wealth, generalship. A man can confer
the greatest of benefits by a right use of these, and inflict
the greatest of injuries by using them wrongly.

It is clear, then, that rhetoric is not bound up with a
single definite class of subjects, but is as universal as dialectic; it is clear, also, that it is useful. It is clear, further,
that its function is not simply to succeed in persuading, 10
but rather to discover the means of coming as near such
success as the circumstances of each particular case allow.
In this it resembles all other arts. For example, it is not
the function of medicine simply to make a man quite
healthy, but to put him as far as may be on the road to
health; it is possible to give excellent treatment even to
those who can never enjoy sound health. Furthermore, it
is plain that it is the function of one and the same art to
discern the real and the apparent means of persuasion, 15

---

[1] [By 'speech' and 'reason' the translator here has done
justice to the twofold meaning of the Greek word 'logos.']

just as it is the function of dialectic to discern the real and the apparent syllogism. What makes a man a 'sophist' is not his faculty, but his moral purpose. In rhetoric, however, the term 'rhetorician' may describe either the speaker's knowledge of the art, or his moral purpose.[1] In dialectic it is different: a man is a 'sophist' because he has a certain kind of moral purpose, a 'dialectician' in respect, not of his moral purpose, but of his faculty.

Let us now try to give some account of the systematic principles of Rhetoric itself—of the right method and means of succeeding in the object we set before us. We must make as it were a fresh start, and before going further define what rhetoric is.

Rhetoric may be defined as the faculty of observing in 2 any given case the available means of persuasion. This is not a function of any other art. Every other art can instruct or persuade about its own particular subject-matter; for instance, medicine about what is healthy and unhealthy, geometry about the properties of magnitudes, arithmetic about numbers, and the same is true of the other arts and sciences. But rhetoric we look upon as the power of observing the means of persuasion on almost any subject presented to us; and that is why we say that, in its technical character, it is not concerned with any special or definite class of subjects.

Of the modes of persuasion some belong strictly to the art of rhetoric and some do not. By the latter I mean such things as are not supplied by the speaker but are there at the outset—witnesses, evidence given under torture, written contracts, and so on. By the former I mean such as we can ourselves construct by means of the principles of rhetoric. The one kind has merely to be used, the other has to be invented.

1356ᵃ　Of the modes of persuasion furnished by the spoken word there are three kinds. The first kind depends on the personal character of the speaker; the second on putting the audience into a certain frame of mind; the third

---

[1] . . . ['Rhetorician,'] in fact, can mean either a *trained speaker* or a *tricky speaker*.

on the proof, or apparent proof, provided by the words of the speech itself. Persuasion is achieved by the speaker's personal character when the speech is so spoken as to make us think him credible. We believe good men more fully and more readily than others: this is true generally whatever the question is, and absolutely true where exact certainty is impossible and opinions are divided. This kind of persuasion, like the others, should be achieved by what the speaker says, not by what people think of this character before he begins to speak. It is not true, as some writers assume in their treatises on rhetoric, that the personal goodness revealed by the speaker contributes nothing to his power of persuasion; on the contrary, his character may almost be called the most effective means of persuasion he possesses. Secondly, persuasion may come through the hearers, when the speech stirs their emotions. Our judgements when we are pleased and friendly are not the same as when we are pained and hostile. It is towards producing these effects, as we maintain, that present-day writers on rhetoric direct the whole of their efforts. This subject shall be treated in detail when we come to speak of the emotions.[1] Thirdly, persuasion is effected through the speech itself when we have proved a truth or an apparent truth by means of the persuasive arguments suitable to the case in question.

There are, then, these three means of effecting persuasion. The man who is to be in command of them must, it is clear, be able (1) to reason logically, (2) to understand human character and goodness in their various forms, and (3) to understand the emotions—that is, to name them and describe them, to know their causes and the way in which they are excited. It thus appears that rhetoric is an offshoot of dialectic and also of ethical studies. Ethical studies may fairly be called political; and for this reason rhetoric masquerades as political science, and the professors of it as political experts—sometimes from want of education, sometimes from ostentation, sometimes owing to other human failings. As a matter of fact, it is a branch

---

[1] ii, cc. 2-11.

of dialectic and similar to it, as we said at the outset.[1] Neither rhetoric nor dialectic is the scientific study of any one separate subject: both are faculties for providing arguments. This is perhaps a sufficient account of their 35 scope and of how they are related to each other.

With regard to the persuasion achieved by proof or 1356[b] apparent proof: just as in dialectic there is induction on the one hand and syllogism or apparent syllogism on the other, so it is in rhetoric. The example is an induction, the enthymeme is a syllogism, and the apparent enthymeme is an apparent syllogism. I call the enthymeme a rhetorical 5 syllogism, and the example a rhetorical induction. Every one who effects persuasion through proof does in fact use either enthymemes or examples: there is no other way. And since every one who proves anything at all is bound to use either syllogisms or inductions (and this is clear to us from the *Analytics*[2]), it must follow that enthymemes 10 are syllogisms and examples are inductions. The difference between example and enthymeme is made plain by the passages in the *Topics*[3] where induction and syllogism have already been discussed. When we base the proof of a proposition on a number of similar cases, this is induction in dialectic, example in rhetoric; when it is shown 15 that, certain propositions being true, a further and quite distinct proposition must also be true in consequence, whether invariably or usually,' this is called syllogism in dialectic, enthymeme in rhetoric. It is plain also that each of these types of oratory has its advantages. Types of oratory, I say: for what has been said in the *Methodics*[4] 20 applies equally well here; in some oratorical styles examples prevail, in others enthymemes; and in like manner, some orators are better at the former and some at the latter. Speeches that rely on examples are as persuasive as the other kind, but those which rely on enthymemes excite the louder applause. The sources of examples and enthy-

---

[1] i. 1. 1354[a]1.
[2] *Anal. Pr.* ii. 23, 24; *Anal. Post.* i. 1. Cp. 68[b]13.
[3] *Top.* i. 1 and 12.
[4] lost logical treatise of Aristotle. . . .

memes,[1] and their proper uses, we will discuss later.[2] Our 25 next step is to define the processes themselves more clearly.

A statement is persuasive and credible either because it is directly self-evident or because it appears to be proved from other statements that are so. In either case it is persuasive because there is somebody whom it persuades. But none of the arts theorize about individual cases. Medicine, for instance, does not theorize about what will help to cure Socrates or Callias, but only about what will help 30 to cure any or all of a given class of patients: this alone is its business: individual cases are so infinitely various that no systematic knowledge of them is possible. In the same way the theory of rhetoric is concerned not with what seems probable to a given individual like Socrates or Hippias, but with what seems probable to men of a given type; and this is true of dialectic also. Dialectic does not 35 construct its syllogisms out of any haphazard materials, such as the fancies of crazy people, but out of materials that call for discussion; and rhetoric, too, draws upon the regular subjects of debate. The duty of rhetoric is to deal 1357ᵃ with such matters as we deliberate upon without arts or systems to guide us, in the hearing of persons who cannot take in at a glance a complicated argument, or follow a long chain of reasoning. The subjects of our deliberation are such as seem to present us with alternative possibil- 5 ities: about things that could not have been, and cannot now or in the future be, other than they are, nobody who takes them to be of this nature wastes his time in deliberation.

It is possible to form syllogisms and draw conclusions from the results of previous syllogisms; or, on the other hand, from premisses which have not been thus proved, and at the same time are so little accepted that they call 10 for proof. Reasonings of the former kind will necessarily be hard to follow owing to their length, for we assume an audience of untrained thinkers; those of the latter kind

---

[1] [An alternate and perhaps better reading would be 'the reason of this.']
[2] ii, cc. 20-4.

will fail to win assent, because they are based on premisses that are not generally admitted or believed.

The enthymeme and the example must, then, deal with 15 what is in the main contingent, the example being an induction, and the enthymeme a syllogism, about such matters. The enthymeme must consist of few propositions, fewer often than those which make up the normal syllogism. For if any of these propositions is a familiar fact, there is no need even to mention it; the hearer adds it himself. Thus, to show that Dorieus has been victor in a 20 contest for which the prize is a crown, it is enough to say 'For he has been victor in the Olympic games', without adding 'And in the Olympic games the prize is a crown', a fact which everybody knows.

There are few facts of the 'necessary' type that can form the basis of rhetorical syllogisms.[1] Most of the things about which we make decisions, and into which therefore 25 we inquire, present us with alternative possibilities. For it is about our actions that we deliberate and inquire, and all our actions have a contingent character; hardly any of them are detennined by necessity. Again, conclusions that state what is merely usual or possible must be drawn from premisses that do the same, just as 'necessary' conclusions must be drawn from 'necessary' premisses; this too is clear 30 to us from the *Analytics*.[2] It is evident, therefore, that the propositions forming the basis of enthymemes, though some of them may be 'necessary', will most of them be only usually true. Now the materials of enthymemes are Probabilities and Signs, which we can see must correspond respectively with the propositions that are generally and those that are necessarily true. A Probability is a thing 35 that usually happens; not, however, as some definitions would suggest, anything whatever that usually happens, but only if it belongs to the class of the 'contingent' or 'variable'. It bears the same relation to that in respect of which it is probable[3] as the universal bears to the particu-

---

[1] ['Material sources' or even 'premisses.']

[2] *An. Pr.* i. 8, 12-14, 27.

[3] i.e. bears the same relation to the conclusion to be reached: 'to that to which its general probability is directed'—to the particular probable case which has to be proved.

lar. Of Signs, one kind bears the same relation to the state- 1357ᵇ
ment it supports as the particular bears to the universal,
the other the same as the universal bears to the particular.
The infallible kind is a 'complete proof' (τεκμήριον); the
fallible kind has no specific name. By infallible signs I
mean those on which syllogisms proper may be based: and 5
this shows us why this kind of Sign is called 'complete
proof': when people think that what they have said cannot
be refuted, they then think that they are bringing forward
a 'complete proof', meaning that the matter has now been
demonstrated and completed (πεπερασμένον); for the word
πέρας has the same meaning (of 'end' or 'boundary') as the
word τέκμαρ in the ancient tongue. Now the one kind of 10
Sign (that which bears to the proposition it supports the
relation of particular to universal) may be illustrated thus.
Suppose it were said, 'The fact that Socrates was wise and
just is a sign that the wise are just'. Here we certainly
have a Sign; but even though the proposition be true, the
argument is refutable, since it does not form a syllogism.
Suppose, on the other hand, it were said, 'The fact that he
has a fever is a sign that he is ill', or, 'The fact that she is 15
giving milk is a sign that she has lately borne a child'.
Here we have the infallible kind of Sign, the only kind that
constitutes a complete proof, since it is the only kind that,
if the particular statement is true, is irrefutable. The other
kind of Sign, that which bears to the proposition it supports the relation of universal to particular, might be illustrated by saying, 'The fact that he breathes fast is a sign
that he has a fever'. This argument also is refutable,
even if the statement about the fast breathing be true, 20
since a man may breathe hard without having a fever.

It has, then, been stated above what is the nature of
a Probability, of a Sign, and of a complete proof, and what
are the differences between them. In the *Analytics*[1] a more
explicit description has been given of these points; it is
there shown why some of these reasonings can be put into
syllogisms and some cannot.

The 'example' has already been described as one kind 25
of induction; and the special nature of the subject-matter

[1] *An. Pr.* ii. 27.

that distinguishes it from the other kinds has also been
stated above. Its relation to the proposition it supports is
not that of part to whole, nor whole to part, nor whole to
whole, but of part to part, or like to like. When two statements are of the same order, but one is more familiar than
30 the other, the former is an 'example'. The argument may,
for instance, be that Dionysius,[1] in asking as he does for
a bodyguard, is scheming to make himself a despot. For
in the past Peisistratus[2] kept asking for a bodyguard in
order to carry out such a scheme, and did make himself
a despot as soon as he got it; and so did Theagenes[3] at
Megara; and in the same way all other instances known
to the speaker are made into examples, in order to show
35 what is not yet known, that Dionysius has the same purpose in making the same request: all these being instances
of the one general principle, that a man who asks for a
1358ᵃ bodyguard is scheming to make himself a despot. We have
now described the sources of those means of persuasion
which are popularly supposed to be demonstrative.

There is an important distinction between two sorts of
enthymemes that has been wholly overlooked by almost
everybody—one that also subsists between the syllogisms
treated of in dialectic. One sort of enthymeme really be-
5 longs to rhetoric, as one sort of syllogism really belongs
to dialectic; but the other sort really belongs to other arts
and faculties, whether to those we already exercise or to
those we have not yet acquired. Missing this distinction,
people fail to notice that the more correctly they handle
their particular subject the further they are getting away
from pure rhetoric or dialectic. This statement will be
10 clearer if expressed more fully. I mean that the proper
subjects of dialectical and rhetorical syllogisms are the
things with which we say the regular or universal Lines of
Argument[4] are concerned, that is to say those lines of
argument that apply equally to questions of right conduct,
natural science, politics, and many other things that have

[1] [Tyrant of Syracuse.]
[2] [Tyrant of Athens.]
[3] [Tyrant of Megara.]
[4] Or Topics, Commonplaces.

nothing to do with one another. Take, for instance, the
line of argument concerned with 'the more or less'.[1] On
this line of argument it is equally easy to base a syllogism 15
or enthymeme about any of what nevertheless are essentially disconnected subjects—right conduct, natural science, or anything else whatever. But there are also those
special Lines of Argument which are based on such propositions as apply only to particular groups or classes of
things. Thus there are propositions about natural science
on which it is impossible to base any enthymeme or syllogism about ethics, and other propositions about ethics on
which nothing can be based about natural science. The 20
same principle applies throughout. The general Lines of
Argument have no special subject-matter, and therefore
will not increase our understanding of any particular class
of things. On the other hand, the better the selection one
makes of propositions suitable for special Lines of Argument, the nearer one comes, unconsciously, to setting up
a science that is distinct from dialectic and rhetoric. One
may succeed in stating the required principles, but one's 25
science will be no longer dialectic or rhetoric, but the science to which the principles thus discovered belong. Most
enthymemes are in fact based upon these particular or
special Lines of Argument; comparatively few on the common or general kind. As in the *Topics*,[2] therefore, so in
this work, we must distinguish. in dealing with enthymemes, the special and the general Lines of Argument on
which they are to be founded. By special Lines of Argument I mean the propositions peculiar to each several
class of things, by general those common to all classes
alike. We may begin with the special Lines of Argument.
But, first of all, let us classify rhetoric into its varieties.
Having distinguished these we may deal with them one by
one, and try to discover the elements of which each is
composed, and the propositions each must employ.   35

3   Rhetoric falls into three divisions, determined by the
    three classes of listeners to speeches. For of the three

---

[1] i.e. the topic of *degree*. [Cp. 1397[b]12 ff.]
[2] Cp. *Top.* i. 10, 14; iii. 5; *Soph. El.* 9.

elements in speech-making—speaker, subject, and person
addressed—it is the last one, the hearer, that determines
1358ᵇ the speech's end and object. The hearer must be either a
judge, with a decision to make about things past or future,
or an observer.[1] A member of the assembly decides about
5 future events, a juryman about past events: while those
who merely decide on the orator's skill are observers. From
this it follows that there are three divisions of oratory—
(1) political, (2) forensic, and (3) the ceremonial oratory
of display.[2]

Political speaking urges us either to do or not to do
something: one of these two courses is always taken by
private counsellors, as well as by men who address public
10 assemblies. Forensic speaking either attacks or defends
somebody: one or other of these two things must always
be done by the parties in a case. The ceremonial oratory
of display either praises or censures somebody. These
three kinds of rhetoric refer to three different kinds of
time. The political orator is concerned with the future: it
15 is about things to be done hereafter that he advises, for or
against. The party in a case at law is concerned with the
past; one man accuses the other, and the other defends
himself, with reference to things already done. The
ceremonial orator is, properly speaking, concerned with
the present, since all men praise or blame in view of the
state of things existing at the time, though they often find
20 it useful also to recall the past and to makes guesses at
the future.

Rhetoric has three distinct ends in view, one for each
of its three kinds. The political orator aims at establish-

---

[1] θεωρός: a mere onlooker, present at a show, where he
decides no grave political or legal issue (cp. 1391ᵇ16-20)
and plays no higher role than that of speech taster or
oratorical connoisseur.—*Political* has been preferred to
deliberative, as being clearer to the English reader. The
oratory of the '(parliamentary) counsellor' is meant.

[2] Or: deliberative (advisory), legal, and epideictic—the
oratory respectively of parliamentary assemblies, of law-
courts, and of ceremonial occasions when there is an element of 'display,' 'show,' 'declamation,' and the result
is a "set speech' or 'harangue.'

ing the expediency or the harmfulness of a proposed course of action; if he urges its acceptance, he does so on the ground that it will do good; if he urges its rejection, he does so on the ground that it will do harm; and all other points, such as whether the proposal is just or unjust, honourable or dishonourable, he brings in as subsidiary 25 and relative to this main consideration. Parties in a law-case aim at establishing the justice or injustice of some action, and they too bring in all other points as subsidiary and relative to this one. Those who praise or attack a man aim at proving him worthy of honour or the reverse, and they too treat all other considerations with reference to this one.

That the three kinds of rhetoric do aim respectively at the three ends we have mentioned is shown by the fact 30 that speakers will sometimes not try to establish anything else. Thus, the litigant will sometimes not deny that a thing has happened or that he has done harm. But that he is guilty of injustice he will never admit; otherwise there would be no need of a trial. So too, political orators often make any concession short of admitting that they are recommending their hearers to take an inexpedient course 35 or not to take an expedient one. The question whether it is not *unjust* for a city to enslave its innocent neighbours often does not trouble them at all. In like manner those who praise or censure a man do not consider whether 1359ᵃ his acts have been expedient or not, but often make it a ground of actual praise that he has neglected his own interest to do what was honourable. Thus, they praise Achilles because he championed his fallen friend Patroclus, though he knew that this meant death, and that otherwise he need not die: yet while to die thus was the nobler thing for him to do, the expedient thing was to live on.[1]   5

It is evident from what has been said that it is these three subjects, more than any others, about which the orator must be able to have propositions at his command. Now the propositions of Rhetoric are Complete Proofs, Probabilities, and Signs. Every kind of syllogism is composed of propositions, and the enthymeme is a particular 10

---

[1] Homer. *Iliad*, xviii. 97 ﬀ.

kind of syllogism composed of the aforesaid propositions.[1]

Since only possible actions, and not impossible ones, can ever have been done in the past or the present, and since things which have not occurred, or will not occur, also cannot have been done or be going to be done, it is neces-
15 sary for the political, the forensic, and the ceremonial speaker alike to be able to have at their command propositions about the possible and the impossible, and about whether a thing has or has not occurred, will or will not occur. Further, all men, in giving praise or blame, in urging us to accept or reject proposals for action, in accusing others or defending themselves, attempt not only
20 to prove the points mentioned but also to show that the good or the harm, the honour or disgrace, the justice or injustice, is great or small, either absolutely or relatively; and therefore it is plain that we must also have at our command propositions about greatness or smallness and the greater or the lesser—propositions both universal and particular. Thus, we must be able to say which is the
25 greater or lesser good, the greater or lesser act of justice or injustice; and so on.

Such, then, are the subjects regarding which we are inevitably bound to master the propositions relevant to them. We must now discuss each particular class of these subjects in turn, namely those dealt with in political, in ceremonial, and lastly in legal, oratory.

30 First, then, we must ascertain what are the kinds of *4* things, good or bad, about which the political orator offers counsel. For he does not deal with all things, but only with such as may or may not take place. Concerning things which exist or will exist inevitably, or which cannot possibly exist or take place, no counsel can be given. Nor, again, can counsel be given about the whole class of things which may or may not take place; for this class includes
35 some good things that occur naturally, and some that occur by accident; and about these it is useless to offer counsel.

---

[1] i.e. of Complete Proofs, Probabilities, and Signs relating to the three subjects of the expedient, the just, and the noble.

Clearly counsel can only be given on matters about which
people deliberate; matters, namely, that ultimately depend
on ourselves, and which we have it in our power to set
going. For we turn a thing over in our mind until we have
reached the point of seeing whether we can do it or not.   1359ᵇ

Now to enumerate and classify accurately the usual
subjects of public business, and further to frame, as far as
possible, true definitions of them, is a task which we must
not attempt on the present occasion. For it does not belong 5
to the art of rhetoric, but to a more instructive art and a
more real branch of knowledge;[1] and as it is, rhetoric has
been given a far wider subject-matter than strictly belongs
to it. The truth is, as indeed we have said already, that
rhetoric is a combination of the science of logic and of 10
the ethical branch of politics;[2] and it is partly like dialectic, partly like sophistical reasoning. But the more we try
to make either dialectic or rhetoric not, what they really
are, practical faculties, but sciences, the more we shall
inadvertently be destroying their true nature; for we shall 15
be re-fashioning them and shall be passing into the region
of sciences dealing with definite subjects rather than
simply with words and forms of reasoning. Even here,
however, we will mention those points which it is of
practical importance to distinguish, their fuller treatment
falling naturally to political science.

The main matters on which all men deliberate and on
which political speakers make speeches are some five in 20
number: ways and means, war and peace, national defence, imports and exports, and legislation.

As to Ways and Means, then, the intending speaker will
need to know the number and extent of the country's
sources of revenue, so that, if any is being overlooked, it 25
may be added, and, if any is defective, it may be increased. Further, he should know all the expenditure of
the country, in order that, if any part of it is superfluous,
it may be abolished, or, if any is too large, it may be
reduced. For men become richer not only by increasing
their existing wealth but also by reducing their expendi-

[1] [To political science.]
[2] [i.e. of ethical theory. Cp. I. 2 1356ᵃ25 ff.]

30 ture. A comprehensive view of these questions cannot be gained solely from experience in home affairs; in order to advise on such matters a man must be keenly interested in the methods worked out in other lands.

As to Peace and War, he must know the extent of the military strength of his country, both actual and potential,
35 and also the nature of that actual and potential strength; and further, what wars his country has waged, and how it has waged them. He must know these facts not only about his own country, but also about neighbouring countries; and also about countries with which war is likely, in order that peace may be maintained with those stronger than his own, and that his own may have power to make war
1360ᵃ or not against those that are weaker. He should know, too, whether the military power of another country is like or unlike that of his own; for this is a matter that may affect their relative strength. With the same end in view he must, besides, have studied the wars of other countries as well as those of his own, and the way they ended; similar
5 causes are likely to have similar results.

With regard to National Defence: he ought to know all about the methods of defence in actual use, such as the strength and character of the defensive force and the positions of the forts—this last means that he must be well acquainted with the lie of the country—in order that a
10 garrison may be increased if it is too small or removed if it is not wanted, and that the strategic points may be guarded with special care.

With regard to the Food Supply: he must know what outlay will meet the needs of his country; what kinds of food are produced at home and what imported; and what articles must be exported or imported. This last he must know in order that agreements and commercial treaties
15 may be made with the countries concerned. There are, indeed, two sorts of state to which he must see that his countrymen give no cause for offence, states stronger than his own, and states with which it is advantageous to trade.

But while he must, for security's sake, be able to take all this into account, he must before all things understand the subject of legislation; for it is on a country's laws that its whole welfare depends. He must, therefore, know how 20 many different forms of constitution there are; under what conditions each of these will prosper and by what internal developments or external attacks each of them tends to be destroyed. When I speak of destruction through internal developments I refer to the fact that all constitutions, except the best one of all, are destroyed both by not being pushed far enough and by being pushed too far. Thus, democracy loses its vigour, and finally passes into 25 oligarchy, not only when it is not pushed far enough, but also when it is pushed a great deal too far;[1] just as the aquiline and the snub nose not only turn into normal noses by not being aquiline or snub enough, but also by being too violently aquiline or snub arrive at a condition in which they no longer look like noses at all.

It is useful, in framing laws, not only to study the past 30 history of one's own country, in order to understand which constitution is desirable for it now, but also to have a knowledge of the constitutions of other nations, and so to learn for what kinds of nation the various kinds of constitution are suited. From this we can see that books of travel are useful aids to legislation, since from these we may learn the laws and customs of different races. The 35 political speaker will also find the researches of historians useful. But all this is the business of political science and not of rhetoric.

These, then, are the most important kinds of information which the political speaker must possess. Let us now 1360[b] go back and state the premises from which he will have to argue in favour of adopting or rejecting measures regarding these and other matters.

5 It may be said that every individual man and all men in common aim at a certain end which determines what 5 they choose and what they avoid. This end, to sum it up briefly, is happiness and its constituents. Let us, then, by way of illustration only, ascertain what is in general the

---

[1] [Aristotle deals more fully with the causes by which constitutions are destroyed or changed into one another in Book V of his *Politics*.]

nature of happiness, and what are the elements of its constituent parts. For all advice to do things or not to do 10 them is concerned with happiness and with the things that make for or against it; whatever creates or increases happiness or some part of happiness, we ought to do; whatever destroys or hampers happiness, or gives rise to its opposite, we ought not to do.[1]

We may define happiness as prosperity combined with 15 virtue; or as independence of life; or as the secure enjoyment of the maximum of pleasure; or as a good condition of property and body, together with the power of guarding one's property and body and making use of them. That happiness is one or more of these things, pretty well everybody agrees.

From this definition of happiness it follows that its con- 20 stituent parts are:—good birth, plenty of friends, good friends, wealth, good children, plenty of children, a happy old age, also such bodily excellences as health, beauty, strength, large stature, athletic powers, together with fame, honour, good luck, and virtue. A man cannot fail to 25 be completely independent if he possesses these internal and these external goods; for besides these there are no others to have. (Goods of the soul and of the body are internal. Good birth, friends, money, and honour are external.) Further, we think that he should possess resources and luck, in order to make his life really secure. As we have already ascertained what happiness in general 30 is, so now let us try to ascertain what each of these parts of it is.

Now good birth in a race or a state means that its members are indigenous or ancient;[2] that its earliest leaders were distinguished men, and that from them have sprung many who were distinguished for qualities that we admire.

The good birth of an individual, which may come either from the male or the female side, implies that both parents 35 are free citizens, and that, as in the case of the state, the

---

[1] [For a more philosophic discussion of 'happiness' see Book I of the *Nicomachean Ethics*.]

[2] [A matter of great pride especially for the Athenians.]

founders of the line have been notable for virtue or wealth or something else which is highly prized, and that many distinguished persons belong to the family, men and women, young and old.

The phrases 'possession of good children' and 'of many children' bear a quite clear meaning. Applied to a community, they mean that its young men are numerous and of good quality: good in regard to bodily excellences, 1361ᵃ such as stature, beauty, strength, athletic powers; and also in regard to the excellences of the soul, which in a young man are temperance and courage. Applied to an individual, they mean that his own children are numerous and 5 have the good qualities we have described. Both male and female are here included; the excellences of the latter are, in body, beauty and stature; in soul, self-command and an industry that is not sordid. Communities as well as individuals should lack none of these perfections, in their 10 women as well as in their men. Where, as among the Lacedaemonians, the state of women is bad, almost half of human life is spoilt.

The constituents of wealth are: plenty of coined money and territory; the ownership of numerous, large, and beautiful estates; also the ownership of numerous and beautiful implements, live stock, and slaves. All these kinds of property are our own, are secure, gentlemanly, 15 and useful. The useful kinds are those that are productive, the gentlemanly kinds are those that provide enjoyment. By 'productive' I mean those from which we get our income; by 'enjoyable', those from which we get nothing worth mentioning except the use of them. The criterion of 'security' is the ownership of property in such places and under such conditions that the use of it is in our 20 power; and it is 'our own' if it is in our own power to dispose of it or keep it. By 'disposing of it' I mean giving it away or selling it. Wealth as a whole consists in using things rather than in owning them; it is really the activity —that is, the use—of property that constitutes wealth.

Fame means being respected by everybody, or having 25 some quality that is desired by all men, or by most, or by the good, or by the wise.

Honour is the token of a man's being famous for doing good. It is chiefly and most properly paid to those who have already done good; but also to the man who can do
30 good in future. Doing good refers either to the preservation of life and the means of life, or to wealth, or to some other of the good things which it is hard to get either always or at that particular place or time—for many gain honour for things which seem small, but the place and the occasion account for it. The constituents of honour are:
35 sacrifices; commemoration, in verse or prose; privileges; grants of land; front seats at civic celebrations; state burial;[1] statues; public maintenance;[2] among foreigners, obeisances and giving place; and such presents as are among various bodies of men regarded as marks of honour. For a present is not only the bestowal of a piece of property, but also a token of honour; which explains why honour-loving as well as money-loving persons desire it.
1361[b] The present brings to both what they want; it is a piece of property, which is what the lovers of money desire; and it brings honour, which is what the lovers of honour desire.

The excellence of the body is health; that is, a condition which allows us, while keeping free from disease, to have the use of our bodies; for many people are 'healthy'
5 as we are told Herodicus[3] was; and these no one can congratulate on their 'health', for they have to abstain from everything or nearly everything that men do.—Beauty varies with the time of life. In a young man beauty is the possession of a body fit to endure the exertion of running and of contests of strength; which means that he is pleas-
10 ant to look at; and therefore all-round athletes are the most beautiful, being naturally adapted both for contests of strength and for speed also. For a man in his prime, beauty is fitness for the exertion of warfare, together with a pleasant but at the same time formidable appearance. For an old man, it is to be strong enough for such exertion

---

[1] Or, (splendid) tombs; sepulchres.
[2] 'Pensions.'
[3] [A physician. His strange health regime is described in Plato, *Republic*, iii 406[a] ff.]

as is necessary, and to be free from all those deformities
of old age which cause pain to others.[1] Strength is the 15
power of moving some one else at will; to do this, you
must either pull, push, lift, pin, or grip him; thus you must
be strong in all of those ways or at least in some. Excellence in size is to surpass ordinary people in height, thick-
ness, and breadth by just as much as will not make one's 20
movements slower in consequence. Athletic excellence of
the body consists in size, strength, and swiftness; swiftness
implying strength. He who can fling forward his legs in
a certain way, and move them fast and far, is good at
running; he who can grip and hold down is good at
wrestling; he who can drive an adversary from his ground 25
with the right blow is a good boxer: he who can do both
the last is a good pancratiast, while he who can do all is
an 'all-round' athlete.

Happiness in old age is the coming of old age slowly
and painlessly; for a man has not this happiness if he
grows old either quickly, or tardily but painfully. It arises
both from the excellences of the body and from good luck.
If a man is not free from disease, or if he is not strong, he
will not be free from suffering; nor can he continue to 30
live a long and painless life unless he has good luck. There
is, indeed, a capacity for long life that is quite independent of health or strength; for many people live long
who lack the excellences of the body; but for our present
purpose there is no use in going into the details of this.

The terms 'possession of many friends' and 'possession 35
of good friends' need no explanation; for we define a
'friend' as one who will always try, for your sake, to do
what he takes to be good for you. The man towards whom
many feel thus has many friends; if these are worthy men,
he has good friends.

'Good luck' means the acquisition or possession of all or
most, or the most important, of those good things which
are due to luck. Some of the things that are due to luck 1362ª
may also be due to artificial contrivance; but many are independent of art, as for example those which are due to
nature—though, to be sure, things due to luck may

[1] [Text and meaning uncertain.]

actually be contrary to nature. Thus health may be due to
artificial contrivance, but beauty and stature are due to
5 nature. All such good things as excite envy are, as a class,
the outcome of good luck. Luck is also the cause of good
things that happen contrary to reasonable expectation: as
when, for instance, all your brothers are ugly, but you are
handsome yourself; or when you find a treasure that everybody else has overlooked; or when a missile hits the next
man and misses you; or when you are the only man not to
10 go to a place you have gone to regularly, while the others
go there for the first time and are killed. All such things
are reckoned pieces of good luck.

As to virtue, it is most closely connected with the subject of Eulogy, and therefore we will wait to define it
until we come to discuss that subject.[1]

15 It is now plain what our aims, future or actual, should 6
be in urging, and what in deprecating, a proposal; the
latter being the opposite of the former. Now the political
or deliberative orator's aim is utility: deliberation seeks
to determine not ends but the means to ends, i.e. what it
20 is most useful to do. Further, utility is a good thing. We
ought therefore to assure ourselves of the main facts about
Goodness and Utility in general.

We may define a good thing as that which ought to be
chosen for its own sake; or as that for the sake of which
we choose something else; or as that which is sought after
by all things, or by all things that have sensation or reason,
or which will be sought after by any things that acquire
25 reason; or as that which must be prescribed for a given
individual by reason generally, or is prescribed for him
by his individual reason, this being his individual good;
or as that whose presence brings anything into a satisfactory and self-sufficing condition; or as self-sufficiency;
or as what produces, maintains, or entails characteristics
of this kind, while preventing and destroying their oppo-
30 sites. One thing may entail another in either of two ways
—(1) simultaneously, (2) subsequently. Thus learning
entails knowledge subsequently, health entails life simul-

[1] i, c. 9.

taneously. Things are productive of other things in three
senses: first, as being healthy produces health; secondly,
as food produces health; and thirdly, as exercise does—
i.e. it does so usually. All this being settled, we now see
that both the acquisition of good things and the removal
of bad things must be good; the latter entails freedom 35
from the evil things simultaneously, while the former
entails possession of the good things subsequently. The
acquisition of a greater in place of a lesser good, or of a
lesser in place of a greater evil, is also good, for in proportion as the greater exceeds the lesser there is acquisition of 1362^b
good or removal of evil.[1] The virtues, too, must be something good; for it is by possessing these that we are in a
good condition, and they tend to produce good works and
good actions. They must be severally named and described 5
elsewhere.[2] Pleasure, again, must be a good thing, since
it is the nature of all animals to aim at it. Consequently
both pleasant and beautiful things must be good things,
since the former are productive of pleasure, while of the
beautiful things some are pleasant and some desirable in
and for themselves.

The following is a more detailed list of things that must 10
be good. Happiness, as being desirable in itself and sufficient by itself, and as being that for whose sake we choose
many other things. Also justice, courage, temperance,
magnanimity,[3] magnificence, and all such qualities, as
being excellences of the soul.[4] Further, health, beauty, and
the like, as being bodily excellences and productive of 15
many other good things: for instance, health is productive
both of pleasure and of life, and therefore is thought the
greatest of goods, since these two things which it causes,

---

[1] . . . Other readings are (1) . . . 'for the difference between the greater and the lesser constitutes acquisition
of good in the one case and removal of evil in the other';
and (2) . . . 'for the acquisition and the removal of the
difference between the greater and the lesser amount to
the acquisition of good and the removal of evil respectively.'

[2] . . . 'separately'; in c. 9.

[3] i.e. loftiness of mind, greatness of spirit.

[4] As such they are treated in the *Nicomachean Ethics*.

pleasure and life, are two of the things most highly prized
by ordinary people. Wealth, again: for it is the excellence
of possession, and also productive of many other good
things. Friends and friendship: for a friend is desirable in
20 himself and also productive of many other good things.
So, too, honour and reputation, as being pleasant, and
productive of many other good things, and usually accompanied by the presence of the good things that cause them
to be bestowed. The faculty of speech and action; since all
such qualities are productive of what is good. Further—
good parts, strong memory, receptiveness, quickness of
25 intuition, and the like, for all such faculties are productive
of what is good. Similarly, all the sciences and arts. And
life: since, even if no other good were the result of life,
it is desirable in itself. And justice, as the cause of good to
the community.

The above are pretty well all the things admittedly
good. In dealing with things whose goodness is disputed,
30 we may argue in the following ways:—That is good of
which the contrary is bad. That is good the contrary of
which is to the advantage of our enemies; for example, if
it is to the particular advantage of our enemies that we
should be cowards, clearly courage is of particular value
to our countrymen. And generally, the contrary of that
which our enemies desire, or of that at which they re-
35 joice, is evidently valuable. Hence the passage beginning:

Surely would Priam exult.[1]

This principle usually holds good, but not always, since
it may well be that our interest is sometimes the same as
that of our enemies. Hence it is said that 'evils draw men
1363[a] together'; that is, when the same thing is hurtful to them
both.

Further: that which is not in excess is good,[2] and that
which is greater than it should be is bad. That also is good

[1] [Sc., if he learned of the Greeks' quarrels amongst themselves.] *Iliad*, i. 255.—The verse-translations throughout
are by Dr. A. S. Way, with occasional adaptations.—
Aristotle, like other Greek writers, often indicates, as
here, a whole passage by a few words taken from it.
[2] . . . The 'mean' is meant.

on which much labour or money has been spent; the mere
fact of this makes it seem good, and such a good is
assumed to be an end—an end reached through a long
chain of means; and any end is a good. Hence the lines 5
beginning:

> And for Priam ⟨and Troy-town's folk⟩ should they
>   leave behind them a boast;[1]

and

>   Oh, it were shame
> To have tarried so long and return empty-handed as
>   erst we came;[2]

and there is also the proverb about 'breaking the pitcher
at the door'.

That which most people seek after, and which is obviously an object of contention, is also a good; for, as has
been shown,[3] that is good which is sought after by everybody, and 'most people' is taken to be equivalent to 'everybody'. That which is praised is good, since no one 10
praises what is not good. So, again, that which is praised
by our enemies [or by the worthless]; for when even those
who have a grievance think a thing good, it is at once felt
that every one must agree with them; our enemies can
admit the fact only because it is evident, just as those must
be worthless whom their friends censure and their enemies
do not. (For this reason the Corinthians conceived them- 15
selves to be insulted by Simonides when he wrote:

> Against the Corinthians hath Ilium no complaint.[4])

Again, that is good which has been distinguished by the
favour of a discerning or virtuous man or woman, as
Odysseus was distinguished by Athena, Helen by Theseus,
Paris by the goddesses, and Achilles by Homer. And,
generally speaking, all things are good which men deliberately choose to do; this will include the things already

---

[1] *Iliad*, ii. 160.
[2] *Illiad*, ii. 298.
[3] 1362ª23.
[4] [Fragm. of Simonides of Keos, famous poet of choral
lyrics (556-468 B.C.)]

20 mentioned, and also whatever may be bad for their
enemies or good for their friends, and at the same time
practicable. Things are 'practicable' in two senses: (1) it is
possible to do them, (2) it is easy to do them. Things are
done 'easily' when they are done either without pain or
quickly: the 'difficulty' of an act lies either in its painful-
ness or in the long time it takes. Again, a thing is good [1]
25 if it is as men wish; and they wish to have either no evil
at all or at least a balance of good over evil. This last will
happen where the penalty is either imperceptible or slight.
Good, too, are things that are a man's very own, possessed
by no one else, exceptional; for this increases the credit of
having them.[2] So are things which befit the possessors,
such as whatever is appropriate to their birth or capacity,
and whatever they feel they ought to have but lack—such
30 things may indeed be trifling, but none the less men deliberately make them the goal of their action. And things
easily effected; for these are practicable (in the sense of
being easy); such things are those in which every one, or
most people, or one's equals, or one's inferiors have succeeded. Good also are the things by which we shall gratify
our friends or annoy our enemies: and the things chosen
35 by those whom we admire: and the things for which we
are fitted by nature or experience, since we think we shall
succeed more easily in these: and those in which no worthless man can succeed, for such things bring greater praise:
and those which we do in fact desire, for what we desire
is taken to be not only pleasant but also better. Further,
1363ᵇ a man of a given disposition makes chiefly for the corresponding things: lovers of victory make for victory,
lovers of honour for honour, money-loving men for money,
and so with the rest. These, then, are the sources from
which we must derive our means of persuasion about
Good and Utility.

5   Since, however, it often happens that people agree that 7
two things are both useful but do not agree about which

---

[1] Or perhaps better, 'Men deliberately choose a thing if it
is. . . .'
[2] Or, 'the value put upon them' (sc. by their possessor).

is the more so, the next step will be to treat of relative
goodness and relative utility.

A thing which surpasses another may be regarded as
being that other thing plus something more, and that other
thing which is surpassed as being what is contained in the
first thing. Now to call a thing 'greater' or 'more' always
implies a comparison of it with one that is 'smaller' or
'less', while 'great' and 'small', 'much' and 'little', are terms 10
used in comparison with normal magnitude. The 'great' is
that which surpasses the normal, the 'small' is that which
is surpassed by the normal; and so with 'many' and 'few'.

Now we are applying the term 'good' to what is desirable for its own sake and not for the sake of something
else;[1] to that at which all things aim; to what they would
choose if they could acquire understanding and practical
wisdom; and to that which tends to produce or preserve 15
such goods, or is always accompanied by them. Moreover,
that for the sake of which things are done is the end (an
end being that for the sake of which all else is done), and
for each individual that thing is a good which fulfils these
conditions in regard to himself. It follows, then, that a
greater number of goods is a greater good than one or
than a smaller number, if that one or that smaller number
is included in the count; for then the larger number surpasses the smaller, and the smaller quantity is surpassed 20
as being contained in the larger.

Again, if the largest member of one class surpasses the
largest member of another, then the one class surpasses
the other; and if one class surpasses another, then the
largest member of the one surpasses the largest member
of the other. Thus, if the tallest man is taller than the
tallest woman, then men in general are taller than women.
Conversely, if men in general are taller than women, then 25
the tallest man is taller than the tallest woman. For the
superiority of class over class is proportionate to the superiority possessed by their largest specimens. Again, where
one good is always accompanied by another, but does
not always accompany it, it is greater than the other,
for the use of the second thing is implied in the use of the 30

[1] Cp. 1362ᵃ24.

first. A thing may be accompanied by another in three ways, either simultaneously, subsequently, or potentially. Life accompanies health simultaneously (but not health life), knowledge accompanies the act of learning subsequently, cheating accompanies sacrilege potentially, since a man who has committed sacrilege is always capable of cheating. Again, when two things each surpass a third, that which does so by the greater amount is the greater of the two; for it must surpass the greater as well as the less of the other two. A thing productive of a greater good 35 than another is productive of is itself a greater good than that other. For this conception of 'productive of a greater' has been implied in our argument.[1] Likewise, that which is produced by a greater good is itself a greater good; thus, if what is wholesome is more desirable and a greater good than what gives pleasure, health too must be a *1364*[a] greater good than pleasure. Again, a thing which is desirable in itself is a greater good than a thing which is not desirable in itself, as for example bodily strength than what is wholesome, since the latter is not pursued for its own sake, whereas the former is; and this was our definition of the good.[2] Again, if one of two things is an end, and the other is not, the former is the greater good, as being chosen for its own sake and not for the sake of something else; as, for example, exercise is chosen for the 5 sake of physical well-being. And of two things that which stands less in need of the other, or of other things, is the greater good, since it is more self-sufficing. (That which stands 'less' in need of others is that which needs either *fewer* or *easier* things.) So when one thing does not exist or cannot come into existence without a second, while the second can exist without the first, the second is the better. That which does not need something else is more self-sufficing than that which does, and presents itself as a greater good for that reason. Again, that which is a begin-

---

[1] i.e. we have already (1363[b]15) said that what is productive of good is good; it follows, then, from our way of looking at 'productivity' and 'degree,' that what is productive of a greater good is a greater good.
[2] 1362[a]22.

ning of other things is a greater good than that which is 10
not, and that which is a cause is a greater good than that
which is not; the reason being the same in each case,
namely that without a cause and a beginning nothing can
exist or come into existence. Again, where there are two
sets of consequences arising from two different beginnings
or causes, the consequences of the more important beginning or cause are themselves the more important; and
conversely, that beginning or cause is itself the more
important which has the more important consequences. 15
Now it is plain, from all that has been said, that one thing
may be shown to be more important than another from
two opposite points of view: it may appear the more
important (1) because it is a beginning and the other
thing is not, and also (2) because it is not a beginning
and the other thing is—on the ground that the end is more
important and is not a beginning.[1] So Leodamas, when
accusing Callistratus, said that the man who prompted
the deed was more guilty than the doer, since it would 20
not have been done if he had not planned it.[2] On the
other hand, when accusing Chabrias he said that the doer
was worse than the prompter, since there would have
been no deed without some one to do it; men, said he,
plot a thing only in order to carry it out.

Further, what is rare is a greater good than what is
plentiful. Thus, gold is a better thing than iron, though
less useful: it is harder to get, and therefore better worth 25
getting. Reversely, it may be argued that the plentiful is
a better thing than the rare, because we can make more
use of it. For what is often useful surpasses what is seldom
useful, whence the saying

---

[1] We might perhaps expect 'on the ground that it is the
end, not the beginning, that matters' . . .

[2] [Leodamas of Acharnae, a famous orator of the 4th
century; Callistratus of Aphidna also a distinguished
Athenian orator and politician. His accusation by Leodamas
here mentioned seems to have been directed against his
conduct in the affairs of Oropus in 366 B.C. in which he
was associated with Chabrias, an Athenian general, and
with him was brought to trial.]

The best of things is water.[1]

More generally: the hard thing is better than the easy,
because it is rarer: and reversely, the easy thing is better
30 than the hard, for it is as we wish it to be. That is the
greater good whose contrary is the greater evil, and whose
loss affects us more. Positive goodness and badness are
more important than the mere *absence* of goodness and
badness: for positive goodness and badness are ends,
which the mere absence of them cannot be. Further, in
proportion as the functions of things are noble or base,
the things themselves are good or bad: conversely, in proportion as the things themselves are good or bad, their
functions also are good or bad; for the nature of results
35 corresponds with that of their causes and beginnings, and
conversely the nature of causes and beginnings corresponds with that of their results. Moreover, those things
are greater goods, superiority in which is more desirable
or more honourable. Thus, keenness of sight is more desirable than keenness of smell, sight generally being more
1364[b] desirable than smell generally; and similarly, unusually
great love of friends being more honourable than unusually great love of money, ordinary love of friends is more
honourable than ordinary love of money. Conversely, if
one of two normal things is better or nobler than the
other, an unusual degree of that thing is better or nobler
than an unusual degree of the other. Again, one thing is
more honourable or better than another if it is more
honourable or better to desire it; the importance of the
5 object of a given instinct corresponds to the importance of
the instinct itself; and for the same reason, if one thing is
more honourable or better than another, it is more honourable and better to desire it. Again, if one science is
more honourable and valuable than another, the activity
with which it deals is also more honourable and valuable;
as is the science, so is the reality that is its object, each
science being authoritative in its own sphere. So, also, the
10 more valuable and honourable the object of a science, the
more valuable and honourable the science itself is in

[1] Pindar. *Olympians*, i, 1.

consequence. Again, that which would be judged, or
which has been judged, a good thing, or a better thing
than something else, by all or most people of understanding, or by the majority of men, or by the ablest, must be
so; either without qualification, or in so far as they use
their understanding to form their judgement. This is indeed a general principle, applicable to all other judgements also; not only the goodness of things, but their
essence, magnitude, and general nature are in fact just 15
what knowledge and understanding will declare them to
be. Here the principle is applied to judgements of goodness, since one definition of 'good' was 'what beings that
acquire understanding will choose in any given case':[1]
from which it clearly follows that that thing is *better*
which understanding declares to be so. That, again, is a
better thing which attaches to better men, either abso- 20
lutely, or in virtue of their being better; as courage is
better than strength. And that is a greater good which
would be chosen by a better man, either absolutely, or in
virtue of his being better: for instance, to suffer wrong
rather than to do wrong, for that would be the choice of
the juster man. Again, the pleasanter of two things is the
better, since *all* things pursue pleasure, and things instinc-
tively desire pleasurable sensation *for its own sake;* and
these are two of the characteristics by which the 'good'
and the 'end' have been defined. One pleasure is greater 25
than another if it is more unmixed with pain, or more
lasting. Again, the nobler thing is better than the less
noble, since the noble is either what is pleasant or what
is desirable in itself. And those things also are greater
goods which men desire more earnestly to bring about for
themselves or for their friends, whereas those things which
they least desire to bring about are greater evils. And
those things which are more lasting are better than those 30
which are more fleeting, and the more secure than the
less; the enjoyment of the lasting has the advantage of
being longer, and that of the secure has the advantage of
suiting our wishes, being there for us whenever we like.
Further, in accordance with the rule of co-ordinate terms

[1] Cp. 1363b14 [and 1362a24].

and inflexions of the same stem, what is true of one such
35 related word is true of all. Thus if the action qualified by
the term 'brave' is more noble and desirable than the
action qualified by the term 'temperate', then 'bravery' is
more desirable than 'temperance' and 'being brave' than
'being temperate'. That, again, which is chosen by all is a
greater good than that which is not, and that chosen by
1365ᵃ the majority than that chosen by the minority. For that
which *all* desire is good, as we have said;[1] and so, the
more a thing is desired, the better it is. Further, that is the
better thing which is considered so by competitors or
enemies, or, again, by authorized judges or those whom
they select to represent them. In the first two cases the
decision is virtually that of every one, in the last two that
of authorities and experts. And sometimes it may be ar-
5 gued that what all share is the better thing, since it is a
dishonour not to share in it; at other times, that what none
or few share is better, since it is rarer. The more praiseworthy things are, the nobler and therefore the better they
are. So with the things that earn greater honours than
others—honour is, as it were, a measure of value; and the
things whose absence involves comparatively heavy penalties; and the things that are better than others admitted
10 or believed to be good. Moreover, things look better
merely by being divided into their parts, since they then
seem to surpass a greater number of things than before.
Hence Homer says that Meleager was roused to battle by
the thought of

All horrors that light on a folk whose city is ta'en of their
    foes,
When they slaughter the men, when the burg is wasted
    with ravening flame,
15 When strangers are haling young children to thraldom,
    ⟨fair women to shame⟩.[2]

The same effect is produced by piling up facts in a climax
after the manner of Epicharmus.[3] The reason is partly the

---

[1] 1363ᵇ14.
[2] *Iliad*, ix. 592-4 (Aristotle seems to quote from memory,
here and elsewhere).
[3] [Sicilian writer of comedies.]

same as in the case of division (for combination too makes the impression of great superiority), and partly that the original thing appears to be the cause and origin of important results. And since a thing is better when it is harder or rare than other things, its superiority may be due to seasons, ages, places, times, or one's natural pow- 20 ers. When a man accomplishes something beyond his natural power, or beyond his years, or beyond the measure of people like him, or in a special way, or at a special place or time, his deed will have a high degree of nobleness, goodness, and justice, or of their opposites. Hence the epigram on the victor at the Olympic games: 25

In time past, bearing a yoke on my shoulders, of wood
    unshaven,
I carried my loads of fish from Argos to Tegea town.[1]

So Iphicrates[2] used to extol himself by describing the low estate from which he had risen. Again, what is natural is better than what is acquired, since it is harder to come by. Hence the words of Homer:

I have learnt from none but myself.[3]   30

And the best part of a good thing is particularly good; as when Pericles in his funeral oration said that the country's loss of its young men in battle was 'as if the spring were taken out of the year'.[4] So with those things which are of service when the need is pressing; for example, in old age and times of sickness. And of two things that which leads more directly to the end in view is the better. So too is that which is better for people generally as well as for a particular individual. Again, what *can* be got is better than 35 what cannot, for it is good in a given case and the other thing is not. And what is at the end of life is better than what is not, since those things are ends in a greater degree

[1] [Fragm. of Simonides.]
[2] [The son of a shoemaker, he became an honored Athenian general, contemporary of Aristotle. He is cited many times in the *Rhetoric*, and must have been a colorful person.]
[3] *Odyssey*, xxii. 347.
[4] Cp. iii, c. 10, 1411ᵃ4. . . . [The funeral oration alluded to is not the one made famous by Thucydides but the one on those fallen in the Samian War, 440 B.C.]

which are nearer the end. What aims at reality is better
1365^b than what aims at appearance. We may define what aims
at appearance as what a man will not choose if nobody is
to know of his having it. This would seem to show that to
receive benefits is more desirable than to confer them,
since a man will choose the former even if nobody is to
know of it, but it is not the general view that he will
choose the latter if nobody knows of it. What a man wants
5 to *be* is better than what a man wants to *seem*, for in aiming at that he is aiming more at reality. Hence men say
that justice is of small value, since it is more desirable to
seem just than to be just, whereas with health it is not so.
That is better than other things which is more useful than
they are for a number of different purposes; for example,
that which promotes life, good life, pleasure, and noble
10 conduct. For this reason wealth and health are commonly
thought to be of the highest value, as possessing all these
advantages. Again, that is better than other things which
is accompanied both with less pain and with actual pleasure; for here there is more than one advantage; and so
here we have the good of feeling pleasure and also the
good of not feeling pain. And of two good things that is
the better whose addition to a third thing makes a better
whole than the addition of the other to the same thing
will make. Again, those things which we are seen to pos-
15 sess are better than those which we are not seen to possess,
since the former have the air of reality. Hence wealth may
be regarded as a greater good if its existence is known to
others. That which is dearly prized is better than what
is not—the sort of thing that some people have only one
of, though others have more like it. Accordingly, blinding
a one-eyed man inflicts worse injury than half-blinding a
man with two eyes; for the one-eyed man has been robbed
of what he dearly prized.

20 The grounds on which we must base our arguments,
when we are speaking for or against a proposal, have now
been set forth more or less completely.

The most important and effective qualification tor suc- 8
cess in persuading audiences and speaking well on public

affairs is to understand all the forms of government and
to discriminate their respective customs, institutions, and
interests. For all men are persuaded by considerations of 25
their interest, and their interest lies in the maintenance of
the established order. Further, it rests with the supreme
authority to give authoritative decisions, and this varies
with each form of government; there are as many different
supreme authorities as there are different forms of government. The forms of government are four—democracy, oligarchy, aristocracy, monarchy. The supreme right to judge 30
and decide always rests, therefore, with either a part or
the whole of one or other of these governing powers.

A Democracy is a form of government under which the
citizens distribute the offices of state among themselves
by lot, whereas under oligarchy there is a property qualification, under aristocracy one of education.[1] By education I mean that education which is laid down by the law;
for it is those who have been loyal to the national institu- 35
tions that hold office under an aristocracy. These are bound
to be looked upon as 'the best men', and it is from this
fact that this form of government has derived its name
('the rule of the best'). Monarchy, as the word implies,
is the constitution in which one man has authority over all. *1366ᵃ*
There are two forms of monarchy: kingship, which is
limited by prescribed conditions, and 'tyranny',[2] which is
not limited by anything.

We must also notice the ends which the various forms
of government pursue, since people choose in practice such
actions as will lead to the realization of their ends. The
end of democracy is freedom; of oligarchy, wealth; of aristocracy, the maintenance of education and national institu- 5
tions; of tyranny, the protection of the tyrant. It is clear,
then, that we must distinguish those particular customs,
institutions, and interests which tend to realize the ideal
of each constitution, since men choose their means
with reference to their ends. But rhetorical persuasion is
effected not only by demonstrative but by ethical argument; it helps a speaker to convince us, if we believe that 10

---

[1] Perhaps 'discipline': with special reference to Sparta.
[2] Despotism, autocracy.

he has certain qualities himself, namely, goodness, or goodwill towards us, or both together. Similarly, we should know the moral qualities characteristic of each form of government, for the special moral character of each is bound to provide us with our most effective means of persuasion in dealing with it. We shall learn the qualities of governments in the same way as we learn the qualities of

15 individuals, since they are revealed in their deliberate acts of choice; and these are determined by the end that inspires them.

We have now considered the objects, immediate or distant, at which we are to aim when urging any proposal, and the grounds on which we are to base our arguments in favour of its utility. We have also briefly considered the means and methods by which we shall gain a good knowl-

20 edge of the moral qualities and institutions peculiar to the various forms of government—only, however, to the extent demanded by the present occasion; a detailed account of the subject has been given in the *Politics*.[1]

We have now to consider Virtue and Vice, the Noble 9 and the Base,[2] since these are the objects of praise and

25 blame. In doing so, we shall at the same time be finding out how to make our hearers take the required view of our own characters—our second method of persuasion.[3] The ways in which to make them trust the goodness of other people are also the ways in which to make them trust our own. Praise, again, may be serious or frivolous;

30 nor is it always of a human or divine being but often of inanimate things, or of the humblest of the lower animals. Here too we must know on what grounds to argue, and must, therefore, now discuss the subject, though by way of illustration only.

The Noble is that which is both desirable for its own sake and also worthy of praise; or that which is both good and also pleasant because good. If this is a true definition

---

[1] *Politics*, iii and iv.
[2] Or (here and elsewhere), 'Goodness and Badness, the Fine and the Mean.'
[3] 1356^{a}2 and 5.

of the Noble, it follows that virtue must be noble, since it 35
is both a good thing and also praiseworthy. Virtue is, according to the usual view, a faculty of providing and preserving good things; or a faculty of conferring many great
benefits, and benefits of all kinds on all occasions. The
forms of Virtue are justice, courage, temperance, magnifi- 1366ᵇ
cence, magnanimity, liberality, gentleness, prudence, wisdom. If virtue is a faculty of beneficence, the highest kinds
of it must be those which are most useful to others, and
for this reason men honour most the just and the coura- 5
geous, since courage is useful to others in war, justice both
in war and in peace. Next comes liberality; liberal people
let their money go instead of fighting for it, whereas other
people care more for money than for anything else. Justice
is the virtue through which everybody enjoys his own
possessions in accordance with the law; its opposite is in- 10
justice, through which men enjoy the possessions of others
in defiance of the law. Courage is the virtue that disposes
men to do noble deeds in situations of danger, in accordance with the law and in obedience to its commands;
cowardice is the opposite. Temperance is the virtue that
disposes us to obey the law where physical pleasures are 15
concerned; incontinence is the opposite. Liberality disposes us to spend money for others' good; illiberality is
the opposite. Magnanimity is the virtue that disposes us
to do good to others on a large scale: [its opposite is meanness of spirit]. Magnificence is a virtue productive of
greatness in matters involving the spending of money. The
opposites of these two are smallness of spirit and meanness respectively. Prudence is that virtue of the under- 20
standing which enables men to come to wise decisions
about the relation to happiness of the goods and evils that
have been previously mentioned.[1]

The above is a sufficient account, for our present purpose, of virtue and vice in general, and of their various
forms. As to further aspects of the subject, it is not difficult to discern the facts; it is evident that things produc- 25
tive of virtue are noble, as tending towards virtue; and

---

[1] Cp. 1362ᵇ10-28. [References to the 'virtues' in the *Nicomachean Ethics*.]

also the effects of virtue, that is, the signs of its presence
and the acts to which it leads. And since the signs of
virtue, and such acts as it is the mark of a virtuous man
to do or have done to him, are noble, it follows that all
30 deeds or signs of courage, and everything done coura-
geously, must be noble things; and so with what is just and
actions done justly. (Not, however, actions justly done to
us; here justice is unlike the other virtues; 'justly' does
not always mean 'nobly'; when a man is punished, it is
more shameful that this should be justly than unjustly
done to him). The same is true of the other virtues. Again,
35 those actions are noble for which the reward is simply
honour, or honour more than money. So are those in which
a man aims at something desirable for some one else's
sake; actions good absolutely, such as those a man does
for his country without thinking of himself; actions good
in their own nature; actions that are not good simply for
the individual, since individual interests are selfish. Noble
1367ª also are those actions whose advantage may be enjoyed
after death, as opposed to those whose advantage is enjoyed during one's lifetime: for the latter are more likely
to be for one's own sake only. Also, all actions done for
the sake of others, since these less than other actions are
done for one's own sake; and all successes which benefit
5 others and not oneself; and services done to one's benefactors, for this is just; and good deeds generally, since
they are not directed to one's own profit. And the opposites of those things of which men feel ashamed, for
men are ashamed of saying, doing, or intending to do
shameful things. So when Alcaeus said

> Something I fain would say to thee,
10   Only shame restraineth me,[1]

Sappho wrote

> If for things good and noble thou wert yearning,
> If to speak baseness were thy tongue not burning,
> No load of shame would on thine eyelids weigh;
> What thou with honour wishest thou wouldst say.[2]

[1] [Fragm. of Alcaeus.]
[2] [Fragm. of Sappho.]

Those things, also, are noble for which men strive anx- 15
iously, without feeling fear; for they feel thus about the
good things which lead to fair fame. Again, one quality or
action is nobler than another if it is that of a naturally
finer being: thus a man's will be nobler than a woman's.
And those qualities are noble which give more pleasure to
other people than to their possessors; hence the nobleness
of justice and just actions. It is noble to avenge oneself
on one's enemies and not to come to terms with them; for 20
requital is just, and the just is noble; and not to surrender
is a sign of courage. Victory, too, and honour belong to
the class of noble things, since they are desirable even
when they yield no fruits, and they prove our superiority
in good qualities. Things that deserve to be remembered
are noble, and the more they deserve this, the nobler they
are. So are the things that continue even after death;
those which are always attended by honour; those which 25
are exceptional; and those which are possessed by one person alone—these last are more readily remembered than
others. So again are possessions that bring no profit, since
they are more fitting than others for a gentleman. So are
the distinctive qualities of a particular people, and the
symbols of what it specially admires, like long hair in
Sparta, where this is a mark of a free man, as it is not easy
to perform any menial task when one's hair is long. Again, 30
it is noble not to practise any sordid craft, since it is the
mark of a free man not to live at another's beck and call.
We are also to assume, when we wish either to praise a
man or blame him, that qualities closely allied to those
which he actually has are identical with them; for instance,
that the cautious man is cold-blooded and treacherous,
and that the stupid man is an honest fellow or the thick- 35
skinned man a good-tempered one. We can always idealize
any given man by drawing on the virtues akin to his actual
qualities; thus we may say that the passionate and excit-
able man is 'outspoken'; or that the arrogant man is 'su-
perb' or 'impressive'. Those who run to extremes will be 1367ᵇ
said to possess the corresponding good qualities; rashness
will be called courage, and extravagance generosity. That
will be what most people think; and at the same time this

method enables an advocate to draw a misleading inference from the motive, arguing that if a man runs into
5 danger needlessly, much more will he do so in a noble
cause; and if a man is open-handed to any one and every
one, he will be so to his friends also, since it is the extreme
form of goodness to be good to everybody.

We must also take into account the nature of our particular audience when making a speech of praise; for, as
Socrates used to say, it is not difficult to praise the Athenians to an Athenian audience.[1] If the audience esteems a
given quality, we must say that our hero has that quality,
10 no matter whether we are addressing Scythians or Spar-
tans or philosophers. Everything, in fact, that is esteemed
we are to represent as noble. After all, people regard the
two things as much the same.

All actions are noble that are appropriate to the man
who does them: if, for instance, they are worthy of his
ancestors or of his own past career. For it makes for happiness, and is a noble thing, that he should add to the
15 honour he already has. Even inappropriate actions are
noble if they are better and nobler than the appropriate
ones would be; for instance, if one who was just an average person when all went well becomes a hero in adver-
sity, or if he becomes better and easier to get on with the
higher he rises. Compare the saying of Iphicrates, 'Think
what I was and what I am'; and the epigram on the victor
at the Olympic games,

In time past, bearing a yoke on my shoulders, of wood
    unshaven[2];

and the encomium of Simonides,

A woman whose father, whose husband, whose brethren
20   were princes all.[3]

Since we praise a man for what he has actually done,
and fine actions are distinguished from others by being in-

---

[1] Cp. Plato, *Menexenus*, 235 D.
[2] Cp. i. 7, 1365ª24-8, for this and the previous quotation.
[3] [Fragm. of Simonides.]

tentionally[1] good, we must try to prove that our hero's noble acts are intentional.[1] This is all the easier if we can make out that he has often acted so before, and therefore we must assert coincidences and accidents to have been intended.[1] Produce a number of good actions, all of the same kind, and people will think that they must have been intended,[1] and that they prove the good qualities of the man who did them.

Praise is the expression in words of the eminence of a man's good qualities, and therefore we must display his actions as the product of such qualities. Encomium refers to what he has actually done; the mention of accessories, such as good birth and education, merely helps to make our story credible—good fathers are likely to have good sons, and good training is likely to produce good character. Hence it is only when a man has already done something that we bestow *encomiums* upon him. Yet the actual deeds are evidence of the doer's character: even if a man has not actually done a given good thing, we shall bestow *praise* on him, if we are sure that he is the sort of man who *would* do it. To call any one blest is, it may be added, the same thing as to call him happy; but these are not the same thing as to bestow praise and encomium upon him; the two latter are a part of 'calling happy', just as goodness is a part of happiness.

To praise a man is in one respect akin to urging a course of action. The suggestions which would be made in the latter case become encomiums when differently 1368ᵃ expressed. When we know what action or character is required, then, in order to express these facts as suggestions for action, we have to change and reverse our form of words. Thus the statement 'A man should be proud not of what he owes to fortune but of what he owes to himself', if put like this, amounts to a suggestion; to make it into praise we must put it thus, 'Since he is proud not of what he owes to fortune but of what he owes to himself.' Consequently, whenever you want to praise any one, think what you would urge people to do; and when you want

---

[1] Deliberate intention, based on moral choice, is meant in all these cases.

to urge the doing of anything, think what you would
praise a man for having done. Since suggestion may or
may not forbid an action, the praise into which we con-
vert it must have one or other of two opposite forms of
expression accordingly.

10   There are, also, many useful ways of heightening the
effect of praise. We must, for instance, point out that a
man is the only one, or the first, or almost the only one
who has done something, or that he has done it better than
any one else; all these distinctions are honourable. And
we must, further, make much of the particular season and
occasion of an action, arguing that we could hardly have
looked for it just then. If a man has often achieved the
same success, we must mention this; that is a strong point;
15 he himself, and not luck, will then be given the credit. So,
too, if it is on his account that observances have been devised and instituted to encourage or honour such achieve-
ments as his own: thus we may praise Hippolochus[1] because the first encomium ever made was for him, or Harmodius and Aristogeiton[2] because their statues were the
first to be put up in the market-place. And we may censure
bad men for the opposite reason.

Again, if you cannot find enough to say of a man him-
20 self, you may pit him against others, which is what Isocrates used to do owing to his want of familiarity with forensic pleading.[3] The comparison should be with famous men;
that will strengthen your case;[4] it is a noble thing to surpass men who are themselves great. It is only natural that
methods of 'heightening the effect'[4] should be attached
particularly to speeches of praise; they aim at proving superiority over others, and any such superiority is a form
of nobleness. Hence if you cannot compare your hero with
25 famous men, you should at least compare him with other

---

[1] [Of Hippolochus nothing is known.]
[2] [Harmodius and Aristogeiton were famous tyrannicides.
Their attempt to kill the sons of Peisistratus in 514 B.C.
only partly succeeded. Cp. Aristotle, *Politics*, viii 10.]
[3] [Some manuscripts have what is perhaps the better reading, 'owing to his familiarity.']
[4] . . . Rhetorical efforts to magnify, extol, amplify. Cp.
1368[b]10 and ii, c. 26.

people generally, since any superiority is held to reveal excellence. And, in general, of the lines of argument which are common to all speeches, this 'heightening of effect' is most suitable for declamations, where we take our hero's actions as admitted facts, and our business is simply to invest these with dignity and nobility. 'Examples' are most suitable to deliberative speeches; for we judge of future 30 events by divination from past events. Enthymemes are most suitable to forensic speeches; it is our doubts about past events that most admit of arguments showing why a thing must have happened or proving that it did happen.

The above are the general lines on which all, or nearly all, speeches of praise or blame are constructed. We have seen the sort of thing we must bear in mind in making such speeches, and the materials out of which encomiums 35 and censures are made. No special treatment of censure and vituperation is needed. Knowing the above facts, we know their contraries; and it is out of these that speeches of censure are made.

10   We have next to treat of Accusation and Defence,[1] and 1368ᵇ to enumerate and describe the ingredients of the syllogisms used therein. There are three things we must ascertain— first, the nature and number of the incentives to wrong-doing; second, the state of mind of wrongdoers; third, the kind of persons who are wronged, and their condition. We 5 will deal with these questions in order. But before that let us define the act of 'wrong-doing'.

We may describe 'wrong-doing' as injury voluntarily inflicted contrary to law. 'Law' is either special or general. By special law I mean that written law which regulates the life of a particular community; by general law, all those unwritten principles which are supposed to be acknowledged everywhere. We do things 'voluntarily' 10 when we do them consciously and without constraint. (Not all voluntary[2] acts are deliberate, but all deliberate acts are conscious[3]—no one is ignorant of what he delib-

---

[1] [It is of two forms of forensic speech.]
[2] i.e. and therefore conscious.
[3] i.e. and therefore voluntary.

erately intends.) The causes of our deliberately intending harmful and wicked acts contrary to law are (1) vice, (2) lack of self-control. For the wrongs a man does to
15 others will correspond to the bad quality or qualities that he himself possesses. Thus it is the mean man who will wrong others about money, the profligate in matters of physical pleasure, the effeminate in matters of comfort, and the coward where danger is concerned—his terror makes him abandon those who are involved in the same danger. The ambitious man[1] does wrong for the sake of
20 honour, the quick-tempered from anger, the lover of victory for the sake of victory, the embittered man for the sake of revenge, the stupid man because he has misguided notions of right and wrong, the shameless man because he does not mind what people think of him; and so with the rest—any wrong that any one does to others corresponds to his particular faults of character.[2]

25   However, this subject has already been cleared up in part in our discussion of the virtues[3] and will be further explained later when we treat of the emotions.[4] We have now to consider the motives and states of mind of wrong-doers, and to whom they do wrong.

    Let us first decide what sort of things people are trying to get or avoid when they set about doing wrong to others. For it is plain that the prosecutor must consider, out of all
30 the aims that can ever induce us to do wrong to our neighbours, how many, and which, affect his adversary; while the defendant must consider how many, and which, do *not* affect him. Now every action of every person either is or is not due to that person himself. Of those not due to himself some are due to chance, the others to necessity;
35 of these latter, again, some are due to compulsion, the others to nature. Consequently all actions that are not due to a man himself are due either to chance or to nature or

----

[1] Greek, 'the honour-loving man.'
[2] Lit., 'and similarly each of the other people (who do wrong to others does it) with reference to his particular part of the subject matter (of bad character).' Cp. . . . 1359^{b}15.
[3] i, c. 9.
[4] ii, cc. 1-11.

to compulsion. All actions that *are* due to a man himself 1369ᵃ
and caused by himself are due either to habit or to rational
or irrational craving. Rational craving is a craving for
good, i.e. a *wish*—nobody wishes for anything unless he
thinks it good. Irrational craving is two fold, viz. anger
and appetite.[1]

Thus every action must be due to one or other of seven 5
causes: chance, nature, compulsion, habit, reasoning,
anger, or appetite. It is superfluous further to distinguish
actions according to the doers' ages, moral states, or the
like; it is of course true that, for instance, young men do
have hot tempers and strong appetites; still, it is not
through youth that they act accordingly, but through 10
anger or appetite. Nor, again, is action due to wealth or
poverty; it is of course true that poor men, being short of
money, do have an appetite for it, and that rich men,
being able to command needless pleasures, do have an
appetite for such pleasures: but here, again, their actions
will be *due* not to wealth or poverty but to appetite. Similarly, with just men, and unjust men, and all others who 15
are said to act in accordance with their moral qualities,
their actions will really be due to one of the causes mentioned—either reasoning or emotion: due, indeed, sometimes to good dispositions and good emotions, and sometimes to bad; but that good qualities should be followed
by good emotions, and bad by bad, is merely an accessory
fact—it is no doubt true that the temperate man, for in- 20
stance, because he is temperate, *is* always and at once
attended by healthy opinions and appetites in regard to
pleasant things, and the intemperate man by unhealthy
ones. So we must ignore such distinctions. Still we must
consider what kinds of actions and of people usually go
together; for while there are no definite kinds of action
associated with the fact that a man is fair or dark, tall or 25
short, it does make a difference if he is young or old, just
or unjust. And, generally speaking, all those accessory
qualities that cause distinctions of human character are
important: e. g. the sense of wealth or poverty, of being

[1] . . . In translating ἐπιθυμία, 'desire' has sometimes been
used, as well as 'appetite.'

lucky or unlucky. This shall be dealt with later[1]—let us
30 now deal first with the rest of the subject before us.

The things that happen by chance are all those whose
cause cannot be determined, that have no purpose, and
that happen neither always nor usually nor in any fixed
way. The definition of chance shows just what they are.
35 Those things happen by nature which have a fixed and
1369[b] internal cause; they take place uniformly, either always or
usually. There is no need to discuss in exact detail the
things that happen contrary to nature, nor to ask whether
they happen in some sense naturally or from some other
cause; it would seem that chance is at least partly the
5 cause of such events. Those things happen through com
pulsion which take place contrary to the desire or reason
of the doer, yet through his own agency. Acts are done
from habit which men do because they have often done
them before. Actions are due to reasoning when, in view
of any of the goods already mentioned,[2] they appear useful either as ends or as means to an end, and are per-
formed for that reason: 'for that reason,' since even licen-
10 tious persons perform a certain number of useful actions,
but because they are pleasant and not because they are
useful. To passion and anger are due all acts of revenge.
Revenge and punishment are different things. Punishment
is inflicted for the sake of the person punished; revenge
for that of the punisher, to satisfy his feelings. (What
anger is will be made clear when we come to discuss the
15 emotions.[3]) Appetite is the cause of all actions that appear
pleasant. Habit, whether acquired by mere familiarity or
by effort, belongs to the class of pleasant things, for there
are many actions not naturally pleasant which men perform with pleasure, once they have become used to them.
To sum up then, all actions due to ourselves either are or
20 seem to be either good or pleasant. Moreover, as all actions due to ourselves are done voluntarily and actions not
due to ourselves are done involuntarily, it follows that all
voluntary actions must either be or seem to be either good

[1] ii, cc. 12-17.
[2] i, c. 6.
[3] ii, c. 2.

or pleasant; for I reckon among goods escape from evils
or apparent evils and the exchange of a greater evil for a
less (since these things are in a sense positively desirable), 25
and likewise I count among pleasures escape from painful
or apparently painful things and the exchange of a greater
pain for a less. We must ascertain, then, the number and
nature of the things that are useful and pleasant. The useful has been previously examined in connexion with political oratory;[1] let us now proceed to examine the pleasant. 30
Our various definitions must be regarded as adequate,
even if they are not exact, provided they are clear.

11   We may lay it down that Pleasure is a movement, a
movement by which the soul as a whole is consciously
brought into its normal state of being; and that Pain is
the opposite.[2] If this is what pleasure is, it is clear that the 1370ᵃ
pleasant is what tends to produce this condition, while
that which tends to destroy it, or to cause the soul to be
brought into the opposite state, is painful. It must therefore be pleasant as a rule to move towards a natural state
of being, particularly when a natural process has achieved
the complete recovery of that natural state. Habits also are 5
pleasant; for as soon as a thing has become habitual, it is
virtually natural; habit is a thing not unlike nature; what
happens often is akin to what happens always, natural
events happening always, habitul events often. Again, that
is pleasant which is not forced on us; for force is unnatural, and that is why what is compulsory is painful, and
it has been rightly said   10

All that is done on compulsion is bitterness unto the soul.[3]

So all acts of concentration, strong effort, and strain are
necessarily painful; they all involve compulsion and force,
unless we are accustomed to them, in which case it is cus-

---

[1] i, c. 6.
[2] [The relation here established between pleasure and the
soul points to a Platonic background. The second part of
the definition may have originated in medical circles; it
is closely paralleled in Plato, *Timaeus,* 64c-65b.]
[3] [Fragm. of Euenus of Paros, elegiac poet and sophist,
contemporary of Socrates.]

tom that makes them pleasant. The opposites to these are
15 pleasant; and hence ease, freedom from toil, relaxation,
amusement, rest, and sleep belong to the class of pleasant
things; for these are all free from any element of compulsion. Everything, too, is pleasant for which we have the
desire within us, since desire is the craving for pleasure.
Of the desires some are irrational, some associated with
reason.[1] By irrational I mean those which do not arise
20 from any opinion held by the mind. Of this kind are those
known as 'natural'; for instance, those originating in the
body, such as the desire for nourishment, namely hunger
and thirst, and a separate kind of desire answering to each
kind of nourishment; and the desires connected with taste
and sex and sensations of touch in general; and those of
25 smell, hearing, and vision. Rational desires are those which
we are induced to have; there are many things we desire
to see or get because we have been told of them and induced to believe them good. Further, pleasure is the consciousness through the senses of a certain kind of emotion;
but imagination[2] is a feeble sort of sensation, and there
will always be in the mind of a man who remembers or
30 expects something an image or picture of what he remembers or expects. If this is so, it is clear that memory and
expectation also, being accompanied by sensation, may be
accompanied by pleasure. It follows that anything pleasant is either present and perceived, past and remembered,
or future and expected, since we perceive present pleasures, remember past ones, and expect future ones. Now
1370ᵇ the things that are pleasant to remember are not only
those that, when actually perceived as present, *were* pleasant, but also some things that were not, provided that
their results have subsequently proved noble and good.
Hence the words

Sweet 'tis when rescued to remember pain,[3]

and

[1] 'are accompanied, or not accompanied, by a rational principle.'
[2] . . . 'mental picturing,' 'fancy,' 'impression.'
[3] Euripides, *Andromeda*, fragm.

Even his griefs are a joy long after to one that remembers 5
All that he wrought and endured.[1]

The reason of this is that it is pleasant even to be merely
free from evil. The things it is pleasant to expect are those
that when present are felt to afford us either great delight or great but not painful benefit. And in general,
all the things that delight us when they are present also
do so, as a rule, when we merely remember or expect 10
them. Hence even being angry is pleasant—Homer said
of wrath that

Sweeter it is by far than the honeycomb dripping with
    sweetness[2]—

for no one grows angry with a person on whom there is
no prospect of taking vengeance, and we feel comparatively little anger, or none at all, with those who are much
our superiors in power. Some pleasant feeling is associated 15
with most of our appetites; we are enjoying either the
memory of a past pleasure or the expectation of a future
one, just as persons down with fever, during their attacks
of thirst, enjoy remembering the drinks they have had and
looking forward to having more. So also a lover enjoys
talking or writing about his loved one, or doing any little 20
thing connected with him; all these things recall him to
memory and make him actually present to the eye of
imagination. Indeed, it is always the first sign of love, that
besides enjoying some one's presence, we remember him
when he is gone, and feel pain as well as pleasure, because
he is there no longer. Similarly there is an element of
pleasure even in mourning and lamentation for the de- 25
parted. There is grief, indeed, at his loss, but pleasure in
remembering him and as it were seeing him before us in
his deeds and in his life. We can well believe the poet
when he says

He spake, and in each man's heart he awakened the love
    of lament.[3]

[1] Cp. *Odyssey*, xv. 400, 401.
[2] *Iliad*, xviii. 109.
[3] *Iliad*, xxiii. 108; *Odyssey*, iv. 183.

Revenge, too, is pleasant; it is pleasant to get anything
30 that it is painful to fail to get, and angry people suffer
extreme pain when they fail to get their revenge; but they
enjoy the prospect of getting it. Victory also is pleasant,
and not merely to 'bad losers', but to every one; the win-
ner sees himself in the light of a champion, and everybody has a more or less keen appetite for being that. The
pleasantness of victory implies of course that combative
1371ª sports and intellectual contests are pleasant (since in these
it often happens that some one wins) and also games like
knucklebones, ball, dice, and draughts. And similarly with
the serious sports; some of these become pleasant when
one is accustomed to them: while others are pleasant from
the first, like hunting with hounds, or indeed any kind of
5 hunting. For where there is competition, there is victory.
That is why forensic pleading and debating contests are
pleasant to those who are accustomed to them and have
the capacity for them. Honour and good repute are among
the most pleasant things of all; they make a man see himself in the character of a fine fellow, especially when he is
10 credited with it by people whom he thinks good judges.
His neighbours are better judges than people at a distance;
his associates and fellow-countrymen better than strangers;
his contemporaries better than posterity; sensible persons
better than foolish ones; a large number of people better
than a small number: those of the former class, in each
case, are the more likely to be good judges of him.
Honour and credit bestowed by those whom you think
15 much inferior to yourself—e.g. children or animals—you
do not value: not for its own sake, anyhow: if you do
value it, it is for some other reason. Friends belong to the
class of pleasant things; it is pleasant to love—if you love
wine, you certainly find it delightful: and it is pleasant to
be loved, for this too makes a man see himself as the pos-
20 sessor of goodness, a thing that every being that has a
feeling for it desires to possess: to be loved means to be
valued for one's own personal qualities. To be admired is
also pleasant, simply because of the honour implied. Flat-
tery and flatterers are pleasant: the flatterer is a man who,
you believe, admires and likes you. To do the same thing

often is pleasant, since, as we saw, anything habitual is [25] pleasant.[1] And to change is also pleasant: change means an approach to nature, whereas invariable repetition of anything causes the excessive prolongation of a settled condition: therefore, says the poet,

Change is in all things sweet.[2]

That is why what comes to us only at long intervals is pleasant, whether it be a person or a thing; for it is a change from what we had before, and, besides, what comes only at long intervals has the value of rarity. Learn- [30] ing things and wondering at things are also pleasant as a rule; wondering implies the desire of learning,[3] so that the object of wonder is an object of desire; while in learn- ing one is brought into one's natural condition. Conferring and receiving benefits belong to the class of pleasant things; to receive a benefit is to get what one desires; to confer a benefit implies both possession and superiority, [1371^b] both of which are things we try to attain. It is because beneficent acts are pleasant that people find it pleasant to put their neighbours straight again and to supply what they lack. Again, since learning and wondering are pleas- ant, it follows that such things as acts of imitation must be [5] pleasant—for instance, painting, sculpture, poetry—and every product of skilful imitation; this latter, even if the object imitated is not itself pleasant; for it is not the ob- ject itself which here gives delight; the spectator draws inferences ('That is a so-and-so') and thus learns some- [10] thing fresh.[4] Dramatic turns of fortune and hairbreadth escapes from perils are pleasant, because we feel all such things are wonderful.

And since what is natural is pleasant, and things akin to each other seem natural to each other, therefore all kindred and similar things are usually pleasant to each other; for instance, one man, horse, or young person is pleasant to another man, horse, or young person. Hence [15]

---

[1] i, c. 10, 1369^{b}16.
[2] Euripides, *Orestes*, 234.
[3] [Text uncertain.]
[4] Cp. *Poetics*, c. 4, 1448^{b}5-19.

the proverbs 'mate delights mate', 'like to like',[1] 'beast knows beast', 'jackdaw to jackdaw', and the rest of them. But since everything like and akin to oneself is pleasant, and since every man is himself more like and akin to himself than any one else is, it follows that all of us must be
20 more or less fond of ourselves. For all this resemblance and kinship is present particularly in the relation of an individual to himself. And because we are all fond of ourselves, it follows that what is our own is pleasant to all of us, as for instance our own deeds and words. That is why we are usually fond of our flatterers, [our lovers,] and honour; also of our children, for our children are our
25 own work. It is also pleasant to complete what is defective, for the whole thing thereupon becomes our own work. And since power over others is very pleasant, it is pleasant to be thought wise, for practical wisdom secures us power over others. (Scientific wisdom is also pleasant, because it is the knowledge of many wonderful things.) Again, since most of us are ambitious, it must be pleasant to disparage our neighbours as well as to have power
30 over them. It is pleasant for a man to spend his time over what he feels he can do best; just as the poet says,

> To that he bends himself,
> To that each day allots most time, wherein
> He is indeed the best part of himself.[2]

Similarly, since amusement and every kind of relaxation and laughter too belong to the class of pleasant things, it follows that ludicrous things are pleasant, whether men,
1372ᵃ words, or deeds. We have discussed the ludicrous separately in the treatise on the *Art of Poetry*.[3]

So much for the subject of pleasant things: by considering their opposites we can easily see what things are unpleasant.

---

[1] *Odyssey*, xvii. 218.

[2] [Euripides, *Antiope*, fragm.]

[3] Not found in the *Poetics*, as it exists today. Aristotle probably analysed the causes and conditions of laughter, when treating of Comedy in his lost Second Book.

12 The above are the motives that make men do wrong
to others; we are next to consider the states of mind in
which they do it, and the persons to whom they do it.   5

They must themselves suppose that the thing can be
done, and done by them: either that they can do it without being found out, or that if they are found out they
can escape being punished, or that if they are punished the
disadvantage will be less than the gain for themselves or
those they care for. The general subject of apparent possibility and impossibility will be handled later on,[1] since
it is relevant not only to forensic but to all kinds of speak- 10
ing. But it may here be said that people think that they
can themselves most easily do wrong to others without
being punished for it if they possess eloquence, or practical ability, or much legal experience, or a large body of
friends, or a great deal of money. Their confidence is
greatest if they personally possess the advantages mentioned: but even without them they are satisfied if they
have friends or supporters or partners who do possess 15
them: they can thus both commit their crimes and escape
being found out and punished for committing them. They
are also safe, they think, if they are on good terms with
their victims or with the judges who try them. Their victims will in that case not be on their guard against being
wronged, and will make some arrangement with them instead of prosecuting; while their judges will favour them 20
because they like them, either letting them off altogether
or imposing light sentences. They are not likely to be
found out if their appearance contradicts the charges that
might be brought against them: for instance, a weakling is
unlikely to be charged with violent assault, or a poor and
ugly man with adultery. Public and open injuries are the
easiest to do, because nobody could at all suppose them
possible, and therefore no precautions are taken. The
same is true of crimes so great and terrible that no man 25
living could be suspected of them: here too no precautions
are taken. For all men guard against ordinary offences, just
as they guard against ordinary diseases; but no one takes
precautions against a disease that nobody has ever had.

[1] ii, c. 19.

You feel safe, too, if you have either no enemies or a great many; if you have none, you expect not to be watched and therefore not to be detected; if you have a great many,
30 you will be watched, and therefore people[1] will think you can never risk an attempt on them, and you can defend your innocence by pointing out that you could never have taken such a risk. You may also trust to hide your crime by the way you do it or the place you do it in, or by some convenient means of disposal.

You may feel that even if you are found out you can stave off a trial, or have it postponed, or corrupt your judges: or that even if you are sentenced you can avoid
35 paying damages, or can at least postpone doing so for a long time: or that you are so badly off that you will have nothing to lose. You may feel that the gain to be got by wrong-doing is great or certain or immediate, and that the
1372[b] penalty is small or uncertain or distant. It may be that the advantage to be gained is greater than any possible retribution: as in the case of despotic power, according to the popular view. You may consider your crimes as bringing you solid profit, while their punishment is nothing more than being called bad names. Or the opposite argument may appeal to you: your crimes may bring you some
5 credit (thus you may, incidentally, be avenging your father or mother, like Zeno),[2] whereas the punishment may amount to a fine, or banishment, or something of that sort. People may be led on to wrong others by either of these motives or feelings; but no man by both—they will affect people of quite opposite characters. You may be encouraged by having often escaped detection or punish-
10 ment already; or by having often tried and failed; for in crime, as in war, there are men who will always refuse to give up the struggle. You may get your pleasure on the spot and the pain later, or the gain on the spot and the loss later. That is what appeals to weak-willed persons— and weakness of will may be shown with regard to all the objects of desire. It may on the contrary appeal to you— as it does appeal to self-controlled and sensible people—

[1] i.e. the victims of the injustice.
[2] [Nothing is known of the man or the case.]

that the pain and loss are immediate, while the pleasure 15
and profit come later and last longer. You may feel able
to make it appear that your crime was due to chance, or
to necessity, or to natural causes, or to habit: in fact, to
put it generally, as if you had failed to do right rather
than actually done wrong. You may be able to trust other
people to judge you equitably. You may be stimulated by
being in want: which may mean that you want neces-
saries, as poor people do, or that you want luxuries, as 20
rich people do. You may be encouraged by having a particularly good reputation, because that will save you from
being suspected: or by having a particularly bad one,
because nothing you are likely to do will make it worse.

The above, then, are the various states of mind in which
a man sets about doing wrong to others. The kind of
people to whom he does wrong, and the ways in which
he does it, must be considered next. The people to whom
he does it are those who have what he wants himself,
whether this means necessities or luxuries and materials 25
for enjoyment. His victims may be far off or near at hand.
If they are near, he gets his profit quickly; if they are far
off, vengeance is slow, as those think who plunder the
Carthaginians. They may be those who are trustful instead
of being cautious and watchful, since all such people are
easy to elude. Or those who are too easy-going to have
enough energy to prosecute an offender. Or sensitive peo- 30
ple, who are not apt to show fight over questions of
money. Or those who have been wronged already by
many people, and yet have not prosecuted; such men
must surely be the proverbial 'Mysian prey'.[1] Or those
who have either never or often been wronged before; in
neither case will they take precautions; if they have never
been wronged they think they never will, and if they have
often been wronged they feel that surely it cannot happen again. Or those whose character has been attacked in 35
the past, or is exposed to attack in the future: they will
be too much frightened of the judges to make up their
minds to prosecute, nor can they win their case if they
do: this is true of those who are hated or unpopular. An- 1373ᵃ

[1] i.e. an easy prey.

other likely class of victim is those who their injurer can pretend have, themselves or through their ancestors or friends, treated badly, or intended to treat badly, the man himself, or his ancestors, or those he cares for; as the proverb says, 'wickedness needs but a pretext'. A man may wrong his enemies, because that is pleasant: he may equally wrong his friends, because that is easy. Then 5 there are those who have no friends, and those who lack eloquence and practical capacity; these will either not attempt to prosecute, or they will come to terms, or failing that they will lose their case. There are those whom it does not pay to waste time in waiting for trial or damages, such as foreigners and small farmers; they will settle for a trifle, and always be ready to leave off. Also those who 10 have themselves wronged others, either often, or in the same way as they are now being wronged themselves—for it is felt that next to no wrong is done to people when it is the same wrong as they have often themselves done to others: if, for instance, you assault a man who has been accustomed to behave with violence to others. So too with those who have done wrong to others, or have meant to, 15 or mean to, or are likely to do so; there is something fine and pleasant in wronging such persons, it seems as though almost no wrong were done. Also those by doing wrong to whom we shall be gratifying our friends, or those we admire or love, or our masters, or in general the people by reference to whom we mould our lives. Also those whom we may wrong and yet be sure of equitable treatment. Also those against whom we have had any grievance, or any previous differences with them, as Callippus had when he behaved as he did to Dion:[1] here too it 20 seems as if almost no wrong were being done. Also those who are on the point of being wronged by others if we fail to wrong them ourselves, since here we feel we have no time left for thinking the matter over. So Aenesidemus[2]

---

[1] [Dion, a friend of Plato, freed Sicily of the tyranny of the older Dionysius and with Plato's assistance attempted to set up an ideal state. In 354 B.C. he was murdered by his former friend and associate Callippus.]

[2] [Tyrant of Leontin.]

is said to have sent the 'cottabus'[1] prize to Gelon,[2] who
had just reduced a town to slavery, because Gelon had
got there first and forestalled his own attempt. Also those
by wronging whom we shall be able to do many righteous
acts; for we feel that we can then easily cure the harm 25
done. Thus Jason the Thessalian[3] said that it is a duty to
do some unjust acts in order to be able to do many just
ones.

Among the kinds of wrong done to others are those that
are done universally, or at least commonly: one expects to
be forgiven for doing these. Also those that can easily be
kept dark, as where things that can rapidly be consumed
like eatables are concerned, or things that can easily be 30
changed in shape, colour, or combination, or things that
can easily be stowed away almost anywhere—portable
objects that you can stow away in small corners, or things
so like others of which you have plenty already that nobody can tell the difference. There are also wrongs of a
kind that shame prevents the victim speaking about, such
as outrages done to the women in his household or to him- 35
self or to his sons. Also those for which you would be
thought very litigious to prosecute any one—trifling
wrongs, or wrongs for which people are usually excused.

The above is a fairly complete account of the circumstances under which men do wrong to others, of the sort
of wrongs they do, of the sort of persons to whom they
do them, and of their reasons for doing them.

13   It will now be well to make a complete classification of 1373[b]
just and unjust actions. We may begin by observing that
they have been defined relatively to two kinds of law, and
also relatively to two classes of persons. By the two kinds
of law I mean particular law and universal law.[4] Particular
law is that which each community lays down and applies
to its own members: this is partly written and partly un- 5

---

[1] [A Sicilian game; the prize was a gift of eggs, cakes, and
sweetmeats.]
[2] [Tyrant of Syracuse.]
[3] [Jason of Pherae, ruler of Thessaly in the 4th cent.]
[4] [Cp. 1368ª8 ff.]

written. Universal law is the law of nature. For there really
is, as every one to some extent divines, a natural justice
and injustice that is binding on all men, even on those who
have no association or covenant with each other. It is this
that Sophocles' Antigone clearly means when she says that
10 the burial of Polyneices was a just act in spite of the pro-
hibition: she means that it was just by nature.

> Not of to-day or yesterday it is,
> But lives eternal: none can date its birth.[1]

And so Empedocles, when he bids us kill no living creature, says that doing this is not just for some people while
15 unjust for others,

> Nay, but, an all-embracing law, through the realms of the
> sky
> Unbroken it stretcheth, and over the earth's immensity.[2]

And as Alcidamas[3] says in his Messeniac Oration. . . .

The actions that we ought to do or not to do have also
20 been divided into two classes as affecting either the whole
community or some one of its members. From this point
of view we can perform just or unjust acts in either of two
ways—towards one definite person, or towards the community. The man who is guilty of adultery or assault is
doing wrong to some definite person; the man who avoids
25 service in the army is doing wrong to the community.

Thus the whole class of unjust actions may be divided
into two classes, those affecting the community, and those
affecting one or more other persons. We will next, before
going further, remind ourselves of what 'being wronged'
means. Since it has already[4] been settled that 'doing a
wrong' must be intentional, 'being wronged' must consist
in having an injury done to you by some one who *intends*

---

[1] Sophocles, *Antigone*, 456-7.
[2] [Fragm. of Empedocles, a physical philosopher of the 5th
cent.]
[3] According to the scholast, the words of Alcidamas [a 5th
cent. sophist and orator] were, 'God has left all men free;
Nature has made no man a slave.' . . .
[4] i. c. 10.

to do it. In order to be wronged, a man must (1) suffer
actual harm, (2) suffer it against his will. The various 30
possible forms of harm are clearly explained by our previous[1] separate discussion of goods and evils. We have
also seen that a voluntary action is one where the doer
knows what he is doing.[2] We now see that every accusation must be of an action affecting either the community
or some individual. The doer of the action must either
understand and intend the action, or not understand and 35
intend it. In the former case, he must be acting either
from deliberate choice or from passion. (Anger will be discussed when we speak of the passions[3]; the motives for
crime and the state of mind of the criminal have already[4]
been discussed.) Now it often happens that a man will 1374^{a}
admit an act, but will not admit the prosecutor's label[5]
for the act nor the facts which that label implies. He will
admit that he took a thing but not that he 'stole' it; that he
struck some one first, but not that he committed 'outrage';
that he had intercourse with a woman, but not that he
committed 'adultery'; that he is guilty of theft, but not that
he is guilty of 'sacrilege', the object stolen not being consecrated; that he has encroached, but not that he has
'encroached on State lands'; that he has been in com- 5
munication with the enemy, but not that he has been
guilty of 'treason'. Here therefore we must be able to distinguish what is theft, outrage, or adultery, from what is
not, if we are to be able to make the justice of our case
clear, no matter whether our aim is to establish a man's
guilt or to establish his innocence. Wherever such charges
are brought against a man, the question is whether he is 10
or is not guilty of a criminal offence. It is deliberate purpose that constitutes wickedness and criminal guilt, and
such names as 'outrage' or 'theft' imply deliberate purpose
as well as the mere action. A blow does not always amount

---

[1] i, c. 6.
[2] i, c. 10.
[3] ii, c. 2.
[4] i, cc. 11 and 12.
[5] . . . a specification or description of the alleged offence,
with a claim for a corresponding penalty.

to 'outrage', but only if it is struck with some such purpose as to insult the man struck or gratify the striker himself. Nor does taking a thing without the owner's knowledge always amount to 'theft', but only if it is taken with the intention of keeping it and injuring the owner. And as with these charges, so with all the others.

We saw that there are two kinds of right and wrong conduct towards others, one provided for by written ordinances, the other by unwritten. We have now discussed the kind about which the laws have something to say. The other kind has itself two varieties. First, there is the conduct that springs from exceptional goodness or badness, and is visited accordingly with censure and loss of honour, or with praise and increase of honour and decorations: for instance, gratitude to, or requital of, our benefactors, readiness to help our friends, and the like. The second kind makes up for the defects of a community's written code of law. This is what we call equity; people regard it as just; it is, in fact, the sort of justice which goes beyond the written law. Its existence partly is and partly is not intended by legislators; not intended, where they have noticed no defect in the law; intended, where they find themselves unable to define things exactly, and are obliged to legislate as if that held good always which in fact only holds good usually; or where it is not easy to be complete owing to the endless possible cases presented, such as the kinds and sizes of weapons that may be used to inflict wounds—a lifetime would be too short to make out a complete list of these. If, then, a precise statement is impossible and yet legislation is necessary, the law must be expressed in wide terms; and so, if a man has no more than a finger-ring on his hand when he lifts it to strike or actually strikes another man, he is guilty of a criminal act according to the written words of the law; 1374ᵇ but he is innocent really, and it is equity that declares him to be so. From this definition of equity it is plain what sort of actions, and what sort of persons, are equitable or the reverse. Equity must be applied to forgivable actions; and it must make us distinguish between criminal acts on the one hand, and errors of judgement, or misfortunes, on

the other. (A 'misfortune' is an act, not due to moral badness, that has unexpected results: an 'error of judgement'
is an act, also not due to moral badness, that has results
that might have been expected: a 'criminal act' has results
that might have been expected, but *is* due to moral badness, for that is the source of all actions inspired by our 10
appetites.) Equity bids us be merciful to the weakness of
human nature; to think less about the laws than about the
man who framed them, and less about what he said than
about what he meant; not to consider the actions of the
accused so much as his intentions; nor this or that detail so much as the whole story; to ask not what a man 15
is now but what he has always or usually been. It bids us
remember benefits rather than injuries, and benefits received rather than benefits conferred; to be patient when
we are wronged; to settle a dispute by negotiation and
not by force; to prefer arbitration to litigation—for an 20
arbitrator goes by the equity of a case, a judge by the
strict law, and arbitration was invented with the express
purpose of securing full power for equity.

The above may be taken as a sufficient account of the
nature of equity.

14 The worse of two acts of wrong done to others is that
which is prompted by the worse disposition. Hence the 25
most trifling acts may be the worst ones; as when Callistratus[1] charged Melanopus with having cheated the temple-
builders of three consecrated half-obols. The converse is
true of just acts. This is because the greater is here potentially contained in the less: there is no crime that a
man who has stolen three consecrated half-obols would
shrink from committing. Sometimes, however, the worse
act is reckoned not in this way but by the greater harm 30
that it does. Or it may be because no punishment for it is
severe enough to be adequate; or the harm done may be
incurable—a difficult and even hopeless crime to defend;[2]

[1] [For Callistratus cp. note to 1364*21. Melanopus was a
political rival; the exact nature of the offence here alluded
to is unknown.]
[2] Or, 'due punishment then being difficult or impossible.'

or the sufferer may not be able to get his injurer legally
punished, a fact that makes the harm incurable, since legal
punishment and chastisement are the proper cure. Or
again, the man who has suffered wrong may have inflicted
some fearful punishment on himself; then the doer of the
35 wrong ought in justice to receive a still more fearful punishment. Thus Sophocles,[1] when pleading for retribution
to Euctemon, who had cut his own throat because of the
1375ᵃ outrage done to him, said he would not fix a penalty less
than the victim had fixed for himself. Again, a man's crime
is worse if he has been the first man, or the only man, or
almost the only man, to commit it: or if it is by no means
the first time he has gone seriously wrong in the same
way: or if his crime has led to the thinking-out and invention of measures to prevent and punish similar crimes
5 —thus in Argos a penalty is inflicted on a man on whose
account a law is passed, and also on those on whose account the prison was built: or if a crime is specially brutal,
or specially deliberate: or if the report of it awakes more
terror than pity. There are also such rhetorically effective
ways of putting it as the following: That the accused has
disregarded and broken not one but many solemn obliga-
10 tions like oaths, promises, pledges, or rights of intermar-
riage between states—here the crime is worse because it
consists of many crimes; and that the crime was committed
in the very place where criminals are punished, as for example perjurers do—it is argued that a man who will commit a crime in a law-court would commit it anywhere.
Further, the worse deed is that which involves the doer
in special shame; that whereby a man wrongs his benefactors— for he does more than one wrong, by not merely
15 doing them harm but failing to do them good; that which
breaks the unwritten laws of justice—the better sort of
man will be just without being forced to be so, and the
written laws depend on force while the unwritten ones do
not. It may however be argued otherwise, that the crime
is worse which breaks the written laws: for the man who

---

[1] [Not the tragedian but a statesman and orator advanced
in years at the end of the Peloponnesian war. The case
mentioned here is unknown.]

commits crimes for which terrible penalties are provided
will not hesitate over crimes for which no penalty is pro- 20
vided at all.—So much, then, for the comparative badness
of criminal actions.

15   There are also the so-called 'non-technical' [1] means of
persuasion; and we must now take a cursory view of these,
since they are specially characteristic of forensic oratory.
They are five in number: laws, witnesses, contracts, tortures, oaths.

First, then, let us take laws and see how they are to be 25
used in persuasion and dissuasion, in accusation and defence. If the written law tells against our case, clearly we[2]
must appeal to the universal law, and insist on its greater
equity and justice. We must argue that the juror's oath 'I
will give my verdict according to my honest opinion'
means that one will not simply follow the letter of the 30
written law. We must urge that the principles of equity
are permanent and changeless, and that the universal law
does not change either, for it is the law of nature, whereas
written laws often do change. This is the bearing of the
lines in Sophocles' *Antigone*, where Antigone pleads that
in burying her brother she had broken Creon's law, but
not the unwritten law:

> Not of to-day or yesterday they are,   1375[b]
> But live eternal: ⟨none can date their birth.⟩
> Not I would fear the wrath of any man,
> ⟨And brave Gods' vengeance⟩ for defying these.[3]

We shall argue that justice indeed is true and profitable,
but that sham justice is not, and that consequently the
written law is not, because it does not fulfil the true purpose of law. Or that justice is like silver, and must be 5
assayed by the judges, if the genuine is to be distinguished

---

[1] Cp. c. 2, *supra*.

[2] Here, and in what follows, 'we' must be taken in a general
sense. More literally, 'tells against his case, clearly the
litigant must. . . . He must argue, &c.' So with 'you' elsewhere: e.g. 1372[a,b].

[3] Sophocles, *Antigone*, 456. . . .

from the counterfeit. Or that the better a man is, the more
he will follow and abide by the unwritten law in pref-
erence to the written. Or perhaps that the law in question contradicts some other highly-esteemed law, or even
contradicts itself. Thus it may be that one law will enact
10 that all contracts must be held binding, while another for-
bids us ever to make illegal contracts. Or if a law is ambiguous, we shall turn it about and consider which construction best fits the interests of justice or utility, and
then follow that way of looking at it. Or if, though the
law still exists, the situation to meet which it was passed
15 exists no longer, we must do our best to prove this and to
combat the law thereby. If however the written law supports our case, we must urge that the oath 'to give my
verdict according to my honest opinion' is not meant to
make the judges give a verdict that is contrary to the law,
but to save them from the guilt of perjury if they mis-
understand what the law really means. Or that no one
chooses what is absolutely good, but every one what is
good for himself.[1] Or that not to use the laws is as bad as
20 to have no laws at all. Or that, as in the other arts, it does
not pay to try to be cleverer than the doctor: for less harm
comes from the doctor's mistakes than from the growing
habit of disobeying authority. Or that trying to be cleverer
than the laws is just what is forbidden by those codes of
law that are accounted best.—So far as the laws are con-
25 cerned, the above discussion is probably sufficient.

As to witnesses, they are of two kinds, the ancient and
the recent; and these latter, again, either do or do not
share in the risks of the trial. By 'ancient' witnesses I mean
the poets and all other notable persons whose judgements
are known to all. Thus the Athenians appealed to Homer[2]
30 as a witness about Salamis; and the men of Tenedos not

[1] Sc., and our written laws, which were made for us, may
not reach the abstract ideal of perfection, but they probably suit us better than if they did.
[2] [Claiming against Megara their ancient right to the possession of Salamis. The *Iliad* verses B 557-58 have often
in antiquity been called an Athenian interpolation.]

long ago appealed to Periander[1] of Corinth in their dispute
with the people of Sigeum; and Cleophon[2] supported his
accusation of Critias by quoting the elegiac verse of Solon,
maintaining that discipline had long been slack in the
family of Critias, or Solon would never have written,

Pray thee, bid the red-haired Critias do what his father
     commands him.[3]

These witnesses are concerned with past events. As to
future events we shall also appeal to soothsayers: thus 1376ᵃ
Themistocles[4] quoted the oracle about 'the wooden wall'
as a reason for engaging the enemy's fleet. Further, proverbs are, as has been said,[5] one form of evidence. Thus
if you are urging somebody not to make a friend of an
old man, you will appeal to the proverb,

Never show an old man kindness.   5

Or if you are urging that he who has made away with
fathers should also make away with their sons, quote,

Fool, who slayeth the father and leaveth his sons to
     avenge him.[6]

'Recent' witnesses are well-known people who have expressed their opinions about some disputed matter: such
opinions will be useful support for subsequent disputants
on the same points: thus Eubulus[7] used in the law-courts

---

[1] [Famous tyrant of Corinth in the 7th cent. B.C. The
     incident referred to is unknown.]
[2] [Cleophon and Ciritas, leaders of opposite parties at the
     end of the Peloponnesian war.]
[3] [Fragm. of Solon, Athenian statesman and elegiac poet of
     6th cent.]
[4] Herodotus, vii. 141, 143. [The engagement was the battle
     of Salamis where Themistocles commanded the Greek
     fleet.]
[5] A general statement, apparently. Or possibly (cp. *Poetics*
     1454ᵃ25) 'proverbs are evidence in the sense indicated,'
     i.e. evidence of the future. But the Greek expression
     usually has the meaning which it bears in (e.g.) 1395ᵇ5.
[6] [Fragm. of the *Cypria* of Stasinus, an early epos.]
[7] [Popular Athenian statesman of 4th cent. Of the case
     mentioned here nothing is known.]

10 against Chares the reply Plato[1] had made to Archibius,[2]
'It has become the regular custom in this country to admit that one is a scoundrel'. There are also those witnesses
who share the risk of punishment if their evidence is pronounced false. These are valid witnesses to the fact that
an action was or was not done, that something is or is not
15 the case; they are not valid witnesses to the quality of an
action, to its being just or unjust, useful or harmful. On
such questions of *quality* the opinion of detached persons
is highly trustworthy. Most trustworthy of all are the
'ancient' witnesses, since they cannot be corrupted.

In dealing with the evidence of witnesses, the following
are useful arguments. If you have no witnesses on your
side, you will argue that the judges must decide from
what is probable; that this is meant by 'giving a verdict in
accordance with one's honest opinion'; that probabilities
20 cannot be bribed to mislead the court; and that probabilities are never convicted of perjury. If you *have* witnesses,
and the other man has not, you will argue that probabilities cannot be put on their trial, and that we could do
without the evidence of witnesses altogether if we need
do no more than balance the pleas advanced on either
side.

The evidence of witnesses may refer either to ourselves
or to our opponent; and either to questions of fact or to
25 questions of personal character: so, clearly, we need never
be at a loss for useful evidence. For if we have no evidence of fact supporting our own case or telling against
that of our opponent, at least we can always find evidence
to prove our own worth or our opponent's worthlessness.
Other arguments about a witness—that he is a friend or an
30 enemy or neutral, or has a good, bad, or indifferent reputation, and any other such distinctions—we must construct
upon the same general lines as we use for the regular
rhetorical proofs.[3]

Concerning contracts argument can be so far employed

---

[1] [May have been the philosopher or the comic poet, contemporary of Aristophanes.]
[2] [Unknown.]
[3] 'enthymemes': cp. ii, c. 23.

as to increase or diminish their importance and their
credibility; we shall try to increase both if they tell in our 1376^b
favour, and to diminish both if they tell in favour of our
opponent. Now for confirming or upsetting the credibility
of contracts the procedure is just the same as for dealing
with witnesses, for the credit to be attached to contracts
depends upon the character of those who have signed
them or have the custody of them. The contract being
once admitted genuine, we must insist on its importance,
if it supports our case. We may argue that a contract is a
law, though of a special and limited kind; and that, while
contracts do not of course make the law binding, the law
does make any lawful contract binding, and that the law
itself as a whole is a sort of contract, so that any one who 10
disregards or repudiates any contract is repudiating the
law itself. Further, most business relations—those, namely,
that are voluntary—are regulated by contracts, and if these
lose their binding force, human intercourse ceases to exist.
We need not go very deep to discover the other appropriate arguments of this kind. If, however, the contract tells
against us and for our opponents, in the first place those 15
arguments are suitable which we can use to fight a law
that tells against us. We do not regard ourselves as bound
to observe a bad law which it was a mistake ever to pass:
and it is ridiculous to suppose that we are bound to observe a bad and mistaken contract. Again, we may argue
that the duty of the judge as umpire is to decide what is 20
just, and therefore he must ask where justice lies, and not
what this or that document means. And that it is impossible to pervert justice by fraud or by force, since it is
founded on nature, but a party to a contract may be the
victim of either fraud or force. Moreover, we must see if
the contract contravenes either universal law or any 25
written law of our own or another country; and also if it
contradicts any other previous or subsequent contract;
arguing that the subsequent is the binding contract, or
else that the previous one was right and the subsequent
one fraudulent—whichever way suits us. Further, we must
consider the question of utility, noting whether the con-

30 tract is against the interest of the judges or not; and so on —these arguments are as obvious as the others.

Examination by torture is one form of evidence, to which great weight is often attached because it is in a sense compulsory. Here again it is not hard to point out the available grounds for magnifying its value, if it happens to tell in our favour, and arguing that it is the only form of evidence that is infallible; or, on the other hand, 1377ᵃ for refuting it if it tells against us and for our opponent, when we may say what is true of torture of every kind alike, that people under its compulsion tell lies quite as often as they tell the truth, sometimes persistently refus-5 ing to tell the truth, sometimes recklessly making a false charge in order to be let off sooner. We ought to be able to quote cases, familiar to the judges, in which this sort of thing has actually happened. [We must say that evidence under torture is not trustworthy, the fact being that many men whether thick-witted, tough-skinned, or stout of heart endure their ordeal nobly, while cowards and timid men are full of boldness till they see the ordeal of these others: so that no trust can be placed in evidence under torture.]

In regard to oaths, a fourfold division can be made. A man may either both offer and accept an oath,[1] or neither, or one without the other—that is, he may offer an oath but 10 not accept one, or accept an oath but not offer one. There is also the situation that arises when an oath has already been sworn either by himself or by his opponent.

If you refuse to offer an oath, you may argue that men do not hesitate to perjure themselves; and that if your opponent does swear, you lose your money, whereas, if he does not, you think the judges will decide against him; and that the risk of an unfavourable verdict is preferable, 15 since you trust the judges and do not trust him.

If you refuse to accept an oath, you may argue that an oath is always paid for; that you would of course have taken it if you had been a rascal, since if you *are* a rascal

---

[1] i.e. both demand an oath from his adversary (call upon him to swear to the truth of his statements) and take an oath himself.

you had better make something by it, and you would in
that case have to swear in order to succeed. Thus your
refusal, you argue, must be due to high principle, not to
fear of perjury: and you may aptly quote the saying of
Xenophanes,

'Tis not fair that he who fears not God should challenge 20
    him who doth.[1]

It is as if a strong man were to challenge a weakling to
strike, or be struck by, him.

If you agree to accept an oath, you may argue that you
trust yourself but not your opponent; and that (to invert
the remark of Xenophanes) the fair thing is for the
impious man to offer the oath and for the pious man to
accept it; and that it would be monstrous if you yourself
were unwilling to accept an oath in a case where you
demand that the judges should do so before giving their 25
verdict. If you wish to offer an oath, you may argue that
piety disposes you to commit the issue to the gods; and
that your opponent ought not to want other judges than
himself, since you leave the decision with him; and that
it is outrageous for your opponents to refuse to swear
about this question, when they insist that others should
do so.

Now that we see how we are to argue in each case
separately, we see also how we are to argue when they
occur in pairs, namely, when you are willing to accept the 30
oath but not to offer it; to offer it but not to accept it;
both to accept and to offer it; or to do neither. These are
of course combinations of the cases already mentioned, 1377ᵇ
and so your arguments also must be combinations of the
arguments already mentioned.

If you have already sworn an oath that contradicts your
present one, you must argue that it is not perjury, since
perjury is a crime, and a crime must be a voluntary action,
whereas actions due to the force or fraud of others are 5
involuntary. You must further reason from this that perjury

---

[1] [Fragm. of Xenophanes of Colophon, traditionally associated with the Eleatic school of philosophy.]

depends on the intention and not on the spoken words. But if it is your opponent who has already sworn an oath that contradicts his present one, you must say that if he does not abide by his oaths he is the enemy of society, and that this is the reason why men take an oath before administering the laws. 'My opponents insist that you, the judges, 10 must abide by the oath you have sworn, and yet they are not abiding by their own oaths.' And there are other arguments which may be used to magnify the importance of the oath.— [So much, then, for the 'non-technical' modes of persuasion.]

BOOK II

We have now considered the materials to be used in 1 supporting or opposing a political measure, in pronouncing eulogies or censures, and for prosecution and defence in the law courts. We have considered the received opinions on which we may best base our arguments so as to convince our hearers—those opinions with which our enthymemes deal, and out of which they are built, in each of 20 the three kinds of oratory, according to what may be called the special needs of each.

But since rhetoric exists to affect the giving of decisions —the hearers decide between one political speaker and another, and a legal verdict *is* a decision—the orator must not only try to make the argument of his speech demonstrative and worthy of belief; he must also make his own character look right and put his hearers, who are to decide, into the right frame of mind. Particularly in political 25 oratory, but also in lawsuits, it adds much to an orator's influence that his own character should look right and that he should be thought to entertain the right feelings towards his hearers; and also that his hearers themselves should be in just the right frame of mind. That the orator's own character should look right is particularly important in political speaking: that the audience should be in the 30 right frame of mind, in lawsuits. When people are feeling friendly and placable, they think one sort of thing; when they are feeling angry or hostile, they think either something totally different or the same thing with a different 1378ᵃ intensity: when they feel friendly to the man who comes before them for judgement, they regard him as having done little wrong, if any; when they feel hostile, they take the opposite view. Again, if they are eager for, and have good hopes of, a thing that will be pleasant if it happens, they think that it certainly will happen and be good for them: whereas if they are indifferent or annoyed, they do 5 not think so.

There are three things which inspire confidence in the orator's own character—the three, namely, that induce us to believe a thing apart from any proof of it: good sense, good moral character, and goodwill. False statements and bad advice are due to one or more of the following 10 three causes. Men either form a false opinion through want of good sense; or they form a true opinion, but because of their moral badness do not say what they really think; or finally, they are both sensible and upright, but not well disposed to their hearers, and may fail in consequence to recommend what they know to be the best course. These are the only possible cases. It follows that any one who is thought to have all three of these good 15 qualities will inspire trust in his audience. The way to make ourselves thought to be sensible and morally good must be gathered from the analysis of goodness already given:[1] the way to establish your own goodness is the same as the way to establish that of others. Good will and friendliness of disposition will form part of our discussion of the emotions,[2] to which we must now turn.

The Emotions are all those feelings that so change men 20 as to affect their judgements, and that are also attended by

[1] i, c. 9.
[2] ii, c. 4.

pain or pleasure. Such are anger, pity, fear and the like, with their opposites. We must arrange what we have to say about each of them under three heads. Take, for instance, the emotion of anger: here we must discover (1) what the state of mind of angry people is, (2) who the
25 people are with whom they usually get angry, and (3) on what grounds they get angry with them. It is not enough to know one or even two of these points; unless we know all three, we shall be unable to arouse anger in any one. The same is true ot the other emotions. So just as earlier in this work we drew up a list of useful propositions for
30 the orator, let us now proceed in the same way to analyse the subject before us.

Anger may be defined as an impulse, accompanied by 2 pain, to a conspicuous revenge for a conspicuous slight directed without justification towards what concerns oneself or towards what concerns one's friends. If this is a proper definition of anger, it must always be felt towards some particular individual, e.g. Cleon, and not 'man' in general. It must be felt because the other has done or in-
1378^b tended to do something to him or one of his friends. It must always be attended by a certain pleasure—that which arises from the expectation of revenge. For since nobody aims at what he thinks he cannot attain, the angry man is aiming at what he can attain, and the belief that
5 you will attain your aim is pleasant. Hence it has been well said about wrath,

Sweeter it is by far than the honeycomb dripping with
  sweetness,
And spreads through the hearts of men.[1]

It is also attended by a certain pleasure because the thoughts dwell upon the act of vengeance, and the images then called up cause pleasure, like the images called up in dreams.
10 Now slighting is the actively entertained opinion of something as obviously of no importance. We think bad

---

[1] *Iliad*, xviii. 109 (cp. i, c. 11, 1370^{b}12 *supra*).

things, as well as good ones, have serious importance; and
we think the same of anything that tends to produce such
things, while those which have little or no such tendency
we consider unimportant. There are three kinds of slighting—contempt, spite, and insolence. (1) Contempt is one
kind of slighting: you feel contempt for what you consider 15
unimportant, and it is just such things that you slight.
(2) Spite is another kind;[1] it is a thwarting another man's
wishes, not to get something yourself but to prevent his
getting it. The slight arises just from the fact that you do
not aim at something for yourself: clearly you do not think
that he can do you harm, for then you would be afraid of 20
him instead of slighting him, nor yet that he can do you
any good worth mentioning, for then you would be anxious
to make friends with him. (3) Insolence is also a form of
slighting, since it consists in doing and saying things that
cause shame to the victim, not in order that anything may
happen to yourself, or because anything has happened 25
to yourself, but simply for the pleasure involved. (Retaliation is not 'insolence', but vengeance.) The cause of the
pleasure thus enjoyed by the insolent man is that he thinks
himself greatly superior to others when ill-treating them.
That is why youths and rich men are insolent; they think
themselves superior when they show insolence. One sort
of insolence is to rob people of the honour due to them;
you certainly slight them thus; for it is the unimportant, 30
for good or evil, that has no honour paid to it. So Achilles
says in anger:

He hath taken my prize for himself and hath done me
    dishonour,

and
                Like an alien honoured by none,[2]

meaning that this is why he is angry. A man expects to
be specially respected by his inferiors in birth, in capacity,
in goodness, and generally in anything in which he[3] is

[1] Or, 'spite seems to show contempt.' . . .
[2] *Iliad*, i. 356; Ib. ix. 648.
[3] . . . Or 'in anything common to them and him in which
he,' &c.

1379ᵃ much their superior: as where money is concerned a
wealthy man looks for respect from a poor man; where
speaking is concerned, the man with a turn for oratory
looks for respect from one who cannot speak; the ruler
demands the respect of the ruled, and the man who thinks
he ought to be a ruler demands the respect of the man
whom he thinks he ought to be ruling. Hence it has been
said

Great is the wrath of kings, whose father is Zeus almighty,

and

5   Yea, but his rancour abideth long afterward also,[1]

their great resentment being due to their great superiority.
Then again a man looks for respect from those who he
thinks owe him good treatment, and these are the people
whom he has treated or is treating well, or means or has
meant to treat well, either himself, or through his friends,
or through others at his request.

It will be plain by now, from what has been said, (1) in
what frame of mind, (2) with what persons, and (3) on
what grounds people grow angry. (1) The frame of mind
10 is that in which any pain is being felt. In that condition,
a man is always aiming at something. Whether, then,
another man opposes him either directly in any way, as by
preventing him from drinking when he is thirsty, or in-
directly, the act appears to him just the same; whether
some one works against him, or fails to work with him,
or otherwise vexes him while he is in this mood, he is
15 equally angry in all these cases. Hence people who are
afflicted by sickness or poverty or love or thirst or any
other unsatisfied desires are prone to anger and easily
roused: especially against those who slight their present
distress. Thus a sick man is angered by disregard of
his illness, a poor man by disregard of his poverty, a man
waging war by disregard of the war he is waging, a lover
20 by disregard of his love, and so throughout, any other sort
of slight being enough if special slights are wanting.

[1] *Iliad*, ii. 196; Ib. i. 82.

Each man is predisposed, by the emotion now controlling him, to his own particular anger. Further, we are angered if we happen to be expecting a contrary result: for a quite unexpected evil is specially painful, just as the quite unexpected fulfilment of our wishes is specially pleasant. Hence it is plain what seasons, times, conditions, and 25 periods of life tend to stir men easily to anger, and where and when this will happen; and it is plain that the more we are under these conditions the more easily we are stirred.

These, then, are the frames of mind in which men are easily stirred to anger. The persons with whom we get angry are those who laugh, mock, or jeer at us, for such conduct is insolent. Also those who inflict injuries upon us that are marks of insolence. These injuries must be such 30 as are neither retaliatory nor profitable to the doers: for only then will they be felt to be due to insolence. Also those who speak ill of us, and show contempt for us, in connexion with the things we ourselves most care about: thus those who are eager to win fame as philosophers get angry with those who show contempt for their philoso- 35 phy; those who pride themselves upon their appearance get angry with those who show contempt for their appearance; and so on in other cases. We feel particularly angry on this account if we suspect that we are in fact, or that people think we are, lacking completely or to an effective extent in the qualities in question. For when we are con- 1379^b vinced that we excel in the qualities for which we are jeered at, we can ignore the jeering. Again, we are angrier with our friends than with other people, since we feel that our friends ought to treat us well and not badly. We are angry with those who have usually treated us with honour or regard, if a change comes and they behave to 5 us otherwise: for we think that they feel contempt for us, or they would still be behaving as they did before. And with those who do not return our kindnesses or fail to return them adequately, and with those who oppose us though they are our inferiors: for all such persons seem to feel contempt for us; those who oppose us seem to think us inferior to themselves, and those who do not return our kindnesses seem to think that those kindnesses were conferred by inferiors. And we feel particularly angry with 10 men of no account at all, if they slight us. For, by our hypothesis, the anger caused by the slight is felt towards people who are not justified in slighting us, and our inferiors are not thus justified. Again, we feel angry with friends if they do not speak well of us or treat us well; and still more, if they do the contrary; or if they do not perceive our needs, which is why Plexippus is angry with 15 Meleager in Antiphon's play;[1] for this want of perception shows that they are slighting us—we do not fail to perceive the needs of those for whom we care. Again, we are angry with those who rejoice at our misfortunes or simply keep cheerful in the midst of our misfortunes, since this shows that they either hate us or are slighting us. Also with those who are indifferent to the pain they give us: 20 this is why we get angry with bringers of bad news. And with those who listen to stories about us or keep on looking at our weaknesses; this seems like either slighting us or hating us; for those who love us share in all our distresses and it must distress any one to keep on looking at his own weaknesses. Further, with those who slight us before five classes of people: namely, (1) our rivals, (2) those whom 25 we admire, (3) those whom we wish to admire us, (4) those for whom we feel reverence, (5) those who feel reverence for us: if any one slights us before such persons, we feel particularly angry. Again, we feel angry with those who slight us in connexion with what we are as honourable men bound to champion—our parents, children, 30 wives, or subjects. And with those who do not return a favour, since such a slight is unjustifiable. Also with those who reply with humorous levity when we are speaking seriously, for such behaviour indicates contempt. And with those who treat us less well than they treat everybody else; it is another mark of contempt that they should think we do not deserve what every one else deserves. Forget- 35 fulness, too, causes anger, as when our own names are forgotten, trifling as this may be; since forgetfulness is

[1] [Fragm. of the *Meleager* of Antiphon, a tragedian of the 4th cent. B.C.]

felt to be another sign that we are being slighted; it is due to negligence, and to neglect us is to slight us.

The persons with whom we feel anger, the frame of mind in which we feel it, and the reasons why we feel it, *1380ᵃ* have now all been set forth. Clearly the orator will have to speak so as to bring his hearers into a frame of mind that will dispose them to anger, and to represent his adversaries as open to such charges and possessed of such qualities as do make people angry.

3 Since growing calm is the opposite of growing angry, 5 and calmness[1] the opposite of anger, we must ascertain in what frames of mind men are calm, towards whom they feel calm, and by what means they are made so. Growing calm may be defined as a settling down or quieting of anger. Now we get angry with those who slight us; and since slighting is a voluntary act, it is plain that we feel calm towards those who do nothing of the kind, or who 10 do or seem to do it involuntarily. Also towards those who intended to do the opposite of what they did do. Also towards those who treat themselves as they have treated us: since no one can be supposed to slight himself. Also towards those who admit their fault and are sorry: since we accept their grief at what they have done as satisfaction, and cease to be angry. The punishment of servants 15 shows this: those who contradict us and deny their offence we punish all the more, but we cease to be incensed against those who agree that they deserved their punishment. The reason is that it is shameless to deny what is obvious, and those who are shameless towards us slight us and show contempt for us: anyhow, we do not feel shame 20 before those of whom we are thoroughly contemptuous. Also we feel calm towards those who humble themselves before us and do not gainsay us; we feel that they thus admit themselves our inferiors, and inferiors feel fear, and nobody can slight any one so long as he feels afraid of him. That our anger ceases towards those who humble themselves before us is shown even by dogs, who do not 25 bite people when they sit down. We also feel calm towards

[1] Or: gentleness, mildness, placability, patience. . . .

those who are serious when we are serious, because then
we feel that we are treated seriously and not contemptu-
ously. Also towards those who have done us more kindnesses than we have done them. Also towards those who
pray to us and beg for mercy, since they humble themselves by doing so. Also towards those who do not insult
30 or mock at or slight any one at all, or not any worthy
person or any one like ourselves. In general, the things
that make us calm may be inferred by seeing what the
opposites are of those that make us angry. We are not
angry with people we fear or respect, as long as we fear
or respect them; you cannot be afraid of a person and also
at the same time angry with him. Again, we feel no anger,
or comparatively little, with those who have done what
35 they did through anger; we do not feel that they have
done it from a wish to slight us, for no one slights people
when angry with them, since slighting is painless, and
1380^b anger is painful. Nor do we grow angry with those who
reverence us.

As to the frame of mind that makes people calm, it is
plainly the opposite to that which makes them angry, as
when they are amusing themselves or laughing or feasting;
when they are feeling prosperous or successful or satisfied; when, in fine, they are enjoying freedom from pain, or
5 inoffensive pleasure, or justifiable hope. Also when time
has passed and their anger is no longer fresh, for time
puts an end to anger. And vengeance previously taken on
one person puts an end to even greater anger felt against
another person. Hence Philocrates,[1] being asked by some
one, at a time when the public was angry with him, 'Why
don't you defend yourself?' did right to reply, 'The time is
10 not yet.' 'Why, when *is* the time?' 'When I see some one
else calumniated.' For men become calm when they have
spent their anger on somebody else. This happened in the
case of Ergophilus:[2] though the people were more irritated
against him than against Callisthenes,[2] they acquitted him
because they had condemned Callisthenes to death the day

[1] [A contemporary political figure.]
[2] [Two Athenian generals of the 4th cent., both commanded
in the Chersonese 362 B.C.]

before. Again, men become calm if they have convicted[1]
the offender; or if he has already suffered worse things 15
than they in their anger would have themselves inflicted
upon him; for they feel as if they were already avenged.
Or if they feel that they themselves are in the wrong and
are suffering justly (for anger is not excited by what is
just), since men no longer think then that they are suffering without justification; and anger, as we have seen,
means this. Hence we ought always to inflict a preliminary
punishment in words: if that is done, even slaves are less 20
aggrieved by the actual punishment. We also feel calm
if we think that the offender will not see that he is
punished on our account and because of the way he has
treated us. For anger has to do with individuals. This is
plain from the definition. Hence the poet has well
written:

> Say that it was Odysseus, sacker of cities,[2]

implying that Odysseus would not have considered himself avenged unless the Cyclops perceived both by whom
and for what he had been blinded. Consequently we do
not get angry with any one who cannot be aware of our 25
anger, and in particular we cease to be angry with people
once they are dead, for we feel that the worst has been
done to them, and that they will neither feel pain nor
anything else that we in our anger aim at making them
feel. And therefore the poet has well made Apollo say, in
order to put a stop to the anger of Achilles against the
dead Hector,

> For behold in his fury he doeth despite to the senseless
> clay.[3]

It is now plain that when you wish to calm others you 30
must draw upon these lines of argument; you must put
your hearers into the corresponding frame of mind, and
represent those with whom they are angry as formidable,
or as worthy of reverence, or as benefactors, or as invol-

---

[1] . . . Or, 'if they pity.'
[2] *Odyssey,* ix. 504.
[3] *Iliad,* xxiv. 54.

untary agents, or as much distressed at what they have
done.

Let us now turn to Friendship[1] and Enmity, and ask *4*
towards whom these feelings are entertained, and why.
35 We will begin by defining friendship and friendly feeling.
We may describe friendly feeling towards any one as wishing for him what you believe to be good things, not for
1381ᵃ your own sake but for his, and being inclined, so far as
you can, to bring these things about. A friend is one who
feels thus and excites these feelings in return: those who
think they feel thus towards each other think themselves
friends. This being assumed, it follows that your friend is
the sort of man who shares your pleasure in what is good
5 and your pain in what is unpleasant, for your sake and for
no other reason. This pleasure and pain of his will be the
token of his good wishes for you, since we all feel glad at
getting what we wish for, and pained at getting what we
do not. Those, then, are friends to whom the same things
are good and evil; and those who are, moreover, friendly
10 or unfriendly to the same people; for in that case they
must have the same wishes, and thus by wishing for each
other what they wish for themselves, they show themselves each other's friends. Again, we feel friendly to
those who have treated us well, either ourselves or those
we care for, whether on a large scale, or readily, or at
some particular crisis; provided it was for our own sake.
And also to those who we think *wish* to treat us well. And
15 also to our friends' friends, and to those who like, or are
liked by, those whom we like ourselves. And also to those
who are enemies to those whose enemies we are, and dislike, or are disliked by, those whom we dislike. For all such
persons think the things good which we think good, so
that they wish what is good for us; and this, as we saw, is
what friends must do. And also to those who are willing
20 to treat us well where money or our personal safety is

---

[1] In this chapter and elsewhere it is difficult to translate
φιλεῖν (and its related words) by any single English
equivalent; 'to be a friend,' 'to like,' 'to love,' may have
to be used in turn. . . .

concerned: and therefore we value those who are liberal, brave, or just. The just we consider to be those who do not live on others; which means those who work for their living, especially farmers and others who work with their own hands. We also like temperate men, because they are not unjust to others; and, for the same reason, those who 25 mind their own business. And also those whose friends we wish to be, if it is plain that they wish to be our friends: such are the morally good, and those well thought of by every one, by the best men, or by those whom we admire or who admire us. And also those with whom it is pleasant to live and spend our days: such are the good-tempered, 30 and those who are not too ready to show us our mistakes, and those who are not cantankerous or quarrelsome—such people are always wanting to fight us, and those who fight us we feel wish for the opposite of what we wish for ourselves—and those who have the tact to make and take a joke; here both parties have the same object in view,[1] when they can stand being made fun of as well as do it 35 prettily themselves. And we also feel friendly towards those who praise such good qualities as we possess, and especially if they praise the good qualities that we are not too sure we *do* possess. And towards those who are cleanly **1381ᵇ** in their person, their dress, and all their way of life. And towards those who do not reproach us with what we have done amiss to them or they have done to help us, for both actions show a tendency to criticize us. And towards those who do not nurse grudges or store up griev- 5 ances, but are always ready to make friends again; for we take it that they will behave to us just as we find them behaving to every one else. And towards those who are not evil speakers and who are aware of neither their neighbours' bad points nor our own, but of our good ones only, as a good man always will be. And towards those who do not try to thwart us when we are angry or in earnest, which would mean being ready to fight us. And towards those 10 who have some serious feeling towards us, such as admiration for us, or belief in our goodness, or pleasure in our company; especially if they feel like this about qualities in

[1] i.e. both wish to pass the time pleasantly.

us for which we especially wish to be admired, esteemed,
or liked. And towards those who are like ourselves in
15 character and occupation, provided they do not get in our
way or gain their living from the same source as we do—
for then it will be a case of 'potter against potter':

Potter to potter and builder to builder begrudge their
reward.[1]

And those who desire the same things as we desire, if it is
possible for us both to share them together; otherwise the
same trouble arises here too. And towards those with
whom we are on such terms that, while we respect their
20 opinions, we need not blush before them for doing what is
conventionally wrong: as well as towards those before
whom we should be ashamed to do anything really wrong.
Again, our rivals, and those whom we should like to envy
us—though without ill-feeling—either we like these people
or at least we wish them to like us. And we feel friendly
towards those whom we help to secure good for themselves, provided we are not likely to suffer heavily by it
25 ourselves. And those who feel as friendly to us when we
are not with them as when we are—which is why all men
feel friendly towards those who are faithful to their dead
friends. And, speaking generally, towards those who are
really fond of their friends and do not desert them in
trouble; of all good men, we feel most friendly to those
who show their goodness as friends. Also towards those
who are honest with us, including those who will tell us of
their own weak points: it has just been said that with our
30 friends we are not ashamed of what is conventionally
wrong, and if we do have this feeling, we do not love
them; if therefore we do not have it, it looks as if we *did*
love them. We also like those with whom we do not feel
frightened or uncomfortable—nobody can like a man of
whom he feels frightened. Friendship has various forms—
comradeship, intimacy, kinship, and so on.
35 Things that cause friendship are: doing kindnesses;
doing them unasked; and not proclaiming the fact when

---

[1] Hesiod, *Works and Days*, 25. . . .

they are done, which shows that they were done for our sake and not for some other reason.

Enmity and Hatred should clearly be studied by refer- 1382ᵃ ence to their opposites. Enmity may be produced by anger or spite or calumny. Now whereas anger arises from offences against oneself, enmity may arise even without that; we may hate people merely because of what we take to be their character. Anger is always concerned with in- dividuals—a Callias or a Socrates—whereas hatred is 5 directed also against classes: we all hate any thief and any informer. Moreover, anger can be cured by time; but hatred cannot. The one aims at giving pain to its object, the other at doing him harm; the angry man wants his victims to feel; the hater does not mind whether they feel or not. All painful things are felt; but the greatest evils, 10 injustice and folly, are the least felt, since their presence causes no pain. And anger is accompanied by pain, hatred is not; the angry man feels pain, but the hater does not. Much may happen to make the angry man pity those who offend him, but the hater under no circumstances wishes to pity a man whom he has once hated: for the one would 15 have the offenders suffer for what they have done; the other would have them cease to exist.

It is plain from all this that we can prove people to be friends or enemies; if they are not, we can make them out to be so; if they claim to be so, we can refute their claim; and if it is disputed whether an action was due to anger or to hatred, we can attribute it to whichever of these we prefer.[1]

5   To turn next to Fear, what follows will show the things and persons of which, and the states of mind in which, we 20 feel afraid. Fear may be defined as a pain or disturbance due to a mental picture of some destructive or painful evil in the future. Of destructive or painful evils only; for there are some evils, e.g. wickedness or stupidity, the prospect of which does not frighten us: I mean only such

---

[1] . . . Or: 'if they dispute . . . with us through anger or through hatred, we can bring them into whichever of the two we prefer (i.e. into greater anger or greater hatred).'

as amount to great pains or losses. And even these only if
25 they appear not remote but so near as to be imminent:
we do not fear things that are a very long way off: for
instance, we all know we shall die, but we are not troubled
thereby, because death is not close at hand. From this
definition it will follow that fear is caused by whatever we
feel has great power of destroying us, or of harming us in
30 ways that tend to cause us great pain. Hence the very
indications of such things are terrible, making us feel that
the terrible thing itself is close at hand; the approach of
what is terrible is just what we mean by 'danger'. Such
indications are the enmity and anger of people who have
power to do something to us; for it is plain that they have
the will to do it, and so they are on the point of doing it. Also
35 injustice in possession of power; for it is the unjust man's
will to do evil that makes him unjust. Also outraged virtue
1382ᵇ in possession of power; for it is plain that, when outraged,
it always has the will to retaliate, and now it has the
power to do so. Also fear felt by those who have the power
to do something to us, since such persons are sure to be
ready to do it. And since most men tend to be bad—
5 slaves to greed, and cowards in danger—it is, as a rule, a
terrible thing to be at another man's mercy; and therefore,
if we have done anything horrible, those in the secret
terrify us with the thought that they may betray or desert
us. And those who can do us wrong are terrible to us
when we are liable to be wronged; for as a rule men do
wrong to others whenever they have the power to do it.
10 And those who have been wronged, or believe themselves
to be wronged, are terrible; for they are always looking
out for their opportunity. Also those who have done people
wrong, if they possess power, since they stand in fear of
retaliation: we have already said that wickedness possessing power is terrible. Again, our rivals for a thing cause us
fear when we cannot both have it at once; for we are
always at war with such men. We also fear those who are
15 to be feared by stronger people than ourselves: if they
can hurt those stronger people, still more can they hurt us;
and, for the same reason, we fear those whom those
stronger people are actually afraid of. Also those who have

destroyed people stronger than we are. Also those who
are attacking people weaker than we are: either they are
already formidable, or they will be so when they have thus
grown stronger. Of those we have wronged, and of our
enemies or rivals, it is not the passionate and outspoken 20
whom we have to fear, but the quiet, dissembling, unscrupulous; since we never know when they are upon us, we
can never be sure they are at a safe distance. All terrible
things are more terrible if they give us no chance of
retrieving a blunder—either no chance at all, or only one
that depends on our enemies and not ourselves. Those
things are also worse which we cannot, or cannot easily, 25
help. Speaking generally, anything causes us to feel fear
that when it happens to, or threatens, others causes us to
feel pity.

The above are roughly, the chief things that are terrible
and are feared. Let us now describe the conditions under
which we ourselves feel fear. If fear is associated with the
expectation that something destructive will happen to us, 30
plainly nobody will be afraid who believes nothing can
happen to him; we shall not fear things that we believe
cannot happen to us, nor people who we believe cannot
inflict them upon us; nor shall we be afraid at times when
we think ourselves safe from them. It follows therefore
that fear is felt by those who believe something to be
likely to happen to them, at the hands of particular per- 35
sons, in a particular form, and at a particular time. People
do not believe this when they are, or think they are, in 1383ᵃ
the midst of great prosperity, and are in consequence insolent, contemptuous, and reckless—the kind of character
produced by wealth, physical strength, abundance of
friends, power: nor yet when they feel they have experi-
enced every kind of horror already and have grown callous
about the future, like men who are being flogged and are
already nearly dead—if they are to feel the anguish of 5
uncertainty, there must be some faint expectation of
escape. This appears from the fact that fear sets us thinking what can be done, which of course nobody does when
things are hopeless. Consequently, when it is advisable
that the audience should be frightened, the orator must

make them feel that they really are in danger of something, pointing out that it has happened to others who
10 were stronger than they are, and is happening, or has
happened, to people like themselves, at the hands of
unexpected people, in an unexpected form, and at an
unexpected time.

Having now seen the nature of fear, and of the things
that cause it, and the various states of mind in which it
is felt, we can also see what Confidence is, about what
15 things we feel it, and under what conditions. It is the opposite of fear, and what causes it is the opposite of what
causes fear; it is, therefore, the expectation associated with
a mental picture of the nearness of what keeps us safe and
the absence or remoteness of what is terrible: it may be
due either to the near presence of what inspires confidence
or to the absence of what causes alarm. We feel it if we
20 can take steps—many, or important, or both—to cure or
prevent trouble; if we have neither wronged others nor
been wronged by them; if we have either no rivals at all
or no strong ones; if our rivals who are strong are our
friends or have treated us well or been treated well by
us; or if those whose interest is the same as ours are the
more numerous party, or the stronger, or both.

25 As for our own state of mind, we feel confidence if we
believe we have often succeeded and never suffered re-
verses, or have often met danger and escaped it safely. For
there are two reasons why human beings face danger
calmly: they may have no experience of it, or they may
30 have means to deal with it: thus when in danger at sea
people may feel confident about what will happen either
because they have no experience of bad weather, or because their experience gives them the means of dealing
with it. We also feel confident whenever there is nothing to
terrify other people like ourselves, or people weaker than
ourselves, or people than whom we believe ourselves to be
stronger—and we believe this if we have conquered them,
35 or conquered others who are as strong as they are, or
stronger. Also if we believe ourselves superior to our
rivals in the number and importance of the advantages
1383ᵇ that make men formidable—wealth, physical strength,

strong bodies of supporters, extensive territory, and the
possession of all, or the most important, appliances of war.
Also if we have wronged no one, or not many, or not those
of whom we are afraid; and generally, if our relations with
the gods are satisfactory, as will be shown especially by 5
signs and oracles. The fact is that anger makes us confident
—that anger is excited by our knowledge that we are not
the wrongers but the wronged, and that the divine power
is always supposed to be on the side of the wronged. Also
when, at the outset of an enterprise, we believe that we
cannot and shall not fail, or that we shall succeed com- 10
pletely.—So much for the causes of fear and confidence.

6   We now turn to Shame and Shamelessness; what follows
will explain the things that cause these feelings, and the
persons before whom, and the states of mind under which,
they are felt. Shame may be defined as pain or disturbance
in regard to bad things, whether present, past, or future, 15
which seem likely to involve us in discredit; and shamelessness as contempt or indifference in regard to these
same bad things. If this definition be granted, it follows
that we feel shame at such bad things as we think are
disgraceful to ourselves or to those we care for. These
evils are, in the first place, those due to moral badness. 20
Such are throwing away one's shield or taking to flight; for
these bad things are due to cowardice. Also, withholding
a deposit or otherwise wronging people about money; for
these acts are due to injustice. Also, having carnal intercourse with forbidden persons, at wrong times, or in wrong
places; for these things are due to licentiousness. Also,
making profit in petty or disgraceful ways, or out of help-
less persons, e.g. the poor, or the dead—whence the
proverb 'He would pick a corpse's pocket'; for all this is 25
due to low greed and meanness. Also, in money matters,
giving less help than you might, or none at all, or accepting help from those worse off than yourself; so also bor-
rowing when it will seem like begging; begging when it
will seem like asking the return of a favour; asking such
a return when it will seem like begging; praising a man
in order that it may seem like begging; and going on 30

begging in spite of failure: all such actions are tokens of meanness. Also, praising people to their face, and praising extravagantly a man's good points and glozing over his weaknesses, and showing extravagant sympathy with
35 his grief when you are in his presence, and all that sort of thing; all this shows the disposition of a flatterer. Also,
1384ª refusing to endure hardships that are endured by people who are older, more delicately brought up, of higher rank, or generally less capable of endurance than ourselves: for all this shows effeminacy. Also, accepting benefits, especially accepting them often, from another man, and then abusing him for conferring them: all this shows a mean, ignoble disposition. Also, talking incessantly about your-
5 self, making loud professions, and appropriating the merits of others; for this is due to boastfulness. The same is true of the actions due to any of the other forms of badness of moral character, of the tokens of such badness, &c.: they are all disgraceful and shameless. Another sort of bad thing at which we feel shame is, lacking a share in the honourable things shared by every one else, or by all or
10 nearly all who are like ourselves. By 'those like ourselves' I mean those of our own race or country or age or family, and generally those who are on our own level. Once we are on a level with others, it is a disgrace to be, say, less well educated than they are; and so with other advantages: all the more so, in each case, if it is seen to be our
15 own fault: wherever we are ourselves to blame for our present, past, or future circumstances, it follows at once that this is to a greater extent due to our moral badness. We are moreover ashamed of having done to us, having had done, or being about to have done to us acts that involve us in dishonour and reproach; as when we surrender our persons, or lend ourselves to vile deeds, e.g. when we submit to outrage. And acts of yielding to the
20 lust of others are shameful whether willing or unwilling (yielding to force being an instance of unwillingness), since unresisting submission to them is due to unmanliness or cowardice.

These things, and others like them, are what cause the feeling of shame. Now since shame is a mental picture of

disgrace, in which we shrink from the disgrace itself and
not from its consequences, and we only care what opinion 25
is held of us because of the people who form that opinion,
it follows that the people before whom we feel shame are
those whose opinion of us matters to us. Such persons are:
those who admire us, those whom we admire, those by
whom we wish to be admired, those with whom we are
competing, and those whose opinion of us we respect. We
admire those, and wish those to admire us, who possess
any good thing that is highly esteemed; or from whom we 30
are very anxious to get something that they are able to
give us—as a lover feels. We compete with our equals.
We respect, as true, the views of sensible people, such as
our elders and those who have been well educated. And
we feel more shame about a thing if it is done openly,
before all men's eyes. Hence the proverb, 'shame dwells in
the eyes'. For this reason we feel most shame before those
who will always be with us and those who notice what we
do, since in both cases eyes are upon us. We also feel it
before those not open to the same imputation as ourselves: 1384ᵇ
for it is plain that their opinions about it are the opposite
of ours. Also before those who are hard on any one whose
conduct they think wrong; for what a man does himself,
he is said not to resent when his neighbours do it: so that
of course he does resent their doing what he does not do 5
himself. And before those who are likely to tell everybody
about you; not telling others is as good as not believing
you wrong. People are likely to tell others about you if
you have wronged them, since they are on the look out to
harm you; or if they speak evil of everybody, for those
who attack the innocent will be still more ready to attack
the guilty. And before those whose main occupation is
with their neighbours' failings—people like satirists and 10
writers of comedy; these are really a kind of evil-speakers
and tell-tales. And before those who have never yet
known us come to grief, since their attitude to us has
amounted to admiration so far: that is why we feel
ashamed to refuse those a favour who ask one for the
first time—we have not as yet lost credit with them. Such
are those who are just beginning to wish to be our friends;

15 for they have seen our best side only (hence the appropriateness of Euripides'[1] reply to the Syracusans): and
such also are those among our old acquaintances who
know nothing to our discredit. And we are ashamed not
merely of the actual shameful conduct mentioned, but also
of the evidences of it: not merely, for example, of actual
sexual intercourse, but also of its evidences; and not
20 merely of disgraceful acts but also of disgraceful talk.
Similarly we feel shame not merely in presence of the
persons mentioned but also of those who will tell them
what we have done, such as their servants or friends. And,
generally, we feel no shame before those upon whose
opinions we quite look down as untrustworthy (no one
feels shame before small children or animals); nor are we
25 ashamed of the same things before intimates as before
strangers, but before the former of what seem genuine
faults, before the latter of what seem conventional ones.

The conditions under which we shall feel shame are
these: first, having people related to us like those before
whom, as has been said,[2] we feel shame. These are, as
was stated, persons whom we admire, or who admire us,
30 or by whom we wish to be admired, or from whom we
desire some service that we shall not obtain if we forfeit
their good opinion. These persons may be actually looking
on (as Cydias represented them in his speech on land
assignments in Samos,[3] when he told the Athenians to
imagine the Greeks to be standing all around them,
actually seeing the way they voted and not merely going
35 to hear about it afterwards): or again they may be near
at hand, or may be likely to find out about what we do.
This is why in misfortune we do not wish to be seen by

---

[1] The scholiast (ed. Rabe, p. 106) tells us that Euripides
was sent to negotiate peace with the Syracusans, and finding them unwilling said: 'You ought, men of Syracuse, to
respect our expressions of esteem if only because we are
new petitioners.' . . .

[2] 1384ᵃ27.

[3] [Of Cydias nothing is known. The speech referred to
must have dealt with the spoliation of Samos after the
reconquest of the island by the Athenians in 440 B.C.]

those who once wished themselves like us; for such a feeling implies admiration. And men feel shame when they have acts or exploits to their credit on which they are 1385[a] bringing dishonour, whether these are their own, or those of their ancestors, or those of other persons with whom they have some close connexion. Generally, we feel shame before those for whose own misconduct we should also feel it—those already mentioned; those who take us as their models; those whose teachers or advisers we have been; 5 or other people, it may be, like ourselves, whose rivals we are.[1] For there are many things that shame before such people makes us do or leave undone. And we feel more shame when we are likely to be continually seen by, and go about under the eyes of, those who know of our disgrace. Hence, when Antiphon the poet was to be cudgelled to death by order of Dionysius,[2] and saw those 10 who were to perish with him covering their faces as they went through the gates, he said, 'Why do you cover your faces? Is it lest some of these spectators should see you *to-morrow?*'

So much for Shame; to understand Shamelessness, we need only consider the converse cases, and plainly we shall 15 have all we need.

7   To take Kindness next: the definition of it will show us towards whom it is felt, why, and in what frames of mind. Kindness—under the influence of which a man is said to 'be kind'—may be defined as helpfulness towards some one in need, not in return for anything, nor for the advantage of the helper himself, but for that of the person helped. Kindness is great if shown to one who is 20 in great need, or who needs what is important and hard to get, or who needs it at an important and difficult crisis; or if the helper is the only, the first, or the chief person to give the help. Natural cravings constitute such needs; and in particular cravings, accompanied by pain, for what

---

[1] Or, 'who resemble, it may be, those whose rivals we are.'
[2] [Antiphon, the tragedian, was flogged to death by Dionysius, the tyrant of Syracuse.]

is not being attained. The appetites are cravings of this kind: sexual desire, for instance, and those which arise
25 during bodily injuries and in dangers; for appetite is active both in danger and in pain. Hence those who stand by us in poverty or in banishment, even if they do not help us much, are yet really kind to us, because our need is great and the occasion pressing; for instance, the man who gave the mat in the Lyceum.[1] The helpfulness must therefore meet, preferably, just this kind of need; and failing just this kind, some other kind as great or greater. We now
30 see to whom, why, and under what conditions kindness is shown; and these facts must form the basis of our arguments. We must show that the persons helped are, or have been, in such pain and need as has been described, and that their helpers gave, or are giving, the kind of help
35 described, in the kind of need described. We can also see how to eliminate the idea of kindness and make our op-
1385[b] ponents appear unkind: we may maintain that they are being or have been helpful simply to promote their own interest—this, as has been stated, is not kindness: or that their action was accidental, or was forced upon them; or that they were not doing a favour, but merely returning one, whether they know this or not—in either case the action *is* a mere return, and is therefore not a kindness even if the doer does *not* know how the case stands. In
5 considering this subject we must look at all the 'categories':[2] an act may be an act of kindness because (1) it is a particular thing, (2) it has a particular magnitude or (3) quality, or (4) is done at a particular time or (5) place. As evidence of the want of kindness, we may point out that a smaller service had been refused to the man in need; or that the same service, or an equal or greater one, has been given to his enemies; these facts show that the service in question was not done for the sake of the person helped. Or we may point out that the thing desired was
10 worthless and that the helper knew it: no one will admit that he is in need of what is worthless.

[1] Particulars unknown. . . . [Probably a reference to an unknown incident in Aristotle's school.]
[2] Cp. *Categ.* 1[b]25 ff.

8 So much for Kindness and Unkindness. Let us now
consider Pity, asking ourselves what things excite pity, and
for what persons, and in what states of our mind pity is
felt. Pity may be defined as a feeling of pain caused by the
sight of some evil, destructive or painful, which befalls one
who does not deserve it, and which we might expect to
befall ourselves or some friend of ours, and moreover to 15
befall us soon. In order to feel pity, we must obviously be
capable of supposing that some evil may happen to us or
some friends of ours, and moreover some such evil as is
stated in our definition or is more or less of that kind. It
is therefore not felt by those completely ruined, who suppose that no further evil can befall them, since the worst 20
has befallen them already; nor by those who imagine
themselves immensely fortunate—their feeling is rather
presumptuous insolence, for when they think they possess
all the good things of life, it is clear that the impossibility
of evil befalling them will be included, this being one of
the good things in question. Those who think evil *may*
befall them are such as have already had it befall them 25
and have safely escaped from it; elderly men, owing to
their good sense and their experience; weak men, especially men inclined to cowardice; and also educated people, since these can take long views. Also those who have
parents living, or children, or wives; for these are our own,
and the evils mentioned above may easily befall them.
And those who are neither moved by any courageous emo- 30
tion such as anger or confidence (these emotions take no
account of the future), nor by a disposition to presumptuous insolence (insolent men, too, take no account of the
possibility that something evil will happen to them), nor
yet by great fear (panic-stricken people do not feel pity,
because they are taken up with what is happening to
themselves); only those feel pity who are between these
two extremes. In order to feel pity we must also believe in 35
the goodness of at least some people; if you think nobody
good, you will believe that everybody deserves evil for- *1386ª*
tune. And, generally, we feel pity whenever we are in the
condition of remembering that similar misfortunes have

happened to us or ours, or expecting them to happen in future.

So much for the mental conditions under which we feel pity. What we pity is stated clearly in the definition. All unpleasant and painful things excite pity if they tend to 5 destroy and annihilate; and all such evils as are due to chance, if they are serious. The painful and destructive evils are: death in its various forms, bodily injuries and afflictions, old age, diseases, lack of food. The evils due to chance are: friendlessness, scarcity of friends (it is a piti- 10 ful thing to be torn away from friends and companions), deformity, weakness, mutilation; evil coming from a source from which good ought to have come; and the frequent repetition of such misfortunes. Also the coming of good when the worst has happened: e.g. the arrival of the Great King's[1] gifts for Diopeithes[2] after his death. Also that 15 either no good should have befallen a man at all, or that he should not be able to enjoy it when it has.

The grounds, then, on which we feel pity are these or like these. The people we pity are: those whom we know, if only they are not very closely related to us—in that case we feel about them as if we were in danger ourselves. For this reason Amasis did not weep, they say, at the 20 sight of his son being led to death, but did weep when he saw his friend begging:[3] the latter sight was pitiful, the former terrible, and the terrible is different from the piti- ful; it tends to cast out pity, and often helps to produce the opposite of pity. Again, we feel pity when the danger is near ourselves.[4] Also we pity those who are like us in 25 age, character, disposition, social standing, or birth; for in all these cases it appears more likely that the same mis- fortune may befall us also. Here too we have to remember the general principle that what we fear for ourselves ex- cites our pity when it happens to others.[5] Further, since

---

[1] [The king of Persia, at that time Artaxerxes III.]
[2] [Commander of the Athenian troops in the Chersonese against Philip of Macedonia in 342-41.]
[3] Cp. *Herod.* iii. 14.
[4] *Or*, . . . 'For our feeling is no longer pity [but terror] when the danger is near ourselves.'
[5] Cp. 1382^{b}26, 27.

it is when the sufferings of others are close to us that they excite our pity (we cannot remember what disasters happened a hundred centuries ago, nor look forward to what will happen a hundred centuries hereafter, and therefore 30 feel little pity, if any, for such things): it follows that those who heighten the effect of their words with suitable gestures, tones, dress, and dramatic action generally, are especially successful in exciting pity: they thus put the disasters before our eyes, and make them seem close to us, just coming or just past. Anything that has just happened, 1386[b] or is going to happen soon, is particularly piteous: so too therefore are the tokens and the actions of sufferers—the garments and the like of those who have already suffered; the words and the like of those actually suffering—of those, for instance, who are on the point of death. Most piteous of all is it when, in such times of trial, the victims 5 are persons of noble character: whenever they are so, our pity is especially excited, because their innocence, as well as the setting of their misfortunes before our eyes, makes their misfortunes seem close to ourselves.

9   Most directly opposed to pity is the feeling called Indignation. Pain at unmerited good fortune is, in one sense, 10 opposite to pain at unmerited bad fortune, and is due to the same moral qualities. Both feelings are associated with good moral character; it is our duty both to feel sympathy and pity for unmerited distress, and to feel indignation at unmerited prosperity; for whatever is undeserved 15 is unjust, and that is why we ascribe indignation even to the gods. It might indeed be thought that envy is similarly opposed to pity, on the ground that envy is closely akin to indignation, or even the same thing. But it is not the same. It is true that it also is a disturbing pain excited by the prosperity of others. But it is excited not by the prosperity of the undeserving but by that of people who are like us or equal with us. The two feelings have this in 20 common, that they must be due not to some untoward thing being likely to befall ourselves, but only to what is happening to our neighbour. The feeling ceases to be envy in the one case and indignation in the other, and becomes

fear, if the pain and disturbance are due to the prospect of something bad for ourselves as the result of the other man's good fortune. The feelings of pity and indignation

25 will obviously be attended by the converse feelings of satisfaction. If you are pained by the unmerited distress of others, you will be pleased, or at least not pained, by their merited distress. Thus no good man can be pained by the punishment of parricides or murderers. These are things we are bound to rejoice at, as we must at the prosperity

30 of the deserving; both these things are just, and both give pleasure to any honest man, since he cannot help expecting that what has happened to a man like him will happen to him too. All these feelings are associated with the same type of moral character. And their contraries are associated with the contrary type; the man who is delighted by others' misfortunes is identical with the man who en-

1387^a vies others' prosperity. For any one who is pained by the occurrence or existence of a given thing must be pleased by that thing's non-existence or destruction. We can now see that all these feelings tend to prevent pity (though they differ among themselves, for the reasons given), so

5 that all are equally useful for neutralizing an appeal to pity.

We will first consider Indignation—reserving the other emotions for subsequent discussion—and ask with whom, on what grounds, and in what states of mind we may be indignant. These questions are really answered by what has been said already. Indignation is pain caused by the sight of undeserved good fortune. It is, then, plain to

10 begin with that there are some forms of good the sight of which cannot cause it. Thus a man may be just or brave, or acquire moral goodness: but we shall not be indignant with him for that reason, any more than we shall pity him for the contrary reason. Indignation is roused by the sight of wealth, power, and the like—by all those things, roughly speaking, which are deserved by good men

15 and by those who possess the goods of nature—noble birth, beauty, and so on. Again, what is long established seems akin to what exists by nature; and therefore we feel more indignation at those possessing a given good if they

have as a matter of fact only just got it and the prosperity
it brings with it. The newly rich give more offence than
those whose wealth is of long standing and inherited. The
same is true of those who have office or power, plenty of 20
friends, a fine family, &c. We feel the same when these
advantages of theirs secure them others. For here again,
the newly rich give us more offence by obtaining office
through their riches than do those whose wealth is of long
standing; and so in all other cases. The reason is that what
the latter have is felt to be really their own, but what the 25
others have is not: what appears to have been always
what it is is regarded as real, and so the possessions of the
newly rich[1] do not seem to be really their own. Further,
it is not any and every man that deserves any given kind
of good; there is a certain correspondence and appropriateness in such things; thus it is appropriate for brave
men, not for just men, to have fine weapons, and for men 30
of family, not for parvenus, to make distinguished mar-
riages. Indignation may therefore properly be felt when
any one gets what is not appropriate for him, though he
may be a good man enough. It may also be felt when any
one sets himself up against his superior, especially against
his superior in some particular respect—whence the lines

Only from battle he shrank with Aias Telamon's son;
Zeus had been angered with him, had he fought with a
   mightier one,[2]

but also, even apart from that, when the inferior in any 1387^b
sense contends with his superior; a musician, for instance,
with a just man, for justice is a finer thing than music.

Enough has been said to make clear the grounds on
which, and the persons against whom, Indignation is felt
—they are those mentioned, and others like them. As for
the people who feel it; we feel it if we do ourselves deserve the greatest possible goods and moreover have them, 5
for it is an injustice that those who are not our equals
should have been held to deserve as much as we have. Or.

---

[1] [The meaning is not certain.]
[2] *Iliad*, xi. 542. The second line is not found in the existing manuscripts of the *Iliad*.

secondly, we feel it if we are really good and honest
people; our judgement is then sound, and we loathe any
kind of injustice. Also if we are ambitious and eager to
10 gain particular ends, especially if we are ambitious for
what others are getting without deserving to get it. And,
generally, if we think that we ourselves deserve a thing
and that others do not, we are disposed to be indignant
with those others so far as that thing is concerned. Hence
servile, worthless, unambitious persons are not inclined to
Indignation, since there is nothing they can believe themselves to deserve.

From all this it is plain what sort of men those are at
15 whose misfortunes, distresses, or failures we ought to feel
pleased, or at least not pained: by considering the facts
described we see at once what their contraries are. If
therefore our speech puts the judges in such a frame of
mind as that indicated and shows that those who claim
pity on certain definite grounds do not deserve to secure
20 pity but do deserve not to secure it, it will be impossible
for the judges to feel pity.

To take Envy next: we can see on what grounds, 1
against what persons, and in what states of mind we feel
it. Envy is pain at the sight of such good fortune as consists of the good things already mentioned; we feel it
towards our equals; not with the idea of getting something
for ourselves, but because the other people have it. We
25 shall feel it if we have, or think we have, equals; and by
'equals' I mean equals in birth, relationship, age, disposition, distinction, or wealth. We feel envy also if we fall
but a little short of having everything; which is why people in high place and prosperity feel it—they think every
one else is taking what belongs to themselves. Also if we
are exceptionally distinguished for some particular thing,
30 and especially if that thing is wisdom or good fortune.
Ambitious men are more envious than those who are not.
So also those who profess wisdom; they are ambitious—to
be thought wise. Indeed, generally, those who aim at a
reputation for anything are envious on this particular
point. And small-minded men are envious, for everything

seems great to them. The good things which excite envy have already been mentioned. The deeds or possessions *1388ᵃ* which arouse the love of reputation and honour and the desire for fame, and the various gifts of fortune, are almost all subject to envy; and particularly if we desire the thing ourselves, or think we are entitled to it, or if having it puts us a little above others, or not having it a little below them. It is clear also what kind of people we envy; that 5 was included in what has been said already: we envy those who are near us in time, place, age, or reputation. Hence the line:

Ay, kin can even be jealous of their kin.[1]

Also our fellow-competitors, who are indeed the people just mentioned—we do not compete with men who lived a hundred centuries ago, or those not yet born, or the dead, or those who dwell near the Pillars of Hercules,[2] or 10 those whom, in our opinion or that of others, we take to be far below us or far above us. So too we compete with those who follow the same ends as ourselves: we compete with our rivals in sport or in love, and generally with those who are after the same things; and it is therefore these whom we are bound to envy beyond all others. Hence the 15 saying:

Potter against potter.[3]

We also envy those whose possession of or success in a thing is a reproach to us: these are our neighbours and equals; for it is clear that it is our own fault we have missed the good thing in question; this annoys us, and excites envy in us. We also envy those who have what we 20 ought to have, or have got what we did have once. Hence old men envy younger men, and those who have spent much envy those who have spent little on the same thing. And men who have not got a thing, or not got it yet, envy those who have got it quickly. We can also see what things

---

[1] [Fragm. of a play by Aeschylus.]
[2] i.e. those who dwell at the farthest limits of the western world.
[3] Hesiod, *Works and Days,* 25. Cp. ii, c. 4, 1381ᵇ17 above.

and what persons give pleasure to envious people, and in
what states of mind they feel it: the states of mind in
25 which they feel pain are those under which they will feel
pleasure in the contrary things. If therefore we ourselves
with whom the decision rests are put into an envious state
of mind, and those for whom our pity, or the award of
something desirable, is claimed are such as have been
described, it is obvious that they will win no pity from
us.

We will next consider Emulation, showing in what fol- 11
lows its causes and objects, and the state of mind in which
30 it is felt. Emulation is pain caused by seeing the presence,
in persons whose nature is like our own, of good things
that are highly valued and are possible for ourselves to
acquire; but it is felt not because others have these goods,
but because we have not got them ourselves. It is therefore a good feeling felt by good persons, whereas envy is
a bad feeling felt by bad persons. Emulation makes us
35 take steps to secure the good things in question, envy
makes us take steps to stop our neighbour having them.
Emulation must therefore tend to be felt by persons who
believe themselves to deserve certain good things that they
1388ᵇ have not got, it being understood that no one aspires to
things which appear impossible.[1] It is accordingly felt by
the young and by persons of lofty disposition. Also by
those who possess such good things as are deserved by
men held in honour—these are wealth, abundance of
5 friends, public office, and the like; on the assumption that
they ought to be good men, they are emulous to gain such
goods because they ought, in their belief, to belong to
men whose state of mind is good. Also by those whom all
others think deserving. We also feel it about anything for
which our ancestors, relatives, personal friends, race, or
country are specially honoured, looking upon that thing
as really our own, and therefore feeling that we deserve
10 to have it. Further, since all good things that are highly
honoured are objects of emulation, moral goodness in its

---

[1] ['It being understood' is the translator's attempt to fill a
lacuna.]

various forms must be such an object, and also all those good things that are useful and serviceable to others: for men honour those who are morally good, and also those who do them service. So with those good things our possession of which can give enjoyment to our neighbours— wealth and beauty rather than health. We can see, too, what persons are the objects of the feeling. They are those who have these and similar things—those already mentioned, as courage, wisdom, public office. Holders of public office—generals, orators,[1] and all who possess such powers —can do many people a good turn. Also those whom many people wish to be like; those who have many acquaintances or friends; those whom many admire, or whom we ourselves admire; and those who have been praised and eulogized by poets or prose-writers. Persons of the contrary sort are objects of contempt: for the feeling and notion of contempt are opposite to those of emulation. Those who are such as to emulate or be emulated by others are inevitably disposed to be contemptuous of all such persons as are subject to those bad things which are contrary to the good things that are the objects of emulation: despising them for just that reason. Hence we often despise the fortunate, when luck comes to them without their having those good things which are held in honour.

This completes our discussion of the means by which the several emotions may be produced or dissipated, and upon which depend the persuasive arguments connected with the emotions.

12   Let us now consider the various types of human character, in relation to the emotions and moral qualities, showing how they correspond to our various ages and fortunes. By emotions I mean anger, desire, and the like; these we have discussed already.[2] By moral qualities I mean virtues and vices; these also have been discussed already,[3] as well as the various things that various types

---

[1] . . . i.e. public speakers, advocates, politicians, statesmen.
[2] ii, cc. 1 ff.
[3] i, c. 9.

of men tend to will and to do.[1] By ages I mean youth,
35 the prime of life, and old age. By fortune I mean birth,
1389ᵃ wealth, power, and their opposites—in fact, good fortune
and ill fortune.

To begin with the Youthful type of character. Young
men have strong passions, and tend to gratify them indiscriminately. Of the bodily desires, it is the sexual by
5 which they are most swayed and in which they show
absence of self-control. They are changeable and fickle
in their desires, which are violent while they last, but
quickly over: their impulses are keen but not deep-rooted,
and are like sick people's attacks of hunger and thirst.
They are hot-tempered and quick-tempered, and apt to
10 give way to their anger; bad temper often gets the better
of them, for owing to their love of honour they cannot
bear being slighted, and are indignant if they imagine
themselves unfairly treated. While they love honour, they
love victory still more; for youth is eager for superiority
over others, and victory is one form of this. They love both
more than they love money, which indeed they love very
15 little, not having yet learnt what it means to be without
it—this is the point of Pittacus' remark about Amphiaraus.[2] They look at the good side rather than the bad,
not having yet witnessed many instances of wickedness.
They trust others readily, because they have not yet often
been cheated. They are sanguine; nature warms their
blood as though with excess of wine; and besides that,
20 they have as yet met with few disappointments. Their lives
are mainly spent not in memory but in expectation; for
expectation refers to the future, memory to the past, and
youth has a long future before it and a short past behind
it: on the first day of one's life one has nothing at all to
remember, and can only look forward. They are easily
25 cheated, owing to the sanguine disposition just mentioned.
Their hot tempers and hopeful dispositions make them
more courageous than older men are; the hot temper pre-

---

[1] [May be tentatively identified with i. 10, 11, 12.]
[2] The remark is unknown. [Pittacus of Mytilene was one
of the Seven Sages. Amphiaraus may be one of the Seven
Against Thebes.]

vents fear, and the hopeful disposition creates confidence; we cannot feel fear so long as we are feeling angry, and any expectation of good makes us confident. They are shy, accepting the rules of society in which they have been trained, and not yet believing in any other standard of 30 honour. They have exalted notions, because they have not yet been humbled by life or learnt its necessary limitations; moreover, their hopeful disposition makes them think themselves equal to great things—and that means having exalted notions. They would always rather do noble deeds than useful ones: their lives are regulated more by moral feeling than by reasoning; and whereas reasoning leads us to choose what is useful, moral goodness leads us to choose what is noble. They are fonder of their friends, in- 35 timates, and companions than older men are, because they *1389*ᵇ like spending their days in the company of others, and have not yet come to value either their friends or anything else by their usefulness to themselves. All their mistakes are in the direction of doing things excessively and vehemently. They disobey Chilon's[1] precept[2] by overdoing everything; they love too much and hate too much, and 5 the same with everything else. They think they know everything, and are always quite sure about it; this, in fact, is why they overdo everything. If they do wrong to others, it is because they mean to insult them, not to do them actual harm. They are ready to pity others, because they think every one an honest man, or anyhow better than he is: they judge their neighbour by their own harmless natures, and so cannot think he deserves to be treated in that way. They are fond of fun and therefore witty, 10 wit being well-bred insolence.

13   Such, then, is the character of the Young. The character of Elderly Men—men who are past their prime—may be said to be formed for the most part of elements that are the contrary of all these. They have lived many years: they have often been taken in, and often made mistakes; 15 and life on the whole is a bad business. The result is that

---

[1] [Chilon of Lacedaemon, another of the Seven Sages.]
[2] . . . '(do) nothing in excess.' 'don't overdo anything.'

they are sure about nothing and *under-do* everything.
They 'think', but they never 'know'; and because of their
hesitation they always add a 'possibly' or a 'perhaps', putting everything this way and nothing positively. They are
20 cynical;[1] that is, they tend to put the worse construction
on everything. Further, their experience makes them dis-
trustful and therefore suspicious of evil. Consequently they
neither love warmly nor hate bitterly, but following the
hint of Bias[2] they love as though they will some day hate
and hate as though they will some day love.[3] They are
25 small-minded, because they have been humbled by life:
their desires are set upon nothing more exalted or unusual
than what will help them to keep alive. They are not
generous, because money is one of the things they must
have, and at the same time their experience has taught
them how hard it is to get and how easy to lose. They
30 are cowardly, and are always anticipating danger; unlike
that of the young, who are warm-blooded, their tempera-
ment is chilly; old age has paved the way for cowardice;
fear is, in fact, a form of chill. They love life; and all the
more when their last day has come, because the object of
all desire is something we have not got, and also because
35 we desire most strongly that which we need most urgently.
They are too fond of themselves; this is one form that
small-mindedness takes. Because of this, they guide their
lives too much by considerations of what is useful and
1390a too little by what is noble—for the useful is what is good
for oneself, and the noble what is good absolutely. They
are not shy, but shameless rather; caring less for what is
noble than for what is useful, they feel contempt for what
people may think of them. They lack confidence in the
future; partly through experience—for most things go
5 wrong, or anyhow turn out worse than one expects; and
partly because of their cowardice. They live by memory
rather than by hope; for what is left to them of life is but

---

[1] Taking up 1389a17, which may be translated 'they are
not cynical but charitable.'

[2] [Bias of Priene, the last of the Seven Sages.]

[3] Or, 'they treat their friends as probable future enemies
and their enemies as probable future friends'; cp. note on
1380b34.

little as compared with the long past; and hope is of the
future, memory of the past. This, again, is the cause of
their loquacity; they are continually talking of the past, 10
because they enjoy remembering it. Their fits of anger are
sudden but feeble. Their sensual passions have either altogether gone or have lost their vigour: consequently they
do not feel their passions much, and their actions are
inspired less by what they do feel than by the love of
gain. Hence men at this time of life are often supposed to
have a self-controlled character; the fact is that their pas- 15
sions have slackened, and they are slaves to the love of
gain. They guide their lives by reasoning more than by
moral feeling; reasoning being directed to utility and moral
feeling to moral goodness. If they wrong others, they
mean to injure them, not to insult them. Old men may feel
pity, as well as young men, but not for the same reason.
Young men feel it out of kindness; old men out of weak- 20
ness, imagining that anything that befalls any one else
might easily happen to them, which, as we saw,[1] is a
thought that excites pity. Hence they are querulous, and
not disposed to jesting or laughter—the love of laughter
being the very opposite of querulousness.

Such are the characters of Young Men and Elderly
Men. People always think well of speeches adapted to, and 25
reflecting, their own character: and we can now see how
to compose our speeches so as to adapt both them and
ourselves to our audiences.

14   As for Men in their Prime, clearly we shall find that
they have a character between that of the young and that
of the old, free from the extremes of either. They have 30
neither that excess of confidence which amounts to rashness, nor too much timidity, but the right amount of
each. They neither trust everybody nor distrust everybody, but judge people correctly. Their lives will be
guided not by the sole consideration either of what is 1390ᵇ
noble or of what is useful, but by both; neither by parsi-
mony nor by prodigality, but by what is fit and proper.
So, too, in regard to anger and desire; they will be brave

[1] ii, c. 8, 1386ᵃ24 and 29

5 as well as temperate, and temperate as well as brave; these virtues are divided between the young and the old; the young are brave but intemperate, the old temperate but cowardly. To put it generally, all the valuable qualities that youth and age divide between them are united in the prime of life, while all their excesses or defects are replaced by moderation and fitness. The body is in its prime from thirty to five-and-thirty; the mind about forty-nine.

So much for the types of character that distinguish 15 youth, old age, and the prime of life. We will now turn to those Gifts of Fortune by which human character is affected. First let us consider Good Birth. Its effect on character is to make those who have it more ambitious; it is the way of all men who have something to start with to add to the pile, and good birth implies ancestral distinction. The well-born man will look down even on those who are as good as his own ancestors, because any far-off distinction is greater than the same thing close to us, and better to boast about. Being well-born, which means coming of a fine stock, must be distinguished from nobility, which means being true to the family nature—a quality not usually found in the well-born, most of whom are poor creatures. In the generations of men as in the fruits of the earth, there is a varying yield; now and then, where the stock is good, exceptional men are produced for a while, and then decadence sets in.[1] A clever stock will degenerate towards the insane type of character, like the descendants of Alcibiades or of the elder Dionysius; a steady stock towards the fatuous and torpid type, like the descendants of Cimon, Pericles, and Socrates.

The type of character produced by Wealth lies on the 16 surface for all to see. Wealthy men are insolent and arrogant; their possession of wealth affects their understanding; they feel as if they had every good thing that exists; wealth becomes a sort of standard of value for everything

[1] . . . 'and then (after an interval of unproductiveness) the families begin again to produce them' (Cope).

else, and therefore they imagine there is nothing it can- *1391ᵃ*
not buy. They are luxurious and ostentatious; luxurious,
because of the luxury in which they live and the prosperity which they display; ostentatious and vulgar, because, like other people's, their minds are regularly occupied with the object of their love and admiration, and also ₅
because they think that other people's idea of happiness is
the same as their own. It is indeed quite natural that they
should be affected thus; for if you have money, there are
always plenty of people who come begging from you.
Hence the saying of Simonides[1] about wise men and rich
men, in answer to Hiero's[2] wife, who asked him whether
it was better to grow rich or wise. 'Why, rich,' he said; ₁₀
'for I see the wise men spending their days at the rich
men's doors.' Rich men also consider themselves worthy to
hold public office; for they consider they already have the
things that give a claim to office. In a word, the type of
character produced by wealth is that of a prosperous fool.
There is indeed one difference between the type of the
newly-enriched and those who have long been rich: the ₁₅
newly-enriched have all the bad qualities mentioned in
an exaggerated and worse form—to be newly-enriched
means, so to speak, *no education in riches*. The wrongs
they do others are not meant to injure their victims, but
spring from insolence or self-indulgence, e.g. those that
end in assault or in adultery.

17   As to Power: here too it may fairly be said that the type ₂₀
of character it produces is mostly obvious enough. Some
elements in this type it shares with the wealthy type,
others are better. Those in power are more ambitious and
more manly in character than the wealthy, because they
aspire to do the great deeds that their power permits them
to do. Responsibility makes them more serious: they have ₂₅
to keep paying attention to the duties their position involves. They are dignified rather than arrogant, for the
respect in which they are held inspires them with dignity

---

[1] [The poet of choral lyrics.]
[2] [Tyrant of Syracuse, at whose court Simonides spent the
last years of his life.]

and therefore with moderation—dignity being a mild and becoming form of arrogance. If they wrong others, they wrong them not on a small but on a great scale.

30   Good fortune in certain of its branches produces the types of character belonging to the conditions just described,[1] since these conditions are in fact more or less the kinds of good fortune that are regarded as most important. It may be added that good fortune leads us to gain all we can in the way of family happiness and bodily

1391[b] advantages.[2] It does indeed make men more supercilious and more reckless; but there is one excellent quality that goes with it—piety, and respect for the divine power, in which they believe because of events which are really the result of chance.

This account of the types of character that correspond

5 to differences of age[3] or fortune[4] may end here; for to arrive at the opposite types to those described, namely, those of the poor, the unfortunate, and the powerless, we have only to ask what the opposite qualities are.

The use of persuasive speech is to lead to decisions. 18 (When we know a thing, and have decided about it, there is no further use in speaking about it.) This is so even if

10 one is addressing a single person and urging him to do or not to do something, as when we scold a man for his conduct or try to change his views: the single person is as much your 'judge' as if he were one of many; we may say, without qualification, that any one is your judge whom you have to persuade. Nor does it matter whether we are arguing against an actual opponent or against a mere proposition; in the latter case we still have to use

15 speech and overthrow the opposing arguments, and we attack these as we should attack an actual opponent. Our principle holds good of ceremonial speeches also; the 'onlookers' for whom such a speech is put together are treated as the judges of it. Broadly speaking, however, the only sort of person who can strictly be called a judge is the man who decides the issue in some matter of public con-

[1] viz. good birth, wealth, and power.
[2] Cp. 1360[b]19-23.   [3] ii, cc. 12-14.   [4] ii, cc. 15-17.

troversy; that is, in law suits and in political debates, in both of which there are issues to be decided. In the section on political oratory an account has already been given of the types of character that mark the different con- 20 stitutions.[1]

The manner and means of investing speeches with moral character may now be regarded as fully set forth.

Each of the main divisions of oratory has, we have seen,[2] its own distinct purpose. With regard to each division, we have noted the accepted views and propositions upon which we may base our arguments—for political,[3] 25 for ceremonial,[4] and for forensic speaking.[5] We have further determined completely by what means speeches may be invested with the required moral character.[6] We are now to proceed to discuss the arguments common to *all* oratory. All orators, besides their special lines of argument, are bound to use, for instance, the topic of the Possible and Impossible; and to try to show that a thing 30 has happened, or will happen in future. Again, the topic of Size is common to all oratory; all of us have to argue that things are bigger or smaller than they seem, whether we are making political speeches, speeches of eulogy or attack, or prosecuting or defending in the law-courts. Hav- 1392a ing analysed these subjects, we will try to say what we can about the general principles of arguing by 'enthymeme' and 'example', by the addition of which we may hope to complete the project with which we set out. Of the above-mentioned general lines of argument, that concerned with Amplification is—as has been already said [7]— most appropriate to ceremonial speeches; that concerned 5 with the Past, to forensic speeches, where the required decision is always about the past; that concerned with Possibility and the Future, to political speeches.

19 Let us first speak of the Possible and Impossible. It may plausibly be argued: That if it is possible for one of a pair of contraries to be or happen, then it is possible

[1] i, c. 8.   [2] i, c. 3.   [3] i, cc. 4-8.
[4] i, c. 9.   [5] i, cc. 10-14.   [6] [ii, cc. 1-18.]
[7] i, c. 9. [1368a10 ff.]

10 for the other: e.g. if a man can be cured, he can also fall ill; for any two contraries are equally possible, in so far as they are contraries. That if of two similar things one is possible, so is the other. That if the harder of two things is possible, so is the easier. That if a thing can come into existence in a good and beautiful form, then it can come into existence generally; thus a house can exist more

15 easily than a beautiful house. That if the beginning of a thing can occur, so can the end; for nothing impossible occurs or begins to occur; thus the commensurability of the diagonal of a square with its side neither occurs nor can begin to occur. That if the end is possible, so is the

20 beginning; for all things that occur have a beginning. That if that which is posterior in essence or in order of generation can come into being, so can that which is prior: thus if a man can come into being, so can a boy, since the boy comes first in order of generation; and if a boy can, so can a man, for the man also is first.[1] That those things are

25 possible of which the love or desire is natural; for no one, as a rule, loves or desires impossibilities. That things which are the object of any kind of science or art are possible and exist or come into existence. That anything is possible the first step in whose production depends on men or things which we can compel or persuade to produce it, by our greater strength, our control of them, or our friendship with them. That where the parts are possible, the

30 whole is possible; and where the whole is possible, the parts are usually possible. For if the slit in front, the toe-piece, and the upper leather can be made, then shoes can

1392ᵇ be made; and if shoes, then also the front slit and toe-piece. That if a whole genus is a thing that can occur, so can the species; and if the species can occur, so can the genus: thus, if a sailing vessel can be made, so also can a trireme; and if a trireme, then a sailing vessel also. That if one of two things whose existence depends on each other is possible, so is the other; for instance, if

5 'double', then 'half', and if 'half', then 'double'. That if a thing can be produced without art or preparation, it can

---

[1] viz. in essence. . . .

be produced still more certainly by the careful application
of art to it. Hence Agathon has said:

> To some things we by art must needs attain,
> Others by destiny or luck we gain.[1]

That if anything is possible to inferior, weaker, and
stupider people, it is more so for their opposites; thus
Isocrates said that it would be a strange thing if he could
not discover a thing that Euthynus had found out.[2] As
for Impossibility, we can clearly get what we want by
taking the contraries of the arguments stated above.

Questions of Past Fact may be looked at in the following ways: First, that if the less likely of two things has
occurred, the more likely must have occurred also. That
if one thing that usually follows another has happened,
then that other thing has happened; that, for instance, if
a man has forgotten a thing, he has also once learnt it.
That if a man had the power and the wish to do a thing,
he has done it; for every one does do whatever he intends
to do whenever he can do it, there being nothing to stop
him. That, further, he has done the thing in question
either if he intended it and nothing external prevented
him; or if he had the power to do it and was angry at the
time; or if he had the power to do it and his heart was
set upon it—for people as a rule do what they long to
do, if they can; bad people through lack of self-control;
good people, because their hearts are set upon good
things. Again, that if a thing was 'going to happen', it
has happened; if a man was 'going to do something', he
has done it, for it is likely that the intention was carried
out. That if one thing has happened which naturally happens before another or with a view to it, the other has
happened; for instance, if it has lightened, it has also
thundered; and if an action has been attempted, it has
been done. That if one thing has happened which naturally happens after another, or with a view to which
that other happens, then that other (that which happens

[2] [Fragm. of Agathon, the tragedian.]
[3] Cp. Isocr. xviii. 15.

first, or happens with a view to this thing) has also hap-
30 pened; thus, if it has thundered it has also lightened, and
if an action has been done it has been attempted. Of all
these sequences some are inevitable and some merely
usual. The arguments for the *non*-occurrence of anything
can obviously be found by considering the opposites of
those that have been mentioned.

1393ᵃ   How questions of Future Fact should be argued is clear
from the same considerations: That a thing will be done
if there is both the power and the wish to do it; or if
along with the power to do it there is a craving for the
result, or anger, or calculation, prompting it. That the
thing will be done, in these cases, if the man is actually
setting about it, or even if he means to do it later—for
5 usually what we mean to do happens rather than what we
do not mean to do. That a thing will happen if another
thing which naturally happens before it has already happened; thus, if it is clouding over, it is likely to rain. That
if the means to an end have occurred, then the end is
likely to occur; thus, if there is a foundation, there will be
a house.

For arguments about the Greatness and Smallness of
10 things, the greater and the lesser, and generally great
things and small, what we have already said will show the
line to take. In discussing deliberative oratory we have
spoken about the relative greatness of various goods, and
about the greater and lesser in general.[1] Since therefore
in each type of oratory the object under discussion is some
kind of good—whether it is utility, nobleness, or justice—
it is clear that every orator must obtain the materials of
15 amplification through these channels. To go further than
this, and try to establish abstract laws of greatness and
superiority, is to argue without an object; in practical life,
particular facts count more than generalizations.

Enough has now been said about these question of pos-
20 sibility and the reverse, of past or future fact, and of the
relative greatness or smallness of things.

[1] i, c. 7.

20   The special forms of oratorical argument having now
been discussed, we have next to treat of those which are
common to all kinds of oratory. These are of two main
kinds, 'Example' and 'Enthymeme'; for the 'Maxim' is part
of an enthymeme.[1]

We will first treat of argument by Example, for it has 25
the nature of induction, which is the foundation of reasoning. This form of argument has two varieties; one consisting in the mention of actual past facts, the other in the
invention of facts by the speaker. Of the latter, again,
there are two varieties, the illustrative parallel and the
fable (e.g. the fables of Aesop, or those from Libya). 30
As an instance of the mention of actual facts, take the
following. The speaker may argue thus: 'We must pre-
pare for war against the king of Persia and not let him
subdue Egypt. For Darius of old did not cross the Aegean 1393ᵇ
until he had seized Egypt; but once he had seized it, he
did cross. And Xerxes, again, did not attack us until he
had seized Egypt; but once he had seized it, he did cross.
If therefore the present king seizes Egypt, he also will
cross, and therefore we must not let him.'

The illustrative parallel is the sort of argument Socrates
used: e.g. 'Public officials ought not to be selected by lot.
That is like using the lot to select athletes, instead of 5
choosing those who are fit for the contest; or using the lot
to select a steersman from among a ship's crew, as if
we ought to take the man on whom the lot falls, and not
the man who knows most about it.'

Instances of the fable are that of Stesichorus[2] about
Phalaris,[3] and that of Aesop in defence of the popular
leader. When the people of Himera had made Phalaris 10
military dictator, and were going to give him a bodyguard,
Stesichorus wound up a long talk by telling them the
fable of the horse who had a field all to himself. Presently
there came a stag and began to spoil his pasturage. The
horse, wishing to revenge himself on the stag, asked a 15

---

[1] i.e. not (as some think) a third main kind. Cp. 1394ᵃ27-9.
[2] [An early poet of choral lyrics, circ. 640-555 B.C.]
[3] [6th cent. tyrant of Acragas, famous for his cruelty.]

man if he could help him to do so. The man said, 'Yes,
if you will let me bridle you and get on to your back with
javelins in my hand'. The horse agreed, and the man
mounted; but instead of getting his revenge on the stag,
the horse found himself the slave of the man. 'You too',
20 said Stesichorus, 'take care lest, in your desire for revenge
on your enemies, you meet the same fate as the horse.
By making Phalaris military dictator, you have already let
yourselves be bridled. If you let him get on to your backs
by giving him a bodyguard, from that moment you will
be his slaves.'

Aesop, defending before the assembly at Samos a popular leader who was being tried for his life, told this story:
25 A fox, in crossing a river, was swept into a hole in the
rocks; and, not being able to get out, suffered miseries for
a long time through the swarms of fleas that fastened on
her. A hedgehog, while roaming around, noticed the fox;
and feeling sorry for her asked if he might remove the
fleas. But the fox declined the offer; and when the hedgehog asked why, she replied, "These fleas are by this time
30 full of me and not sucking much blood; if you take them
away, others will come with fresh appetites and drink up
all the blood I have left.' 'So, men of Samos', said Aesop,
'my client will do you no further harm; he is wealthy already. But if you put him to death, others will come along
1394ª who are not rich, and their peculations will empty your
treasury completely.'

Fables are suitable for addresses to popular assemblies;
and they have one advantage—they are comparatively
easy to invent, whereas it is hard to find parallels among
actual past events. You will in fact frame them just as you
5 frame illustrative parallels: all you require is the power of
thinking out your analogy, a power developed by intellectual training. But while it is easier to supply parallels by
inventing fables, it is more valuable for the political
speaker to supply them by quoting what has actually happened, since in most respects the future will be like what
the past has been.

Where we are unable to argue by Enthymeme, we must
10 try to demonstrate our point by this method of Example,

and to convince our hearers thereby. If we *can* argue by
Enthymeme, we should use our Examples as subsequent
supplementary evidence. They should not precede the
Enthymemes: that will give the argument an inductive air,
which only rarely suits the conditions of speech-making.[1]
If they follow the enthymemes, they have the effect of
witnesses giving evidence, and this always tells. For the
same reason, if you put your examples first you must give 15
a large number of them; if you put them last, a single one
is sufficient; even a single witness will serve if he is a
good one. It has now been stated how many varieties of
argument by Example there are, and how and when they
are to be employed.

21   We now turn to the use of Maxims, in order to see upon
what subjects and occasions, and for what kind of speaker, 20
they will appropriately form part of a speech. This will
appear most clearly when we have defined a maxim. It is
a statement; not about a particular fact, such as the character of Iphicrates,[2] but of a general kind; nor is it about
any and every subject—e.g. 'straight is the contrary of
curved' is not a maxim—but only about questions of
practical conduct, courses of conduct to be chosen or 25
avoided. Now an Enthymeme is a syllogism dealing with
such practical subjects. It is therefore roughly true that
the premisses or conclusions of Enthymemes, considered
apart from the rest of the argument, are Maxims: e.g.

Never should any man whose wits are sound
Have his sons taught more wisdom than their fellows.[3]   30

Here we have a Maxim; add the reason or explanation,
and the whole thing is an Enthymeme; thus—

It makes them idle; and therewith they earn
Ill-will and jealousy throughout the city.[4]

Again,   *1394*

---

[1] Perhaps, 'which does not suit skilled orators except before
a small audience.'
[2] [Cp. 1365ª28.]   [3] Euripides, *Medea*, 295.   [4] Ib. 297.

> There is no man in all things prosperous,[1]

and

> There is no man among us all is free,

5 are maxims; but the latter, taken with what follows it, **is**
an Enthymeme—

> For all are slaves of money or of chance.[2]

From this definition of a maxim it follows that there are
four kinds of maxims. In the first place, the maxim may
or may not have a supplement. Proof is needed where the
statement is paradoxical [3] or disputable; no supplement
10 is wanted where the statement contains nothing paradoxical,[3] either because the view expressed is already a
known truth, e.g.

> Chiefest of blessings is health for a man, as it seemeth
> to me,[4]

this being the general opinion: or because, as soon as **the**
15 view is stated, it is clear at a glance, e.g.

> No love is true save that which loves for ever.[5]

Of the Maxims that do have a supplement attached, some
are part of an Enthymeme, e.g.

> Never should any man whose wits are sound, &c.[6]

Others have the essential character of Enthymemes, but
are not stated as parts of Enthymemes; these latter are
20 reckoned the best; they are those in which the reason for
the view expressed is simply implied, e.g.

> O mortal man, nurse not immortal wrath.[7]

To say 'it is not right to nurse immortal wrath' is a maxim;

[1] Euripides, fragm. 661, N.²
[2] Euripides, *Hecuba*, 864 f.
[3] Surprising, startling, heretical, unorthodox.
[4] Possibly a fragment of Epicharmus. . . .
[5] Euripides, *Troades*, 1051.
[6] Euripides, *Medea*, 295.
[7] [From an unidentified tragedy.]

the added words 'O mortal man' give the reason. Similarly, with the words

Mortal creatures ought to cherish mortal, not immortal
    thoughts.[1]

What has been said has shown us how many kinds of 25
Maxim there are, and to what subjects the various kinds
are appropriate. They must not be given without supplement if they express disputed or paradoxical views: we
must, in that case, either put the supplement first and
make a maxim of the conclusion, e.g. you might say, 'For
my part, since both unpopularity and idleness, are un- 30
desirable, I hold that it is better not to be educated'; or
you may say this first, and then add the previous clause.
Where a statement, without being paradoxical, is not obviously true, the reason should be added as concisely as
possible. In such cases both laconic and enigmatic sayings
are suitable: thus one might say what Stesichorus said to 1395ᵃ
the Locrians, 'Insolence is better avoided, lest the cicalas
chirp on the ground'.[2]

The use of Maxims is appropriate only to elderly men,
and in handling subjects in which the speaker is experi-
enced. For a young man to use them is—like telling stories
—unbecoming; to use them in handling things in which
one has no experience is silly and ill-bred: a fact suffi- 5
ciently proved by the special fondness of country fellows
for striking out maxims, and their readiness to air them.

To declare a thing to be universally true when it is not
is most appropriate when working up feelings of horror
and indignation in our hearers; especially by way of preface, or after the facts have been proved. Even hackneyed
and commonplace maxims are to be used, if they suit one's 10
purpose: just because they are commonplace, every one
seems to agree with them, and therefore they are taken
for truth. Thus, any one who is calling on his men to risk
an engagement without obtaining favourable omens may
quote

[1] Epicharmus?
[2] [Cp. 1393ᵇ9.] . . . The cicalas would have to chirp on
the ground if an enemy cut down the trees.

One omen of all is best, that we fight for our fatherland.[1]

Or, if he is calling on them to attack a stronger force—

15   The War-God showeth no favour.[2]

Or, if he is urging people to destroy the innocent children of their enemies—

Fool, who slayeth the father and leaveth his sons to avenge him.[3]

Some proverbs are also maxims, e.g. the proverb 'An Attic neighbour'.[4] You are not to avoid uttering maxims that contradict such sayings as have become public property 20 (I mean such sayings as 'know thyself' and 'nothing in excess'), if doing so will raise your hearers' opinion of your character, or convey an effect of strong emotion— e. g. an angry speaker might well say, 'It is not true that we ought to know ourselves: anyhow, if this man had known himself, he would never have thought himself fit for an army command.' It will raise people's opinion of our 25 character to say, for instance, 'We ought not to follow the saying that bids us treat our friends as future enemies: much better to treat our enemies as future friends.'[5] The moral purpose should be implied partly by the very wording of our maxim. Failing this, we should add our reason: e.g. having said 'We should treat our friends, not as the saying advises, but as if they were going to be our friends always', we should add 'for the other behaviour is 30 that of a traitor': or we might put it, 'I disapprove of that saying. A true friend will treat his friend as if he were going to be his friend for ever'; and again, 'Nor do I approve of the saying "nothing in excess": we are bound to hate bad men excessively.'

1395[b]   One great advantage of Maxims to a speaker is due to the want of intelligence in his hearers, who love to hear him succeed in expressing as a universal truth the opinions which they hold themselves about particular cases. I

---

[1] *Iliad*, xii. 243.   [2] Ib. xviii. 309.   [3] Cp. i, c. 15, 1376[a]7.
[4] ['An Attic neighbour' is a restless neighbor.]
[5] Cp. ii, c. 13, 1389[b]23-5.

will explain what I mean by this, indicating at the same
time how we are to hunt down the maxims required. The
maxim, as has been already said, is a general statement, 5
and people love to hear stated in general terms what they
already believe in some particular connexion: e.g. if a
man happens to have bad neighbours or bad children, he
will agree with any one who tells him 'Nothing is more
annoying than having neighbours', or, 'Nothing is more
foolish than to be the parent of children.' The orator has
therefore to guess the subjects on which his hearers really 10
hold views already, and what those views are, and then
must express, as general truths, these same views on these
same subjects. This is one advantage of using maxims.
There is another which is more important—it invests a
speech with moral character. There is moral character in
every speech in which the moral purpose is conspicuous:
and maxims always produce this effect, because the utterance of them amounts to a general declaration of moral 15
principles: so that, if the maxims are sound, they display
the speaker as a man of sound moral character. So much
for the Maxim—its nature, varieties, proper use, and advantages.

22   We now come to the Enthymemes, and will begin the 20
subject with some general consideration of the proper way
of looking for them, and then proceed to what is a distinct
question, the lines of argument to be embodied in them.
It has already[1] been pointed out that the Enthymeme is
a syllogism, and in what sense it is so. We have also
noted the differences between it and the syllogism of
dialectic. Thus we must not carry its reasoning too far
back, or the length of our argument will cause obscurity: 25
nor must we put in all the steps that lead to our conclusion, or we shall waste words in saying what is mani-
fest. It is this simplicity that makes the uneducated more
effective than the educated when addressing popular audiences—makes them, as the poets[2] tell us, 'charm the
crowd's ears more finely'. Educated men lay down broad 30

[1] i, c. 2, 1356^{b}3, 1357^{a}16.
[2] Cp. Euripides, *Hippolytus*, 989.

general principles; uneducated men argue from common
knowledge and draw obvious conclusions. We must not,
therefore, start from any and every accepted opinion, but
only from those we have defined—those accepted by our
1396ᵃ judges or by those whose authority they recognize: and
there must, moreover, be no doubt in the minds of most,
if not all, of our judges that the opinions put forward
really are of this sort. We should also base our arguments
upon probabilities as well as upon certainties.

The first thing we have to remember is this. Whether
5 our argument concerns public affairs or some other subject, we must know some, if not all, of the facts about the
subject on which we are to speak and argue. Otherwise
we can have no materials out of which to construct arguments. I mean, for instance, how could we advise the
Athenians whether they should go to war or not, if we did
not know their strength, whether it was naval or military
10 or both, and how great it is; what their revenues amount
to; who their friends and enemies are; what wars, too,
they have waged, and with what success; and so on? Or
how could we eulogize them if we knew nothing about the
sea-fight at Salamis, or the battle of Marathon, or what
they did for the Heracleidae,[1] or any other facts like that?
15 All eulogy is based upon the noble deeds—real or imaginary—that stand to the credit of those eulogized. On
the same principle, invectives are based on facts of the
opposite kind: the orator looks to see what base deeds—
real or imaginary—stand to the discredit of those he is
attacking, such as treachery to the cause of Hellenic freedom, or the enslavement of their gallant allies against the
20 barbarians (Aegina,[2] Potidaea,[3] &c.), or any other mis-
deeds of this kind that are recorded against them. So, too,
in a court of law: whether we are prosecuting or defending,
we must pay attention to the existing facts of the case.
It makes no difference whether the subject is the Lace-

---

[1] [These are some of the historical and mythical merits
claimed by the Athenians mentioned in all praises of
their city and their ancestors.]

[2] Cp. Thucyd. ii. 27; iv. 57.

[3] Cp. Thucyd. ii. 70.

daemonians or the Athenians, a man or a god; we must do
the same thing. Suppose it to be Achilles whom we are 25
to advise, to praise or blame, to accuse or defend; here too
we must take the facts, real or imaginary; these must be
our material, whether we are to praise or blame him for
the noble or base deeds he has done, to accuse or defend
him for his just or unjust treatment of others, or to advise
him about what is or is not to his interest. The same thing 30
applies to any subject whatever. Thus, in handling the
question whether justice is or is not a good, we must start
with the real facts about justice and goodness. We see,
then, that this is the only way in which any one ever
proves anything, whether his arguments are strictly cogent 1396ᵇ
or not: not all facts can form his basis, but only those
that bear on the matter in hand: nor, plainly, can proof
be effected otherwise by means of the speech. Consequently, as appears in the *Topics*,[1] we must first of all
have by us a selection of arguments about questions that 5
may arise and are suitable for us to handle; and then we
must try to think out arguments of the same type for special needs as they emerge; not vaguely and indefinitely,
but by keeping our eyes on the actual facts of the subject
we have to speak on, and gathering in as many of them
as we can that bear closely upon it: for the more actual
facts we have at our command, the more easily we prove 10
our case; and the more closely they bear on the subject,
the more they will seem to belong to that speech only
instead of being commonplaces. By 'commonplaces' I mean,
for example, eulogy of Achilles because he is a human
being or a demi-god, or because he joined the expedition
against Troy: these things are true of many others, so that
this kind of eulogy applies no better to Achilles than to
Diomede. The special facts here needed are those that are 15
true of Achilles alone; such facts as that he slew Hector,
the bravest of the Trojans, and Cycnus the invulnerable,
who prevented all the Greeks from landing, and again
that he was the youngest man who joined the expedition,
and was not bound by oath to join it, and so on.

Here, then, we have our first principle of selection of 20

[1] Cp. *Top.* i, c. 14.

Enthymemes—that which refers to the lines of argument selected. We will now consider the various elementary classes of enthymemes. (By an 'elementary class' of enthymeme I mean the same thing as a 'line of argument'.) We will begin, as we must begin, by observing that there 25 are two kinds of enthymemes. One kind proves some affirmative or negative proposition; the other kind disproves one. The difference between the two kinds is the same as that between syllogistic proof and disproof in dialectic. The demonstrative enthymeme is formed by the conjunction of compatible propositions; the refutative, by the conjunction of incompatible propositions.

We may now be said to have in our hands the lines of argument for the various *special* subjects that it is useful 30 or necessary to handle, having selected the propositions suitable in various cases. We have, in fact, already ascertained the lines of argument applicable to enthymemes about good and evil, the noble and the base, justice and injustice, and also to those about types of character, emotions, and moral qualities.[1] Let us now lay hold of certain 1397ª facts about the whole subject, considered from a different and more general point of view. In the course of our discussion we will take note of the distinction between lines of proof and lines of disproof:[2] and also of those lines of argument used in what seem to be enthymemes, but are not, since they do not represent valid syllogisms.[3] Having made all this clear, we will proceed to classify Objections 5 and Refutations, showing how they can be brought to bear upon enthymemes.[4]

1. One line of positive proof is based upon considera- 23 tion of the opposite of the thing in question. Observe whether that opposite has the opposite quality. If it has not, you refute the original proposition; if it has, you 10 establish it. E.g. 'Temperance is beneficial; for licentiousness is hurtful'. Or, as in the Messenian speech,[5] 'If war is

---

[1] i, cc. 4-14; ii, cc. 1-18.   [2] ii, c. 23.
[3] ii, c. 24.   [4] ii, c. 25.
[5] Cp. 1373ᵇ18. [A speech attributed to Alcidamas, a fifth century sophist and orator.]

the cause of our present troubles, peace is what we need
to put things right again'. Or—

> For if not even evil-doers should
> Anger us if they meant not what they did,
> Then can we owe no gratitude to such
> As were constrained to do the good they did us.[1]   15

Or—

> Since in this world liars may win belief,
> Be sure of the opposite likewise—that this world
> Hears many a true word and believes it not.[2]

2. Another line of proof is got by considering some
modification of the key-word, and arguing that what can 20
or cannot be said of the one, can or cannot be said of the
other: e.g. 'just' does not always mean 'beneficial', or
'justly' would always mean 'beneficially', whereas it is *not*
desirable to be justly put to death.[3]

3. Another line of proof is based upon correlative
ideas. If it is true that one man *gave* noble or just treatment to another, you argue that the other must have
received noble or just treatment; or that where it is right
to command obedience, it must have been right to obey
the command. Thus Diomedon, the tax-farmer, said of the 25
taxes: 'If it is no disgrace for you to sell them,[4] it is no
disgrace for us to buy them'. Further, if 'well' or 'justly'
is true of the person to whom a thing is done, you argue
that it is true of the doer. But it is possible to draw a false
conclusion here. It may be just that A should be treated
in a certain way, and yet *not* just that he should be so 30
treated by B. Hence you must ask yourself two distinct
questions: (1) Is it right that A should be thus treated? *1397*ᵇ
(2) Is it right that B should thus treat him? and apply
your results properly, according as your answers are Yes
or No. Sometimes in such a case the two answers differ:

---

[1] [From an unidentified tragedy.]
[2] Fragm. of Euripides, *Thyestes*.
[3] Cp. i, c. 9, 1366ᵇ33.
[4] i.e. the right of collecting them.

you may quite easily have a position like that in the
Alcmaeon of Theodectes:

And was there none to loathe thy mother's crime?[1]
to which question Alcmaeon in reply says,

Why, there are two things to examine here.

5 And when Alphesiboea asks what he means, he rejoins:

They judged *her* fit to die, not *me* to slay her.

Again there is the lawsuit about Demosthenes[2] and the
men who killed Nicanor; as they were judged to have
killed him justly, it was thought that he was killed justly.
And in the case of the man who was killed at Thebes,[3]
10 the judges were requested to decide whether it was unjust that he should be killed, since if it was not, it was
argued that it could not have been unjust to kill him.

4. Another line of proof is the *a fortiori*. Thus it may
be argued that if even the gods are not omniscient, certainly human beings are not. The principle here is that,
if a quality does not in fact exist where it is *more* likely
to exist, it clearly does not exist where it is *less* likely.
15 Again, the argument that a man who strikes his father
also strikes his neighbours follows from the principle that,
if the less likely thing is true, the more likely thing is true
also; for a man is less likely to strike his father than to
strike his neighbours. The argument, then, may run thus.
Or it may be urged that, if a thing is not true where it is
more likely, it is not true where it is less likely; or that, if
it is true where it is less likely, it is true where it is more
likely: according as we have to show that a thing *is* or
is *not* true.[4] This argument might also be used in a case
of parity, as in the lines:

[1] i.e. was there nobody who thought the slaying a just act?
[Fragm. of the *Alcmaeon* of Theodectes. The tragedian
and orator was a personal friend of Aristotle.]

[2] [Probably not the famous orator. Nicanor is unknown.]

[3] [Xenophon, *Hellen.* viii. 3.]

[4] The reasoning in the text shows confusion, and the text is
uncertain. We might rather have expected the following
connexion of thought: 'The argument, then, may run thus
—that if the less likely is true the more likely is true; or
as before—that if the more likely is not true, the less
likely is not true: according as we have to show, &c.'

Thou hast pity for *thy* sire, who has lost his sons:
Hast none for Oeneus, whose brave son is dead?[1]   20

And, again, 'if Theseus did no wrong, neither did Paris';
or 'if the sons of Tyndareus did no wrong, neither did
Paris'; or 'if Hector did well to slay Patroclus, Paris did
well to slay Achilles'.[2] And 'if other followers of an art
are not bad men, neither are philosophers'. And 'if generals are not bad men because it often happens that they
are condemned to death, neither are sophists'. And the 25
remark that 'if each individual among you ought to think
of his own city's reputation, you ought all to think of the
reputation of Greece as a whole'.

5. Another line of argument is based on considerations
of time. Thus Iphicrates, in the case against Harmodius,
said, 'if before doing the deed I had bargained that, if I
did it, I should have a statue, you would have given
me one. Will you not give me one now that I *have* done
the deed? You must not make promises when you are 30
expecting a thing to be done for you, and refuse to fulfil
them when the thing has been done.'[3] And, again, to
induce the Thebans to let Philip pass through their territory into Attica, it was argued[4] that 'if he had insisted 1398ᵉ
on this before he helped them against the Phocians, they
would have promised to do it. It is monstrous, therefore,
that just because he threw away his advantage then, and
trusted their honour, they should not let him pass through
now'.

6. Another line is to apply to the other speaker what
he has said against yourself. It is an excellent turn to give

---

[1] [Fragm. probably from a play about Meleager.]
[2] [From a speech of the rhetorician Polycrates.]
[3] [Iphicrates, the general, was granted a statue for his defeat of the Lacedaemonians in 392 B.C. He claimed his
statue only after his retirement in 371 B.C. Harmodius, a
political opponent, opposed the honor.]
[4] [In 339 B.C. Philip of Macedonia sent an embassy to the
Thebans requesting passage through their territory into
Attica. An Athenian counter-embassy persuaded the Thebans to refuse the request. The words here quoted are
words of the Macedonian ambassadors, not of Philip.]

to a debate, as may be seen in the *Teucer*.[1] It was employed by Iphicrates in his reply to Aristophon. 'Would
you', he asked, 'take a bribe to betray the fleet?' 'No', said
Aristophon; and Iphicrates replied, 'Very good: if you,
who are Aristophon, would not betray the fleet, would
I, who am Iphicrates?'[2] Only, it must be recognized be-
forehand that the other man is more likely than you are
to commit the crime in question. Otherwise you will make
yourself ridiculous; if it is Aristeides[3] who is prosecuting,
you cannot say that sort of thing to him. The purpose is
to discredit the prosecutor, who as a rule would have it
appear that his character is better than that of the defendant, a pretension which it is desirable to upset. But
the use of such an argument is in all cases ridiculous if
you are attacking others for what you do or would do
yourself, or are urging others to do what you neither do
nor would do yourself.

7. Another line of proof is secured by defining your
terms. Thus, 'What is the supernatural? Surely it is either
a god or the work of a god. Well, any one who believes
that the work of a god exists, cannot help also believing
that gods exist'.[4] Or take the argument of Iphicrates,
'Goodness is true nobility; neither Harmodius nor Aristogeiton had any nobility before they did a noble deed'.
He also argued that he himself was more akin to Harmodius and Aristogeiton than his opponent was. 'At any
rate, my deeds are more akin to those of Harmodius and
Aristogeiton than yours are.'[5] Another example may be

---

[1] Of Sophocles; cp. iii, c. 15, 1416^{b}1.
[2] [Aristophon, a celebrated orator of the century, prosecuted Iphicrates in 355 B.C. for a failure in a recent war.]
[3] [An Athenian political leader of the 5th cent., famous for
his justice and integrity.]
[4] Cp. Plato, *Apol.* 27 c-e.
[5] [Another example taken from Iphicrates' speech against
Harmodius (cp. 1397^{b}28 ff.) who claimed descent from
Harmodius, the tyrannicide. The argument seems to have
been: personal merit, not family relationship, conveys true
nobility. On account of my merit I am closer to the
tyrannicides than you, their descendant.]

found in the *Alexander*.[1] 'Every one will agree that by
incontinent people we mean those who are not satisfied
with the enjoyment of one love.' A further example is to
be found in the reason given by Socrates for not going
to the court of Archelaus. He said that 'one is *insulted* 25
by being unable to requite benefits, as well as by being
unable to requite injuries'.[2] All the persons mentioned
define their term and get at its essential meaning, and
then use the result when reasoning on the point at issue.

8. Another line of argument is founded upon the various senses of a word. Such a word is 'rightly', as has been
explained in the *Topics*.[3]

9. Another line is based upon logical division. Thus,
'All men do wrong from one of three motives, A, B, or C: 30
in my case A and B are out of the question, and even the
accusers do not allege C'.

10. Another line is based upon induction. Thus from
the case of the woman of Peparethus it might be argued
that women everywhere can settle correctly the facts about
their children. Another example of this occurred at Athens *1398ᵇ*
in the case between the orator Mantias[4] and his son, when
the boy's mother revealed the true facts: and yet another
at Thebes, in the case between Ismenias and Stilbon, when
Dodonis proved that it was Ismenias who was the father of
her son Thettaliscus, and he was in consequence always
regarded as being so.[5] A further instance of induction may
be taken from the *Law* of Theodectes:[6] 'If we do not hand 5
over our horses to the care of men who have mishandled
other people's horses, nor ships to those who have wrecked
other people's ships, and if this is true of everything else

---

[1] From some rhetorical essay on Alexander (viz. Paris),
possibly by Polycrates. [Cp. 1393ᵇ23.] . . .

[2] Cp. Xenophon, *Apol. Socr.* 17; Diog. Laert., *Vit. Socr.* ii.
5, 25.

[3] . . . [Or,] 'in the *Topics* the right use of words has been
discussed.' Cp. *Topics,* i, c. 15 and ii, c. 3.

[4] [Possibly the person mentioned in Demosth. *Or.* xviii. 7,
10.]

[5] [Nothing known of the case and the people.]

[6] [The tragedian, rhetor, and friend of Aristotle.]

alike, then men who have failed to secure other people's
safety are not to be employed to secure our own.' Another
instance is the argument of Alcidamas.[1] 'Every one hon-
10 ours the wise. Thus the Parians have honoured Archilochus, in spite of his bitter tongue; the Chians Homer,
though he was not their countryman; the Mytilenaeans
Sappho, though she was a woman; the Lacedaemonians
actually made Chilon a member of their senate, though
they are the least literary of men; the Italian Greeks honoured Pythagoras; the inhabitants of Lampsacus gave pub-
15 lic burial to Anaxagoras, though he was an alien, and
honour him even to this day. (It may be argued that peo-
ples for whom philosophers legislate are always prosperous) on the ground that the Athenians became prosperous
under Solon's laws and the Lacedaemonians under those
of Lycurgus, while at Thebes no sooner did the leading
men become philosophers than the country began to prosper.

11. Another line of argument is founded upon some decision already pronounced, whether on the same subject
20 or on one like it or contrary to it. Such a proof is most
effective if every one has always decided thus; but if not
every one, then at any rate most people; or if all, or most,
wise or good men have thus decided, or the actual judges
of the present question, or those whose authority they
accept, or any one whose decision they cannot gainsay because he has complete control over them, or those whom
it is not seemly to gainsay, as the gods, or one's father,
or one's teachers. Thus Autocles[2] said, when attacking
25 Mixidemides, that it was a strange thing that the Dread
Goddesses could without loss of dignity submit to the
judgement of the Areopagus, and yet Mixidemides could
not. Or as Sappho said, 'Death is an evil thing; the gods
have so judged it, or they would die'.[3] Or again as Aris-

---

[1] [The sophist and orator.]

[2] [Autocles, an Athenian political figure and versatile orator, contemporary of Aristotle. Of the case and Mixidemides nothing is known. The reference is to the Erinys as
seen in Aeschylus' play 'The Eumenides' where they submit to the judgement of Areopagus.]

[3] [Fragm. of Sappho.]

tippus[1] said in reply to Plato when he spoke somewhat
too dogmatically, as Aristippus thought: 'Well, anyhow, 30
our *friend*', meaning Socrates, 'never spoke like that'. And
Hegesippus, having previously consulted Zeus at Olym-
pia, asked Apollo at Delphi 'whether his opinion was the
same as his father's', implying that it would be shameful 1399ᵃ
for him to contradict his father. Thus too Isocrates argued
that Helen must have been a good woman, because Theseus decided that she was; and Paris a good man, because
the goddesses chose him before all others; and Evagoras
also, says Isocrates, was good, since when Conon met with 5
his misfortune he betook himself to Evagoras without trying any one else on the way.[2]

12. Another line of argument consists in taking separately the parts of a subject. Such is that given in the
Topics: [3] 'What *sort* of motion is the soul? for it must be
this or that.' The *Socrates* of Theodectes provides an example: 'What temple has he profaned? What gods recognized by the state has he not honoured?' [4]

13. Since it happens that any given thing usually has
both good and bad consequences, another line of argu- 10
ment consists in using those consequences as a reason for
urging that a thing should or should not be done, for prosecuting or defending any one, for eulogy or censure. E.g.
education leads both to unpopularity, which is bad, and
to wisdom, which is good. Hence you either argue, 'It is
therefore not well to be educated, since it is not well to 15
be unpopular': or you answer, 'No, it is well to be educated, since it is well to be wise'. The *Art of Rhetoric* of
Callippus[5] is made up of this line of argument, with the

---

[1] [Aristippus of Cyrene, pupil of Socrates, founder of the
Cyrenaic school of philosophy and as such a rival of
Plato.]

[2] Isocrates, *Helen*, 18-38; Ibid., 41-8 . . . ; Isocrates, *Evagoras*, 51 ff.

[3] Cp. *Top.* ii. 4; iv. 1.

[4] [Fragm. of *Defense of Socrates* by Theodectes.]

[5] [Calippus is quoted again in 1400ᵃ4. Nothing is known
of him or his work. He may have been an early pupil of
Isocrates.]

addition of those of Possibility and the others of that kind already described.[1]

14. Another line of argument is used when we have to urge or discourage a course of action that may be done in either of two opposite ways, and have to apply the method just mentioned to both. The difference between this one 20 and the last is that, whereas in the last any two things are contrasted, here the things contrasted are opposites. For instance, the priestess enjoined upon her son not to take to public speaking: 'For', she said, 'if you say what is right, men will hate you; if you say what is wrong, the gods will hate you.' The reply might be, 'On the contrary, you *ought* to take to public speaking: for if you say what is right, the gods will love you; if you say what is wrong, 25 men will love you.' This amounts to the proverbial 'buying the marsh with the salt'. It is just this situation, viz. when each of two opposites has both a good and a bad consequence opposite respectively to each other, that has been termed *divarication*.

15. Another line of argument is this: The things people approve of openly are not those which they approve of secretly: openly, their chief praise is given to justice and 30 nobleness; but in their hearts they prefer their own advantage. Try, in face of this, to establish the point of view which your opponent has not adopted. This is the most effective of the forms of argument that contradict common opinion.

16. Another line is that of rational correspondence. E.g. Iphicrates, when they were trying to compel his son, a youth under the prescribed age, to perform one of the 35 state duties because he was tall, said 'If you count tall boys men, you will next be voting short men boys'.[2] And 1399ᵇ Theodectes in his *Law*[3] said, 'You make citizens of such mercenaries[4] as Strabax and Charidemus, as a reward of

---

[1] ii, c. 19.   [2] [For Iphicrates cp. 1397ᵇ28 and 1398ª19.]
[3] Cp. 1398ᵇ6.

[4] [The mercenaries were a problem for the Greek cities from the beginning of the 4th cent. Charidemus, their celebrated leader in the middle of the century, served Athens and was rewarded by being made a citizen. Strabax is less well known but also was made an Athenian citizen.]

their merits; will you not make exiles of such citizens as
those who have done irreparable harm among the mercenaries?'

17. Another line is the argument that if two results are
the same their antecedents are also the same. For instance, 5
it was a saying of Xenophanes that to assert that the gods
had birth is as impious as to say that they die; the consequence of both statements is that there is a time when
the gods do not exist.[1] This line of proof assumes generally
that the result of any given thing is always the same: e.g.
'you are going to decide not about Isocrates, but about
the value of the whole profession of philosophy.'[2] Or, 'to 10
give earth and water' means slavery; or, 'to share in the
Common Peace' means obeying orders. We are to make
either such assumptions or their opposite, as suits us best.

18. Another line of argument is based on the fact that
men do not always make the same choice on a later as
on an earlier occasion, but reverse their previous choice.
E.g. the following enthymeme: 'When we were exiles, we 15
fought in order to return; now we have returned, it would
be strange to choose exile in order not to have to fight.'[3]
On one occasion, that is, they chose to be true to their
homes at the cost of fighting, and on the other to avoid
fighting at the cost of deserting their homes.

19. Another line of argument is the assertion that some
possible motive for an event or state of things is the *real*
one: e.g. that a gift was given in order to cause pain by 20
its withdrawal. This notion underlies the lines:

> God gives to many great prosperity,
> Not of good will towards them, but to make
> The ruin of them more conspicuous.[4]

Or take the passage from the *Meleager* of Antiphon: 25

---

[1] [Fragm. of Xenophanes the Eleatic philosopher. Cp.
1377ᵃ20.]

[2] [The manuscripts read 'Socrates' but the passage has been
identified in the *Antidosis* speech (173) of Isocrates.]

[3] [From a speech of Lysias.]

[4] [From an unidentified tragedy.]

To slay no boar, but to be witnesses
Of Meleager's prowess unto Greece.[1]

Or the argument in the *Ajax* of Theodectes, that Diomede
chose out Odysseus[2] not to do him honour, but in order
that his companion might be a lesser man than himself—
30 such a motive for doing so is quite possible.

20. Another line of argument is common to forensic and
deliberative oratory, namely, to consider inducements and
deterrents, and the motives people have for doing or avoiding the actions in question. These are the conditions which
make us bound to act if they are for us, and to refrain
from action if they are against us: that is, we are bound to
act if the action is possible, easy, and useful to ourselves
35 or our friends or hurtful to our enemies; this is true even
if the action entails loss, provided the loss is outweighed
by the solid advantage. A speaker will urge action by
pointing to such conditions, and discourage it by pointing
1400[a] to the opposite. These same arguments also form the
materials for accusation or defence—the deterrents being
pointed out by the defence, and the inducements by the
prosecution. As for the defence, . . . This topic forms the
whole *Art of Rhetoric* both of Pamphilus and of Callippus.[3]

5   21. Another line of argument refers to things which are
supposed to happen and yet seem incredible. We may argue that people could not have believed them, if they had
not been true or nearly true: even that they are the more
likely to be true because they are incredible. For the
things which men believe are either facts or probabilities:
if, therefore, a thing that *is* believed is improbable and
even incredible, it must be true, since it is certainly not
believed because it is at all probable or credible. An example is what Androcles of the deme Pitthus said in his
well-known arraignment of the law. The audience tried to
10 shout him down when he observed that the laws required

---

[1] [Fragm. from the *Meleager* of Antiphon.]
[2] Cp. *Iliad*, x. 218-54.
[3] [Both rhetoricians of the 5th cent. of whom nothing is
known.]

a law to set them right. 'Why,' he went on, 'fish need salt, improbable and incredible as this might seem for creatures reared in salt water; and olive-cakes need oil, incredible as it is that what produces oil should need it.'

22. Another line of argument is to refute our opponent's case by noting any contrasts or contradictions of dates, acts, or words that it anywhere displays; and this in any of the three following connexions. (1) Referring to our opponent's conduct, e.g. 'He says he is devoted to you, yet he conspired with the Thirty.' (2) Referring to our own conduct, e.g. 'He says I am litigious, and yet he cannot prove that I have been engaged in a single lawsuit.' (3) Referring to both of us together, e.g. '*He* has never even *lent* any one a penny, but *I* have *ransomed* quite a number of you.'

23. Another line that is useful for men and causes that have been really or seemingly slandered, is to show why the facts are not as supposed; pointing out that there is a reason for the false impression given. Thus a woman, who had palmed off her son on another woman, was thought to be the lad's mistress because she embraced him; but when her action was explained the charge was shown to be groundless. Another example is from the *Ajax* of Theodectes, where Odysseus tells Ajax the reason why, though he is really braver than Ajax, he is not thought so.

24. Another line of argument is to show that if the *cause* is present, the *effect* is present, and if absent, absent. For by proving the cause you at once prove the effect, and conversely nothing can exist without its cause. Thus Thrasybulus accused Leodamas of having had his name recorded as a criminal on the slab in the Acropolis, and of erasing the record in the time of the Thirty Tyrants: to which Leodamas replied, 'Impossible: for the Thirty would have trusted me all the more if my quarrel with the commons had been inscribed on the slab.'[1]

25. Another line is to consider whether the accused

---

[1] [Thrasybulus freed Athens in 403 B.C. from the rule of the Thirty Tyrants. Leodamas is probably the famous orator.]

person can take or could have taken a better[1] course than
that which he is recommending or taking, or has taken. If
1400[b] he has *not* taken this better course, it is clear that he is
not guilty, since no one deliberately and consciously
chooses what is bad. This argument is, however, fallacious,
for it often becomes clear after the event how the action
could have been done better, though before the event this
was far from clear.

26. Another line is, when a contemplated action is in-
5 consistent with any past action, to examine them both
together. Thus, when the people of Elea asked Xenophanes[2] if they should or should not sacrifice to Leucothea and
mourn for her, he advised them not to mourn for her if
they thought her a goddess, and not to sacrifice to her if
they thought her a mortal woman.

27. Another line is to make previous mistakes the
grounds of accusation or defence. Thus, in the *Medea* of
10 Carcinus[3] the accusers allege that Medea has slain her
children; 'at all events', they say, 'they are not to be seen'
—Medea having made the mistake of sending her children
away. In defence she argues that it is not her children, but
Jason, whom she would have slain; for it would have been
a mistake on her part not to do this if she *had* done the
15 other. This special line of argument for enthymeme forms
the whole of the *Art of Rhetoric* in use before Theodorus.[4]

28. Another line is to draw meanings from names.
Sophocles, for instance, says,

O steel in heart as thou art steel in name.[5]

This line of argument is common in praises of the gods.
Thus, too, Conon[6] called Thrasybulus[7] *rash in counsel*.

---

[1] i.e. better suited to effect the evil purpose with which he
is charged.
[2] [Cp. 1399[b]6.]
[3] [A tragedian, contemporary of Aristotle.]
[4] [Theodorus of Byzantium, outstanding teacher of rhetoric
of 5th cent.]
[5] [Fragm. from the *Tyro* of Sophocles.]
[6] [The victor of Cnidus (394 B.C.).]
[7] [The liberator of Athens in 403 B.C.]

And Herodicus[1] said of Thrasymachus,[2] 'You are always *bold in battle'*; of Polus,[2] 'you are always *a colt';* and of the legislator Draco[3] that his laws were those not of a human being but of a *dragon*, so savage were they. And, in Euripides, Hecuba says of Aphrodite,

> Her name and Folly's (ἀφροσύνης) rightly begin alike,[4]

and Chaeremon writes

> Pentheus—a name foreshadowing grief (πένθος) to come.[5]

The Refutative Enthymeme has a greater reputation than the Demonstrative, because within a small space it works out two opposing arguments, and arguments put side by side are clearer to the audience. But of all syllogisms, whether refutative or demonstrative, those are most applauded of which we foresee the conclusions from the beginning, so long as they are not obvious at first sight—for part of the pleasure we feel is at our own intelligent anticipation; or those which we follow well enough to see the point of them as soon as the last word has been uttered.

24 Besides genuine syllogisms, there may be syllogisms that look genuine but are not; and since an enthymeme is merely a syllogism of a particular kind, it follows that, besides genuine enthymemes, there may be those that look genuine but are not.

1. Among the lines of argument that form the Spurious Enthymeme the first is that which arises from the particular words employed.

(a) One variety of this is when—as in dialectic, without having gone through any reasoning process, we make a final statement as if it were the conclusion of such a process, 'Therefore so-and-so is not true', 'Therefore also

[1] [The physician (cp. 1361ᵇ5).]
[2] [Thrasymachus and Polus, sophists and rhetoricians, are introduced by Plato in *Republic* I and in the *Gorgias*.]
[3] [The almost mythical Athenian lawgiver of the 7th cent.]
[4] Euripides, *Troades*, 990.
[5] [Fragm. of Chaeremon, a tragedian of the 4th cent.]

so-and-so must be true'—so too in rhetoric a compact and
antithetical utterance passes for an enthymeme, such language being the proper province of enthymeme, so that it
is seemingly the form of wording here that causes the illusion mentioned. In order to produce the effect of genuine reasoning by our form of wording it is useful to summarize the results of a number of previous reasonings: as
'some he saved—others he avenged—the Greeks he freed'.[1]
Each of these statements has been previously proved from
other facts; but the mere collocation of them gives the
impression of establishing some fresh conclusion.

(*b*) Another variety is based on the use of similar words
for different things; e.g. the argument that the mouse
must be a noble creature, since it gives its name to the
most august of all religious rites—for such the Mysteries
are.[2] Or one may introduce, into a eulogy cf the dog, the
dog-star; or Pan, because Pindar said:

> O thou blessed one!
> Thou whom they of Olympus call
> The hound of manifold shape
> That follows the Mother of Heaven:[3]

or we may argue that, because there is much disgrace in
there *not* being a dog about, there is honour in *being* a
dog.[4] Or that Hermes is readier than any other god to go
shares, since we never say 'shares all round' except of
him.[5] Or that speech is a very excellent thing, since good
men are not said to be worth money but to be worthy of
esteem[6]—the phrase 'worthy of esteem' also having the
meaning of 'worth speech'.

2. Another line is to assert of the whole what is true
of the parts, or of the parts what is true of the whole. A
whole and its parts are supposed to be identical, though

---

[1] Isocrates, *Evagoras*, 65-9.
[2] [A pun on the similarity of the Greek words *mys* and *mysterion*.]
[3] [Fragm. of Pindar.]
[4] viz. a dog-philosopher, a Cynic.
[5] [Alluding to a proverb.]
[6] The same Greek word (λόγος) is here used for 'speech' and 'esteem': hence what follows.

often they are not. You have therefore to adopt whichever
of these two lines better suits your purpose. That is how
Euthydemus argues:[1] e.g. that any one knows that there
is a trireme in the Peiraeus, since he knows the separate
details that make up this statement. There is also the argument that one who knows the letters knows the whole
word, since the word is the same thing as the letters which
compose it; or that, if a double portion of a certain thing 30
is harmful to health, then a single portion must not be
called wholesome, since it is absurd that two good things
should make one bad thing. Put thus, the enthymeme is
refutative; put as follows, demonstrative: 'For one good
thing cannot be made up of two bad things.' The whole
line of argument is fallacious. Again, there is Polycrates'
saying that Thrasybulus put down thirty tyrants, where
the speaker adds them up one by one. Or the argument
in the *Orestes* of Theodectes, where the argument is from 35
part to whole:

'Tis right that she who slays her lord should die.

'It is right, too, that the son should avenge his father. Very
good: these two things are what Orestes has done.' Still, 1401[b]
perhaps the two things, once they are put together, do not
form a right act. The fallacy might also be said to be due
to omission, since the speaker fails to say by whose hand
a husband-slayer should die.

3. Another line is the use of indignant language,
whether to support your own case or to overthrow your
opponent's. We do this when we paint a highly-coloured 5
picture of the situation without having proved the facts of
it: if the defendant does so, he produces an impression of
his innocence; and if the prosecutor goes into a passion,
he produces an impression of the defendant's guilt. Here
there is no genuine enthymeme: the hearer infers guilt or
innocence, but no proof is given, and the inference is fallacious accordingly.

4. Another line is to use a 'Sign', or single instance, as

[1] [A sophist known for his captious arguments. Cp. Plato's
dialogue *Euthydemus*. The argument of Euthydemus was
some kind of fallacy.]

certain evidence; which, again, yields no valid proof. Thus,
10 it might be said that lovers are useful to their countries,
since the love of Harmodius and Aristogeiton caused the
downfall of the tyrant Hipparchus.[1] Or, again, that Dionysius is a thief, since he is a vicious man—there is, of
course, no valid proof here; not every vicious man is a
thief, though every thief is a vicious man.

5. Another line represents the accidental as essential.
15 An instance is what Polycrates says of the mice, that they
'came to the rescue' because they gnawed through the
bowstrings.[2] Or it might be maintained that an invitation
to dinner is a great honour for it was because he was *not*
invited that Achilles was angered' with the Greeks at
Tenedos.[3] As a fact, what angered him was the *insult* involved; it was a mere accident that this was the particular
form that the insult took.

6. Another is the argument from consequence. In the
20 *Alexander*,[4] for instance, it is argued that Paris must have
had a lofty disposition, since he despised society and lived
by himself on Mount Ida: because lofty people do this
kind of thing, therefore Paris too, we are to suppose, had
a lofty soul. Or, if a man dresses fashionably and roams
around at night, he is a rake, since that is the way rakes
25 behave. Another similar argument points out that beggars
sing and dance in temples, and that exiles can live where-
ever they please, and that such privileges are at the disposal of those we account happy; and therefore every one
might be regarded as happy if only he has those privileges.
What matters, however, is the *circumstances* under which
the privileges are enjoyed. Hence this line too falls under
the head of fallacies by omission.

30 7. Another line consists in representing as causes things
which are not causes, on the ground that they happened
along with or before the event in question. They assume
that, because B happens *after* A, it happens *because* of

[1] Cp. Plato, *Symposium*, 182 B, C.
[2] [From Polycrates', the sophist's, encomium on mice.]
[3] [Incident in a lost play of Sophocles.]
[4] [A speech probably by the sophist Polycrates. Cp. 1397*21, 1398*22, 1399*3, 1401*34.]

A. Politicians are especially fond of taking this line. Thus Demades said that the policy of Demosthenes was the cause of all the mischief, 'for after it the war occurred'.[1]

8. Another line consists in leaving out any mention of time and circumstances. E.g. the argument that Paris was justified in taking Helen, since her father left her free to choose: here the freedom was presumably not perpetual; it could only refer to her first choice, beyond which her father's authority could not go.[2] Or again, one might say 1402^a that to strike a free man is an act of wanton outrage; but it is not so in every case—only when it is unprovoked.

9. Again, a spurious syllogism may, as in 'eristical' discussions, be based on the confusion of the absolute with that which is not absolute but particular. As, in dialectic, for instance, it may be argued that what-is-not *is*, on the ground that what-is-not *is* what-is-not; or that the unknown can be known, on the ground that it can be known to *be* unknown: so also in rhetoric a spurious enthymeme may be based on the confusion of some particular probability with absolute probability. Now no particular probability is universally probable: as Agathon says,

> One might perchance say this was probable—   10
> That things improbable oft will hap to men.[3]

For what is improbable does happen, and therefore it is probable that improbable things *will* happen. Granted this, one might argue that 'what is improbable is probable'. But this is not true absolutely. As, in eristic, the imposture comes from not adding any clause specifying relationship or reference or manner; so here it arises because the probability in question is not general but specific. It is of this line of argument that Corax's[4] *Art of Rhetoric* is composed.

[1] [Demades, the orator, arranged the peace between Philip of Macedonia and Athens after the Athenian defeat at Chaironea and thereafter was the representative of the Macedonian party in Athens and an adversary of Demosthenes, the great orator.]

[2] [Probably again from the *Alexander* of Polycrates. Cp. 1401^b20.]

[3] [Fragm. from a tragedy by Agathon.]

[4] [One of the earliest Sicilian teachers of rhetoric.]

If the accused is not open to the charge—for instance if
a weakling be tried for violent assault—the defence is that
20 he was not likely to do such a thing. But if he *is* open to
the charge—i.e. if he is a *strong* man—the defence is still
that he was not likely to do such a thing, since he could
be sure that people would think he *was* likely to do it.
And so with any other charge: the accused must be either
open or not open to it: there is in either case an appearance of probable innocence, but whereas in the latter case
the probability is genuine, in the former it can only be as-
serted in the special sense mentioned.[1] This sort of argument illustrates what is meant by making the worse argument seem the better. Hence people were right in objecting
25 to the training Protagoras[2] undertook to give them. It was
a fraud; the probability it handled was not genuine but
spurious, and has a place in no art except Rhetoric[3] and
Eristic.

Enthymemes, genuine and apparent, have now been de- 25
30 scribed; the next subject is their Refutation.
An argument may be refuted either by a counter-syllogism or by bringing an objection. It is clear that counter-syl-
logisms can be built up from the same lines of arguments
as the original syllogisms: for the materials of syllogisms
are the ordinary opinions of men, and such opinions often
contradict each other. Objections, as appears in the *Top-*
35 *ics,*[4] may be raised in four ways—either by directly attacking your opponent's own statement, or by putting forward another statement like it, or by putting forward a
statement contrary to it, or by quoting previous decisions.
1. By 'attacking your opponent's own statement' I mean,
for instance, this: if his enthymeme should assert that love
1402[b] is always good, the objection can be brought in two ways,
either by making the general statement that 'all want is
an evil', or by making the particular one that there would

---

[1] [Or 'in the former not simply so!']
[2] [The famous sophist. Cp. Plato's dialogue *Protagoras*.]
[3] [This remark entails no approval on the part of Aristotle.]
[4] Cp. *Topics*, viii. 10. . . .

be no talk of 'Caunian love' [1] if there were not evil loves as well as good ones.

2. An objection 'from a contrary statement' is raised when, for instance, the opponent's enthymeme having concluded that a good man does good to all his friends, you object, 'That proves nothing, for a bad man does not do evil to all his friends'.

3. An example of an objection 'from a like statement' is, the enthymeme having shown that ill-used men always hate their ill-users, to reply, 'That proves nothing, for well-used men do not always love those who used them well'.

4. The 'decisions' mentioned are those proceeding from well-known men; for instance, if the enthymeme employed has concluded that 'Some allowance ought to be made for drunken offenders, since they did not know what they were doing', the objection will be, 'Pittacus,[2] then, deserves no approval, or he would not have prescribed specially severe penalties for offences due to drunkenness'.

Enthymemes are based upon one or other of four kinds of alleged fact: (1) Probabalities, (2) Examples, (3) Infallible Signs, (4) Ordinary Signs.[3] (1) Enthymemes based upon Probabilities are those which argue from what is, or is supposed to be, usually true. (2) Enthymemes based upon Example are those which proceed by induction from one or more similar cases, arrive at a general proposition, and then argue deductively to a particular inference. (3) Enthymemes based upon Infallible Signs are those which argue from the inevitable and invariable. (4) Enthymemes based upon ordinary Signs are those which argue from some universal or particular proposition, true or false.

Now (1) as a Probability is that which happens usually but not always. Enthymemes founded upon Probabilities can, it is clear, always be refuted by raising some objection. The refutation is not always genuine: it may be spurious: for it consists in showing not that your opponent's premiss is not probable, but only in showing that

---

[1] The incestuous love of Byblis for her brother Caunus.
[2] [One of the Seven Sages.]
[3] Fallible signs.

it is not inevitably true. Hence it is always in defence
rather than in accusation that it is possible to gain an advantage by using this fallacy. For the accuser uses probabilities to prove his case: and to refute a conclusion as
improbable is not the same thing as to refute it as not inevitable. Any argument based upon what usually happens
is always open to objection: otherwise it would not be a
30 probability but an invariable and necessary truth. But the
judges think, if the refutation takes this form, either that
the accuser's case is not probable or that they must not decide it; which, as we said, is a false piece of reasoning. For
they ought to decide by considering not merely what *must*
be true but also what is *likely* to be true: this is, indeed,
the meaning of 'giving a verdict in accordance with one's
honest opinion'. Therefore it is not enough for the defendant to refute the accusation by proving that the charge is
35 not *bound* to be true: he must do so by showing that it is
not *likely* to be true. For this purpose his objection must
state what is more usually true than the statement attacked. It may do so in either of two ways: either in
respect of frequency or in respect of exactness. It will be
most convincing if it does so in both respects; for if the
1403ª thing in question *both* happens *oftener* as we represent it
and happens more *as* we represent it, the probability is
particularly great.

(2) Fallible Signs, and Enthymemes based upon them,
can be refuted even if the facts are correct, as was said
at the outset.[1] For we have shown in the *Analytics*[2] that
no Fallible Sign can form part of a valid logical proof.

5   (3) Enthymemes depending on examples may be refuted in the same way as probabilities. If we have a negative instance, the argument is refuted, in so far as it is
proved not inevitable, even though the positive examples
are more similar and more frequent. And if the positive
examples *are* more numerous and more frequent, we must
contend that the present case is dissimilar, or that its conditions are dissimilar, or that it is different in some way or
other.

[1] i, c. 2, 1357ᵇ13,14.
[2] *Anal. Pr.*, ii. 27.

(4) It will be impossible to refute Infallible Signs, 10 and Enthymemes resting on them, by showing in any way that they do not form a valid logical proof: this, too, we see from the *Analytics*.[1] All we can do is to show that the fact alleged does not exist. If there is no doubt that it does, and that it is an Infallible Sign, refutation now be- 15 comes impossible: for this is equivalent to a demonstration which is clear in every respect.

26   Amplification and Depreciation are not an element of enthymeme. By 'an element of enthymeme' I mean the same thing as 'a line of enthymematic argument'[2]—a general class embracing a large number of particular kinds of enthymeme. Amplification and Depreciation are one kind of enthymeme, viz. the kind used to show that a thing is 20 great or small; just as there are other kinds used to show that a thing is good or bad, just or unjust, and anything else of the sort. All these things are the *subject-matter* of syllogisms and enthymemes; none of these is the line of argument of an enthymeme; no more, therefore, are Amplification and Depreciation.

Nor are Refutative Enthymemes a different species from 25 Constructive. For it is clear that refutation consists either in offering positive proof or in raising an objection. In the first case we prove the opposite of our adversary's statements. Thus, if he shows that a thing has happened, we show that it has not; if he shows that it has not happened, we show that it has. This, then, could not be the distinction if there were one, since the same means are employed 30 by both parties, enthymemes being adduced to show that the fact is or is not so-and-so. An objection, on the other hand, is not an enthymeme at all, but, as was said in the *Topics*,[3] it consists in stating some accepted opinion from which it will be clear that our opponent has not reasoned correctly or has made a false assumption.

Three points must be studied in making a speech; and

---

[1] *Anal. Pr.*, ii, 27.
[2] [As treated in ii, 23.]
[3] Cp. *Top.*, viii. 10.

35 we have now completed the account of (1) Examples, Maxims, Enthymemes, and in general the *thought*-element 2403^b —the way to invent and refute arguments. We have next to discuss (2) Style, and (3) Arrangement.

BOOK III

In making a speech one must study three points: first, 1 the means of producing persuasion; second, the style, or language, to be used; third, the proper arrangement of the various parts of the speech. We have already specified the sources of persuasion. We have shown that these are three 10 in number;[1] what they are; and why there are only these three: for we have shown that persuasion must in every case be effected either (1) by working on the emotions of the judges themselves, (2) by giving them the right impression of the speakers' character, or (3) by proving the truth of the statements made.

Enthymemes also have been described, and the sources from which they should be derived; there being both special and general lines of argument for enthymemes.

15   Our next subject will be the style of expression. For it is not enough to know *what* we ought to say; we must also say it *as* we ought; much help is thus afforded towards producing the right impression of a speech. The first question to receive attention was naturally the one that comes first naturally—how persuasion can be produced from the facts themselves. The second is how to set these facts out 20 in language. A third would be the proper method of delivery; this is a thing that affects the success of a speech greatly; but hitherto the subject has been neglected. Indeed, it was long before it found a way into the arts of

[1] i, c. 2.

tragic drama and epic recitation: at first poets acted[1] their
tragedies themselves. It is plain that delivery has just as
much to do with oratory as with poetry. (In connexion 25
with poetry, it has been studied by Glaucon of Teos[2]
among others.) It is, essentially, a matter of the right
management of the voice to express the various emotions
—of speaking loudly, softly, or between the two; of high,
low, or intermediate pitch; of the various rhythms that 30
suit various subjects. These are the three things—volume
of sound, modulation of pitch, and rhythm—that a speaker
bears in mind. It is those who *do* bear them in mind who
usually win prizes in the dramatic contests; and just as in
drama the actors now count for more than the poets, so
it is in the contests of public life, owing to the defects of
our political institutions. No systematic treatise upon the 35
rules of delivery has yet been composed;[3] indeed, even
the study of language made no progress till late in the
day. Besides, delivery is—very properly—not regarded as
an elevated subject of inquiry.[4] Still, the whole business 1404ᵃ
of rhetoric being concerned with appearances, we must
pay attention to the subject of delivery, unworthy though
it is, because we cannot do without it. The right thing in
speaking really is that we should be satisfied not to annoy
our hearers, without trying to delight them: we ought in
fairness to fight our case with no help beyond the bare 5
facts: nothing, therefore, should matter except the proof
of those facts. Still, as has been already said, other things
affect the result considerably, owing to the defects of our
hearers. The arts of language cannot help having a small
but real importance, whatever it is we have to expound to
others: the way in which a thing is said does affect its in- 10
telligibility. Not, however, so much importance as people
think. All such arts are fanciful and meant to charm the

[1] Or, 'delivered.'
[2] [Probably the rhapsode mentioned in Plato's dialogue *Ion*,
530 D.]
[3] [Aristotle's pupil Theophrastus was the first to provide a
theory of delivery.]
[4] Or, 'is thought to be vulgar, when viewed from a lofty
standpoint,' 'on any noble view.'

hearer. Nobody uses fine language when teaching geometry.

When the principles of delivery have been worked out,
they will produce the same effect as on the stage.[1] But only
very slight attempts to deal with them have been made
and by a few people, as by Thrasymachus in his 'Appeals
15 to Pity'.[2] Dramatic ability is a natural gift, and can hardly
be systematically taught. The principles of good diction
can be so taught, and therefore we have men of ability in
this direction too, who win prizes in their turn, as well as
those speakers who excel in delivery—speeches of the written or literary kind owe more of their effect to their diction than to their thought.

20 It was naturally the poets who first set the movement
going; for words represent things, and they had also the
human voice at their disposal, which of all our organs can
best represent other things. Thus the arts of recitation and
acting were formed, and others as well. Now it was because poets seemed to win fame through their fine language when their thoughts were simple enough, that the
25 language of oratorical prose at first took a poetical colour,
e.g. that of Gorgias.[3] Even now most uneducated people
think that poetical language makes the finest discourses.
That is not true: the language of prose is distinct from
that of poetry. This is shown by the state of things to-day,
when even the language of tragedy has altered its char-
30 acter. Just as iambics were adopted, instead of tetrameters,
because they are the most prose-like of all metres, so tragedy has given up all those words, not used in ordinary
talk, which decorated the early drama and are still used
by the writers of hexameter poems. It is therefore ridicu-
35 lous to imitate a poetical manner which the poets themselves have dropped; and it is now plain that we have not
to treat in detail the whole question of style, but may con-

[1] [A rendering now favored is 'when the principles of style
have been worked out they will produce the same effect
as delivery.']
[2] [Thrasymachus of Chalcedon, sophist and teacher of rhetoric, sharply criticized by Plato.]
[3] [Another leading teacher of rhetoric of the 5th cent.]

fine ourselves to that part of it which concerns our present subject, rhetoric. The other—the poetical—part of it
has been discussed in the treatise on the *Art of Poetry*.[1]
2   We may, then, start from the observations there made, 1404[b]
including the definition of style. Style to be good must be
clear, as is proved by the fact that speech which fails to
convey a plain meaning will fail to do just what speech
has to do. It must also be appropriate, avoiding both
meanness and undue elevation; poetical language is certainly free from meanness, but it is not appropriate to 5
prose.[2] Clearness is secured by using the words (nouns
and verbs alike) that are current and ordinary. Freedom
from meanness, and positive adornment too, are secured by
using the other words mentioned in the *Art of Poetry*.[3]
Such variation from what is usual makes the language
appear more stately. People do not feel towards strangers
as they do towards their own countrymen, and the same 10
thing is true of their feeling for language. It is therefore
well to give to everyday speech an unfamiliar air: people
like what strikes them, and are struck by what is out of
the way. In verse such effects are common, and there they
are fitting: the persons and things there spoken of are
comparatively remote from ordinary life. In prose passages
they are far less often fitting because the subject-matter is 15
less exalted. Even in poetry, it is not quite appropriate
that fine language should be used by a slave or a very
young man, or about very trivial subjects: even in poetry
the style, to be appropriate, must sometimes be toned
down, though at other times heightened. We can now see
that a writer must disguise his art and give the impression
of speaking naturally and not artificially. Naturalness is
persuasive, artificiality is the contrary; for our hearers are 20
prejudiced and think we have some design against them,
as if we were mixing their wines for them. It is like the
difference between the quality of Theodorus'[4] voice and
the voices of all other actors: his really seems to be that

[1] *Poetics*, cc. 20-2.
[2] [Cp. beginning of *Poetics* 22.]
[3] *Poetics*, cc. 21, 22.
[4] [A celebrated actor of the time.]

of the character who is speaking, theirs do not. We can hide our purpose successfully by taking the single words of our composition from the speech of ordinary life. This 25 is done in poetry by Euripides, who was the first to show the way to his successors.

Language is composed of nouns and verbs. Nouns are of the various kinds considered in the treatise on Poetry.[1] Strange words, compound words, and invented words must be used sparingly and on few occasions: on *what* occa- 30 sions we shall state later.[2] The reason for this restriction has been already indicated: they depart from what is suitable, in the direction of excess. In the language of prose, besides the regular and proper terms for things, metaphorical terms only can be used with advantage. This we gather from the fact that these two classes of terms, the proper or regular and the metaphorical—these and no 35 others—are used by everybody in conversation. We can now see that a good writer can produce a style that is distinguished without being obtrusive, and is at the same time clear, thus satisfying our definition of good oratorical prose. Words of ambiguous meaning are chiefly useful to enable the sophist to mislead his hearers. Synonyms are useful to the poet, by which I mean words whose ordinary 1405ª meaning is the same, e.g. πορεύεσθαι (*advancing*) and βαδίξειν (*proceeding*); these two are ordinary words and have the same meaning.

In the *Art of Poetry*,[3] as we have already said, will be found definitions of these kinds of words; a classification of Metaphors; and mention of the fact that metaphor is of 5 great value both in poetry and in prose. Prose-writers must, however, pay specially careful attention to metaphor, because their other resources are scantier than those of poets. Metaphor, moreover, gives style clearness, charm, and distinction as nothing else can: and it is not a thing whose use can be taught by one man to another. Metaphors, like epi- 10 thets, must be fitting, which means that they must fairly correspond to the thing signified: failing this, their inap-

[1] *Poetics*, c. 21.
[2] iii, cc. 3, 7.
[3] Cp. *Poetics*, cc. 21, 22.

propriateness will be conspicuous: the want of harmony between two things is emphasized by their being placed side by side. It is like having to ask ourselves what dress will suit an old man; certainly not the crimson cloak that suits a young man. And if you wish to pay a compliment, you must take your metaphor from something better in the 15 same line; if to disparage, from something worse. To illustrate my meaning: since opposites are in the same class, you do what I have suggested if you say that a man who begs 'prays', and a man who prays 'begs'; for praying and begging are both varieties of asking. So Iphicrates[1] called Callias a 'mendicant priest' instead of a 'torch- 20 bearer', and Callias replied that Iphicrates must be uninitiated or he would have called him not a 'mendicant priest' but a 'torch-bearer'. Both are religious titles, but one is honourable and the other is not. Again, somebody calls actors 'hangers-on of Dionysus', but they call themselves 'artists': each of these terms is a metaphor, the one intended to throw dirt at the actor, the other to dignify 25 him. And pirates now call themselves 'purveyors'. We can thus call a crime a mistake, or a mistake a crime. We can say that a thief 'took' a thing, or that he 'plundered' his victim. An expression like that of Euripides' Telephus,[2]

King of the oar, on Mysia's coast he landed,

is inappropriate; the word 'king' goes beyond the dignity 30 of the subject, and so the art is *not* concealed. A metaphor may be amiss because the very syllables of the words conveying it fail to indicate sweetness of vocal utterance. Thus Dionysius the Brazen[3] in his elegies calls poetry 'Calliope's screech'. Poetry and screeching are both, to be sure, vocal utterances. But the metaphor is bad, because the sounds of 'screeching', unlike those of poetry, are dis-

---

[1] [Iphicrates, the Athenian general (cp. 1365ª28). Callias, a vain, foolish Athenian aristocrat in whose family the office of 'torchbearer' was hereditary. The 'torchbearer' led the procession from Athens to Eleusis on the fifth day of the Great Eleusinian.]
[2] [A lost play.]
[3] [Poet and rhetorician of the 5th cent.]

cordant and unmeaning. Further, in using metaphors to
give names to nameless things, we must draw them not
35 from remote but from kindred and similar things, so that
the kinship is clearly perceived as soon as the words are
said. Thus in the celebrated riddle

1405^b I marked how a man glued bronze with fire to another
man's body,

the process is nameless; but both it and gluing are a kind
of application, and that is why the application of the cup-
ping-glass is here called a 'gluing'. Good riddles do, in
general, provide us with satisfactory metaphors: for meta-
5 phors imply riddles, and therefore a good riddle can furnish a good metaphor. Further, the materials of metaphors
must be beautiful; and the beauty, like the ugliness, of
all words may, as Licymnius says, lie in their sound or in
their meaning.[1] Further, there is a third consideration—
one that upsets the fallacious argument of the sophist
Bryson, that there is no such thing as foul language, be-
10 cause in whatever words you put a given thing your meaning is the same. This is untrue. One term may describe
a thing more truly than another, may be more like it, and
set it more intimately before our eyes. Besides, two different words will represent a thing in two different lights;
so on this ground also one term must be held fairer or
15 fouler than another. For both of two terms will indicate
what *is* fair, or what *is* foul, but not simply their fairness
or their foulness, or if so, at any rate not in an equal degree. The materials of metaphor must be beautiful to the
ear, to the understanding, to the eye or some other physical sense. It is better, for instance, to say 'rosy-fingered
20 morn', than 'crimson-fingered' or, worse still, 'red-fingered
morn'. The epithets that we apply, too, may have a bad
and ugly aspect, as when Orestes is called a 'mother-
slayer'; or a better one, as when he is called his 'father's
avenger'. Simonides,[2] when the victor in the mule-race
offered him a small fee, refused to write him an ode,

---

[1] [A teacher of rhetoric and a dithyrambic poet.]
[2] [The lyric poet.]

because, he said, it was so unpleasant to write odes to 25
half-asses: but on receiving an adequate fee, he wrote

Hail to you, daughters of storm-footed steeds,

though of course they were daughters of asses too. The
same effect is attained by the use of diminutives, which
make a bad thing less bad and a good thing less good.
Take, for instance, the banter of Aristophanes in the *Bab-* 30
ylonians[1] where he uses 'goldlet' for 'gold', 'cloaklet' for
'cloak', 'scofflet' for 'scoff', and 'plaguelet'. But alike in using epithets and in using diminutives we must be wary
and must observe the mean.

3 Bad taste in language may take any of four forms:—
(1) The misuse of compound words. Lycophron,[2] for 35
instance, talks of the '*many-visaged* heaven' above the
'*giant-crested* earth', and again the '*strait-pathed* shore';
and Gorgias[2] of the '*pauper-poet* flatterer' and 'oath-break- 1406ᵃ
ing and *over-oath-keeping*'. Alcidamas[2] uses such expressions as 'the soul filling with rage and face becoming
flame-flushed', and 'he thought their enthusiasm would be
issue-fraught' and '*issue-fraught* he made the persuasion of
his words', and '*sombre-hued* is the floor of the sea'. The 5
way all these words are compounded makes them, we feel,
fit for verse only. This, then, is one form in which bad
taste is shown.
(2) Another is the employment of strange words. For
instance, Lycophron talks of 'the *prodigious* Xerxes' and
'*spoliative* Sciron'; Alcidamas of 'a *toy* for poetry' and 'the
witlessness of nature', and says '*whetted* with the *unmiti-* 10
gated temper of his spirit'.
(3) A third form is the use of long, unseasonable, or
frequent epithets. It is appropriate enough for a poet to
talk of 'white milk', but in prose such epithets are sometimes lacking in appropriateness or, when spread too
thickly, plainly reveal the author turning his prose into
poetry. Of course we must use some epithets, since they

[1] [A lost play.]
[2] [Lycophron, Georgias, Alcidamas, authoritative teachers of
rhetoric in the 5th and 4th cent.]

15 lift our style above the usual level and give it an air of distinction. But we must aim at the due mean, or the result will be worse than if we took no trouble at all; we shall get something actually bad instead of something merely not good. That is why the epithets of Alcidamas seem so tasteless; he does not use them as the seasoning of the meat, but as the meat itself, so numerous and swollen and
20 aggressive are they. For instance, he does not say 'sweat', but 'the *moist* sweat'; not 'to the Isthmian games', but 'to the *world-concourse* of the Isthmian games'; not 'laws', but 'the laws *that are monarchs of states*'; not 'at a run', but '*his heart impelling him to speed of foot*'; not 'a school of the Muses', but '*Nature's* school of the Muses had he in-
25 herited'; and so '*frowning* care of heart', and 'achiever' not of 'popularity' but of '*universal* popularity', and '*dispenser* of pleasure to his audience', and 'he concealed it' not 'with boughs' but 'with boughs *of the forest trees*', and 'he
30 clothed' not 'his body' but '*his body's nakedness*', and 'his soul's desire was *counter-imitative*' (this is at one and the same time a compound and an epithet, so that it seems a poet's effort), and 'so *extravagant* the excess of his wickedness'. We thus see how the inappropriateness of such poetical language imports absurdity and tastelessness into speeches, as well as the obscurity that comes from all this
35 verbosity—for when the sense is plain, you only obscure and spoil its clearness by piling up words.

The ordinary use of compound words is where there is no term for a thing and some compound can be easily formed, like 'pastime' ($\chi\rho o\nu o\tau\rho\iota\beta\epsilon\hat{\iota}\nu$); but if this is much
1406^b done, the prose character disappears entirely. We now see why the language of compounds is just the thing for writers of dithyrambs, who love sonorous noises; strange words for writers of epic poetry, which is a proud and stately affair; and metaphor for iambic verse, the metre which (as has been already[1] said) is widely used to-day.

5 (4) There remains the fourth region in which bad taste may be shown, metaphor. Metaphors like other things may be inappropriate. Some are so because they are ridiculous;

---

[1] [iii, c. 1, 1404^a30.]

they are indeed used by comic as well as tragic poets. Others are too grand and theatrical; and these, if they are far-fetched, may also be obscure. For instance, Gorgias talks of 'events that are green and full of sap', and says 'foul was the deed you sowed and evil the harvest you reaped'. That is too much like poetry. Alcidamas, again, called philosophy 'a fortress that threatens the power of law', and the *Odyssey* 'a goodly looking-glass of human life', and talked about 'offering no such toy to poetry': all these expressions fail, for the reasons given, to carry the hearer with them. The address of Gorgias to the swallow, when she had let her droppings fall on him as she flew overhead, is in the best tragic manner. He said, 'Nay, shame, O Philomela'. Considering her as a bird, you could not call her act shameful; considering her as a girl, you could; and so it was a good gibe to address her as what she was once and not as what she is.

4   The Simile also is a metaphor; the difference is but slight. When the poet says of Achilles that he

Leapt on the foe as a lion,[1]

this is a simile; when he says of him 'the lion leapt', it is a metaphor—here, since both are courageous, he has transferred to Achilles the name of 'lion'. Similes are useful in prose as well as in verse; but not often, since they are of the nature of poetry. They are to be employed just as metaphors are employed, since they are really the same thing except for the difference mentioned.

The following are examples of similes. Androtion[2] said of Idrieus that he was like a terrier let off the chain, that flies at you and bites you—Idrieus too was savage now that he was let out of *his* chains. Theodamas compared Archidamus to an Euxenus[3] who could not do geometry— a proportional[4] simile, implying that Euxenus is an Archi-

---

[1] Cp. *Iliad*, xx. 164.

[2] [Androtion, an Athenian orator of the 4th cent., was sent on an embassy to Mausolus, prince of Caria. Idrieus was the brother and successor (351 B.C.) of Mausolus.]

[3] [Nothing known of these three persons.]

[4] A 'rule-of-three' simile, an 'analogical' simile.

damus who *can* do geometry. In Plato's *Republic* those who strip the dead are compared to curs which bite the stones thrown at them but do not touch the thrower,[1] and there is the simile about the Athenian people, who are
35 compared to a ship's captain who is strong but a little deaf;[2] and the one about poets' verses, which are likened to persons who lack beauty but possess youthful freshness —when the freshness had faded the charm perishes, and
1407ᵃ so with verses when broken up into prose.[3] Pericles compared the Samians to children who take their pap but go on crying; and the Boeotians to holm-oaks, because they were ruining one another by civil wars just as one oak
5 causes another oak's fall. Demosthenes[4] said that the Athenian people were like sea-sick men on board ship. Again, Democrates[5] compared the political orators to nurses who swallow the bit of food themselves and then smear the children's lips with the spittle. Antisthenes[6] compared the
10 lean Cephisodotus[7] to frankincense, because it was his consumption that gave one pleasure. All these ideas may be expressed either as similes or as metaphors; those which succeed as metaphors will obviously do well also as similes, and similes, with the explanation omitted, will appear as metaphors. But the proportional metaphor must always
15 apply reciprocally to either of its co-ordinate terms. For instance, if a drinking-bowl is the shield of Dionysus, a shield may fittingly be called the brinking-bowl of Ares.[8]

Such, then, are the ingredients of which speech is com- 5 posed. The foundation of good style is correctness of language which falls under five heads. (1) First, the proper
20 use of connecting words, and the arrangement of them in the natural sequence which some of them require. For in-

[1] Plato, *Rep.*, v. 469 E.
[2] Ib., vi. 488 A.
[3] Cp. Ib., x. 601 B.
[4] [By general consent not the great orator; more probably the general of the Peloponnesian war.]
[5] [Probably active in Athenian political life of the 4th cent.]
[6] [Most likely the Cynic philosopher.]
[7] [One of the best speakers of the time.]
[8] [Fragm. of Timotheus, the dithyrambic poet.]

stance, the connective μέν (e.g. ἐγὼ μέν) requires the correlative δέ (e.g. ὁ δέ). The answering word must be
brought in before the first has been forgotten, and not be
widely separated from it; nor, except in the few cases
where this is appropriate, is another connective to be in-25
troduced before the one required. Consider the sentence,
'But I, as soon as he told me (for Cleon had come begging and praying), took them along and set out.' [1] In this
sentence many connecting words are inserted in front of
the one required to complete the sense; and if there is a
long interval before 'set out', the result is obscurity. One
merit, then, of good style lies in the right use of connect-30
ing words. (2) The second lies in calling things by their
own special names and not by vague general ones. (3)
The third is to avoid ambiguities; unless, indeed, you def-
initely desire to be ambiguous, as those do who have nothing to say but are pretending to mean something. Such
people are apt to put that sort of thing into verse. Em-35
pedocles,[2] for instance, by his long circumlocutions imposes
on his hearers; these are affected in the same way as most
people are when they listen to diviners, whose ambiguous
utterances are received with nods of acquiescence—

Croesus by crossing the Halys will ruin a mighty realm.[3]

Diviners use these vague generalities about the matter in *1407*[b]
hand because their predictions are thus, as a rule, less
likely to be falsified. We are more likely to be right, in
the game of 'odd and even', if we simply guess 'even' or
'odd' than if we guess at the actual number; and the
oracle-monger is more likely to be right if he simply says
that a thing will happen than if he says *when* it will happen, and therefore he refuses to add a definite date. All [5]
these ambiguities have the same sort of effect,[4] and are to
be avoided unless we have some such object as that mentioned. (4) A fourth rule is to observe Protagoras' classi-

---

[1] [The text of the two preceding sentences is subject to
  considerable doubt.]
[2] [The physical philosopher.]
[3] Cp. Herod., i. 53, 91.
[4] i.e. are equally destructive of clearness.

fication of nouns into male, female, and inanimate; for
these distinctions also must be correctly given. 'Upon her
arrival she said her say and departed (ἡ δ' ἐλθοῦσα καὶ
διαλεχθεῖσα ᾤχετο).' (5) A fifth rule is to express plurality,
10 fewness, and unity by the correct wording, e.g. 'Having
come, they struck me (οἱ δ' ἐλθόντες ἔτυπτόν με).'

It is a general rule that a written composition should
be easy to read and therefore easy to deliver.[1] This cannot
be so where there are many connecting words or clauses,
or where punctuation is hard, as in the writings of Heracleitus.[2] To punctuate Heracleitus is no easy task, because we often cannot tell whether a particular word
15 belongs to what precedes or what follows it. Thus, at the
outset of his treatise he says, 'Though this truth is always
men understand it not', where it is not clear with which
of the two clauses the word 'always' should be joined by
the punctuation. Further, the following fact leads to sole-
cism, viz. that the sentence does not work out properly if
you annex to two terms a third which does not suit them
20 both.[3] Thus either 'sound' or 'colour' will fail to work out
properly with some verbs: 'perceive' will apply to both,
'see' will not. Obscurity is also caused if, when you intend
to insert a number of details, you do not first make your
meaning clear; for instance, if you say, 'I meant, after telling him this, that, and the other thing, to set out', rather
than something of this kind 'I meant to set out after tell-
25 ing him; then this, that, and the other thing occurred.'

The following suggestions will help to give your lan- 6
guage impressiveness.[4] (1) Describe a thing instead of
naming it: do not say 'circle', but 'that surface which ex-
tends equally from the middle every way'. To achieve conciseness, do the opposite—put the name instead of the

---

[1] Or, 'easy to understand.' . . .
[2] [Heracleitus of Ephesus, pre-Socratic philosopher. His obscurity is frequently mentioned and criticized in antiquity.]
[3] [This is based on the Greek text as reconstructed by
W. D. Ross.]
[4] [The Greek word sometimes means 'inflated diction,' 'bom-
bast,' 'pomp,' 'grandiloquence,' rather than 'dignity.']

description. When mentioning anything ugly or unseemly, use its name if it is the description that is ugly, and de- 30 scribe it if it is the name that is ugly. (2) Represent things with the help of metaphors and epithets, being careful to avoid poetical effects. (3) Use plural for singular, as in poetry, where one finds

> Unto havens Achaean,[1]

though only one haven is meant,
and

> Here are my letter's many-leavèd folds.[2]

(4) Do not bracket two words under one article, but put 35 one article with each; e.g. τῆς γυναικὸς τῆς ἡμετέρας.[3] The reverse to secure conciseness; e.g. τῆς ἡμετέρας γυναικός.[3] (5) Use plenty of connecting words; conversely, to secure conciseness, dispense with connectives, while still preserving connexion; e.g. 'having gone and spoken', and 'having 1408ᵇ gone, I spoke', respectively. (6) And the practice of Antimachus, too, is useful—to describe a thing by mentioning attributes it does not possess; as he does in talking of Teumessus—

> There is a little wind-swept knoll . . .[4]

A subject can be developed indefinitely along these lines. You may apply this method of treatment by negation either to good or to bad qualities, according to which your 5 subject requires. It is from this source that the poets draw expressions such as the 'stringless' or 'lyreless' melody, thus forming epithets out of negations. This device is popular

---

[1] [Fragm. from an unidentified tragedy.]
[2] Euripides, *Iph. Taur.* 727: more literally, 'here are the tablet's folds with many doors.'
[3] [These are two ways of expressing 'our wife.']
[4] [Fragm. from the lengthy epos *Thebais* of Antimachus of Colophon, contemporary of Plato. Describing the expedition of the Seven Against Thebes he mentions Theumessus, a village of Boeotia in the plain of Thebes, standing upon a low rocky hill of the same name, and continues this description for many lines.]

in proportional metaphors, as when the trumpet's note is called 'a lyreless melody'.[1]

10 Your language will be *appropriate* if it expresses emo- 7 tion and character, and if it corresponds to its subject. 'Correspondence to subject' means that we must neither speak casually about weighty matters, nor solemnly about trivial ones; nor must we add ornamental epithets to commonplace nouns, or the effect will be comic, as in the 15 works of Cleophon,[2] who can use phrases as absurd as 'O queenly fig-tree'. To express emotion, you will employ the language of anger in speaking of outrage; the language of disgust and discreet reluctance to utter a word when speaking of impietv or foulness; the language of exultation for a tale of glory, and that of humiliation for a tale of pity; and so in all other cases.

20 This aptness of language is one thing that makes people believe in the truth of your story: their minds draw the false conclusion that you are to be trusted from the fact that others behave as you do when things are as you describe them; and therefore they take your story to be true, whether it is so or not. Besides, an emotional speaker always makes his audience feel with him, even when there is nothing in his arguments; which is why many speakers 25 try to overwhelm their audience by mere noise.

Furthermore, this way of proving your story by displaying these signs of its genuineness expresses your personal character. Each class of men, each type of disposition, will have its own appropriate way of letting the truth appear. Under 'class' I include differences of age, as boy, man, or old man; of sex, as man or woman; of nationality, as Spartan or Thessalian. By 'dispositions' I here mean those dispositions only which determine the 30 character of a man's life, for it is not every disposition that does this. If, then, a speaker uses the very words which

[1] The Greek word for 'melody' is appropriate to the lyre and not to the trumpet.
[2] [An Athenian writer of tragedies. Cp. *Poetics* ii. 5.]

are in keeping with a particular disposition, he will reproduce the corresponding character; for a rustic and an
educated man will not say the same things nor speak in
the same way. Again, some impression is made upon an
audience by a device which speech-writers employ to
nauseous excess, when they say 'Who does not know
this?' or 'It is known to everybody.' The hearer is ashamed
of his ignorance, and agrees with the speaker, so as to 35
have a share of the knowledge that everybody else possesses.

All the variations of oratorical style are capable of being 1408ᵇ
used in season or out of season. The best way to counteract any exaggeration is the well-worn device by which the
speaker puts in some criticism of himself; for then people
feel it must be all right for him to talk thus, since he certainly knows what he is doing. Further, it is better not
to have everything always just corresponding to everything
else—your hearers will see through you less easily thus. 5
I mean for instance, if your words are harsh, you should
not extend this harshness to your voice and your counte-
nance and have everything else in keeping. If you do, the
artificial character of each detail becomes apparent;
whereas if you adopt one device and not another, you are
using art all the same and yet nobody notices it. (To be
sure, if mild sentiments are expressed in harsh tones and
harsh sentiments in mild tones, you become comparatively unconvincing.) Compound words, fairly plentiful 10
epithets, and strange words best suit an emotional speech.
We forgive an angry man for talking about a wrong as
'heaven-high' or 'colossal'; and we excuse such language
when the speaker has his hearers already in his hands and
has stirred them deeply either by praise or blame or anger
or affection, as Isocrates, for instance, does at the end of 15
his *Panegyric,* with his 'name and fame' and 'in that they
brooked'. Men do speak in this strain when they are
deeply stirred, and so, once the audience is in a like
state of feeling, approval of course follows. This is why
such language is fitting in poetry, which is an inspired
thing. This language, then, should be used either under

20 stress of emotion, or ironically, after the manner of Gorgias and of the passages in the *Phaedrus*.[1]

The form of a prose composition should be neither 8 metrical nor destitute of rhythm. The metrical form destroys the hearer's trust by its artificial appearance, and at the same time it diverts his attention, making him watch 25 for metrical recurrences, just as children catch up the herald's question, 'Whom does the freedman choose as his advocate?', with the answer 'Cleon!' On the other hand, unrhythmical language is too unlimited; we do not want the limitations of metre, but some limitation we must have, or the effect will be vague and unsatisfactory. Now it is number that limits all things; and it is the numerical limitation of the form of a composition that constitutes rhythm, of which metres are definite sections.

30 Prose, then, is to be rhythmical, but not metrical, or it will become not prose but verse. It should not even have too precise a prose rhythm, and therefore should only be rhythmical to a certain extent.

Of the various rhythms, the heroic has dignity, but lacks the tones of the spoken language.[2] The iambic is the very language of ordinary people, so that in common 35 talk iambic lines occur oftener than any others: but in a speech we need dignity and the power of taking the hearer out of his ordinary self. The trochee is too much akin to wild dancing: we can see this in tetrameter verse, 1409ᵃ which is one of the trochaic rhythms.[3]

There remains the paean, which speakers began to use in the time of Thrasymachus, though they had then no name to give it.[4] The paean is a third class of rhythm, closely akin to both the two already mentioned; it has in it the ratio of three to two, whereas the other two kinds 5 have the ratio of one to one, and two to one respectively.

---

[1] Cp. Plato, *Phaedrus*, 238 D, 241 E. *Irony* is attributed to Gorgias, with an illustration in the *Politics*, iii. 2, 1275ᵇ27.
[2] [The soundness of the Greek text is not above doubt.]
[3] Or, 'which is a tripping rhythm.' . . .
[4] [Thrasymachus of Chalcedon, the sophist and rhetorician. Cp. 1404ᵃ14.]

Between the two last ratios comes the ratio of one-and-a-half to one, which is that of the paean.

Now the other two kinds of rhythm must be rejected in writing prose, partly for the reasons given, and partly because they are too metrical; and the paean must be adopted, since from this alone of the rhythms mentioned no definite metre arises, and therefore it is the least obtrusive of them. At present the same form of paean is employed at the beginning as at the end of sentences, whereas the end should differ from the beginning. There are two opposite kinds of paean, one of which is suitable to the beginning of a sentence, where it is indeed actually used; this is the kind that begins with a long syllable and ends with three short ones, as

$$\bar{\Delta}\breve{\alpha}\breve{\lambda}o\gamma\epsilon\nu\grave{\epsilon}\varsigma \mid \bar{\epsilon}\breve{\iota}\tau\epsilon \; \Lambda\nu\kappa\acute{\iota}\big|\alpha\nu,^1$$

and

$$\bar{X}\rho\nu\sigma\epsilon o\kappa\acute{o}\mu\big|\bar{\alpha} \; \text{"}E\kappa\alpha\tau\epsilon \mid \pi\alpha\hat{\iota} \; \Delta\iota\acute{o}\varsigma.^2$$

The other paean begins, conversely, with three short syllables and ends with a long one, as

$$\breve{\mu}\epsilon\tau\grave{\alpha} \; \delta\grave{\epsilon} \; \gamma\hat{\alpha}\nu \mid \breve{\upsilon}\delta\breve{\alpha}\tau\breve{\alpha} \; \tau' \; \bar{\omega}\kappa\big|\epsilon\alpha\nu\grave{o}\nu \; \bar{\eta}\big|\phi\acute{\alpha}\nu\iota\sigma\epsilon \; \nu\acute{\upsilon}\xi.^3$$

This kind of paean makes a real close: a short syllable can give no effect of finality, and therefore makes the rhythm appear truncated. A sentence should break off with the long syllable: the fact that it is over should be indicated not by the scribe, or by his period-mark in the margin, but by the rhythm itself.

We have now seen that our language must be rhythmical and not destitute of rhythm, and what rhythms, in what particular shape, make it so.

9　The language of prose must be either free-running, with its parts united by nothing except the connecting words,

---

[1] 'O Delos-born, or if perchance Lycia (thou callest thy birthplace).'

[2] 'Golden-haired Archer, Son of Zeus.'

[3] After earth and its waters, night shrouded the Ocean from sight.' This line and the two which precede it are [by some regarded as] fragments of the *Paeans* of Simonides. . . .

25 like the preludes in dithyrambs; or compact and antithetical, like the strophes of the old poets. The free-running style is the ancient one, e.g. 'Herein is set forth the
inquiry of Herodotus the Thurian.' [1] Every one used this
method formerly; not many do so now. By 'free-running'
style I mean the kind that has no natural stopping-places,
30 and comes to a stop only because there is no more to
say of that subject. This style is unsatisfying just because
it goes on indefinitely—one always likes to sight a stop-
ping-place in front of one: it is only at the goal that
men in a race faint and collapse; while they see the end
of the course before them, they can keep going. Such,
then, is the free-running kind of style; the compact is
35 that which is in periods. By a period I mean a portion of
speech that has in itself a beginning and an end, being at
the same time not too big to be taken in at a glance.
1409^b Language of this kind is satisfying and easy to follow.
It is satisfying, because it is just the reverse of indefinite;
and moreover, the hearer always feels that he is grasping
something and has reached some definite conclusion;
whereas it is unsatisfactory to see nothing in front of you
and get nowhere. It is easy to follow, because it can easily
be remembered; and this because language when in
5 periodic form can be numbered,[2] and number is the
easiest of all things to remember. That is why verse, which
is measured, is always more easily remembered than prose,
which is not: the measures of verse can be numbered. The
period must, further, not be completed until the sense is
complete: it must not be capable of breaking off abruptly,
as may happen with the following iambic lines of
Sophocles—

20   Calydon's soil is this; of Pelops' land
    ⟨The smiling plains face us across the strait⟩.[3]

[1] Herodotus, i, 1, init. Aristotle intends to indicate the first
complete sentence, or more than that.[Our Mss. of Herodotus read 'Herodotus the Halicarnassian.']
[2] i.e. is recognized as consisting of a countable number of
parts or divisions.
[3] [According to the scholiast the line is a fragm. from the
Meleager of Euripides.]

By a wrong division[1] of the words the hearer may take
the meaning to be the reverse of what it is: for instance,
in the passage quoted, one might imagine that Calydon
is in the Peloponnesus.

A Period may be either divided into several members[2]
or simple. The period of several members is a portion of
speech (1) complete in itself, (2) divided into parts, and
(3) easily delivered at a single breath—as a whole, that
is; not by fresh breath being taken at the division.[3] A member is one of the two parts of such a period. By a
'simple' period, I mean that which has only one member.
The members, and the whole periods, should be neither
curt nor long. A member which is too short often makes
the listener stumble; he is still expecting the rhythm to go
on to the limit his mind has fixed for it; and if meanwhile he is pulled back by the speaker's stopping, the
shock is bound to make him, so to speak, stumble. If, on
the other hand, you go on too long, you make him feel left
behind, just as people who when walking pass beyond
the boundary before turning back leave their companions
behind. So too if a period is too long you turn it into
a speech, or something like a dithyrambic prelude. The
result is much like the preludes that Democritus of Chios[4]
jeered at Melanippides[4] for writing instead of antistrophic
stanzas—

> He that sets traps for another man's feet
>   Is like to fall into them first;
> And long-winded preludes do harm to us all,
>   But the preluder catches it worst.[5]

Which applies likewise to long-membered[6] orators. Periods

[1] i.e. by coming to an abrupt stop at the end of the first
line and making no pause in its middle.
[2] [The Greek means 'limbs.']
[3] [The text is quite uncertain. Aristotle's meaning seems to
be that the 'colic' period must not merely consist of parts
that are easily delivered at a single breath.]
[4] [Democritus of Chios, a musician of late 5th cent.; Melanippides of Melos, a poet of dithyrambs of late 5th cent.]
[5] [A parody of Hesiod, *Works and Days* 263.]
[6] i.e. long-winded framers of long-membered periods. . . .

whose members are altogether too short are not periods at
all; and the result is to bring the hearer down with a crash.

The periodic style which is divided into members is
of two kinds. It is either simply divided, as in 'I have
often wondered at the conveners of national gatherings
35 and the founders of athletic contests';[1] or it is antithetical,
where, in each of the two members, one of one pair of
opposites is put along with one of another pair, or the
1410ᵃ same word is used to bracket two opposites, as 'They
aided both parties—not only those who stayed behind but
those who accompanied them: for the latter they acquired
new territory larger than that at home, and to the former
they left territory at home that was large enough'. Here
the contrasted words are 'staying behind' and 'accompany-
ing', 'enough' and 'larger'. So in the example, 'Both to
5 those who want to get property and to those who desire
to enjoy it' where 'enjoyment' is contrasted with 'getting'.
Again, 'it often happens in such enterprises that the wise
men fail and the fools succeed'; 'they were awarded the
prize of valour immediately, and won the command of
the sea not long afterwards'; 'to sail through the main-
10 land and march through the sea, by bridging the Helles-
pont and cutting through Athos'; 'nature gave them their
country and law took it away again'; 'some of them
perished in misery, others were saved in disgrace'; 'Athenian citizens keep foreigners in their houses as servants,
while the city of Athens allows her allies by thousands
15 to live as the foreigner's slaves'; and 'to possess in life
or to bequeath at death'. There is also what some one said
about Peitholaus[2] and Lycophron[2] in a law-court, 'These
men used to sell you when they were at home, and now
they have come to you here and bought you'.[2] All
these passages have the structure described above. Such

---

[1] [This and all the following illustrations are taken from
the *Panegyricus* of Isocrates.]

[2] [Peitholaus and Lycophron, after the murder of their
brother-in-law rulers of Pherae, were defeated by Philip
of Macedonia (353-352 B.C.) and thereafter became leaders
of mercenaries. Place, circumstances and speaker of the
quotation are unknown.]

a form of speech is satisfying, because the significance 20
of contrasted ideas is easily felt, especially when they are
thus put side by side, and also because it has the effect
of a logical argument; it is by putting two opposing conclusions side by side that you prove one of them false.

Such, then, is the nature of *antithesis*. *Parisosis* is making the two members of a period equal in length. *Paromoeosis* is making the extreme words of both members
like each other. This must happen either at the beginning 25
or at the end of each member. If at the beginning, the
resemblance must always be between whole words; at the
end, between final syllables or inflexions of the same word
or the same word repeated. Thus, at the beginning

$$\text{ἀγρὸν γὰρ ἔλαβεν ἀργὸν παρ' αὐτοῦ}^1$$

and

$$\text{δωρητοί τ' ἐπέλοντο παράρρητοί τ' ἐπέεσσιν.}^2$$

At the end

$$\text{οὐκ ᾠήθησαν αὐτὸν παιδίον τετοκέναι, ἀλλ' αὐτοῦ}\qquad 30$$
$$\text{αἴτιον γεγονέναι,}^3$$

and

$$\text{ἐν πλείσταις δὲ φροντίσι καὶ ἐν ἐλαχίσταις ἐλπίσιν.}^4$$

An example of inflexions of the same word is

$$\text{ἄξιος δὲ σταθῆναι χαλκοῦς, οὐκ ἄξιος ὢν χαλκοῦ;}^5$$

Of the same word repeated,

[1] Aristophanes, fragm. (Kock, *Comicorum Atticorum Frag-
menta*, i, p. 553.) 'A field he took from him, a fallow
field.'
[2] *Iliad*, ix. 526, 'Yet might they by presents be won, and
by pleadings be pacified.'
[3] *Auct. Inc.* With οὐκ, the meaning will be 'they didn't
imagine that he *had borne* the child, but that he was the
cause of its *having been borne.*' Presumably a humorous
remark in a paternity case. . . .
[4] *Inc.* 'In the midst of plenteous cares and exiguous hopes.
[5] *Inc.* 'Is he worthy to have a copper statue, when he is not
worth a copper?'

σὺ δ' αὐτὸν καὶ ζῶνατ ἔλεγες κακῶς καὶ νῦν γράφεις κακῶς.[1]

Of one syllable,

35 τί δ' ἂν ἔπαθες δεινόν, εἰ ἄνδρ' εἶδες ἀργόν;[2]

It is possible for the same sentence to have all these
1410[b] features together—*antithesis, parison,* and *homoeoteleuton.*
(The possible beginnings of periods have been pretty fully
enumerated in the *Theodectea.*)[3] There are also spurious
antitheses, like that of Epicharmus—

5   There one time I as their guest did stay,
      And they were my hosts on another day.[4]

We may now consider the above points settled, and pass 10
on to say something about the way to devise lively and
taking sayings. Their actual invention can only come
through natural talent or long practice; but this treatise
may indicate the way it is done. We may deal with them
by enumerating the different kinds of them. We will begin
10 by remarking that we all naturally find it agreeable to get
hold of new ideas easily: words express ideas, and therefore those words are the most agreeable that enable us to
get hold of new ideas. Now strange words simply puzzle
us; ordinary words convey only what we know already;
it is from metaphor that we can best get hold of something fresh. When the poet calls old age 'a withered
stalk',[5] he conveys a new idea, a new fact, to us by means
15 of the general notion of 'lost bloom', which is common to
both things. The similes of the poets do the same, and
therefore, if they are good similes, give an effect of bril-
liance. The simile, as has been said before,[6] is a metaphor,
differing from it only in the way it is put; and just because

---

[1] *Inc.* 'When he was alive you spoke evil of him, and now
you write evil of him.'
[2] *Inc.* 'Would it have been very shocking to you if you had
seen a man idling?'
[3] [This seems to be the rhetorical system of Aristotle's
friend Theodectes.]
[4] [Fragm. of Epicharmus, Sicilian writer of comedies.]
[5] *Odyssey,* xiv. 213, 'stubble.'
[6] iii, c. 4 init.

it is longer it is less attractive. Besides, it does not say
outright that 'this' *is* 'that', and therefore the hearer is
less interested in the idea. We see, then, that both speech 20
and reasoning are lively in proportion as they make us
seize a new idea promptly. For this reason people are not
much taken either by obvious arguments (using the word
'obvious' to mean what is plain to everybody and needs
no investigation), nor by those which puzzle us when we
hear them stated, but only by those which convey their
information to us as soon as we hear them, provided we
had not the information already; or which the mind only 25
just fails to keep up with. These two kinds do convey to us
a sort of information: but the obvious and the obscure
kinds convey nothing, either at once or later on. It is
these qualities, then, that, so far as the meaning of what
is said is concerned, make an argument acceptable. So far
as the style is concerned, it is the antithetical form that
appeals to us, e.g. 'judging that the peace common to all
the rest was a war upon their own private interests,' [1] 30
where there is an antithesis between war and peace. It is
also good to use metaphorical words; but the metaphors
must not be far-fetched, or they will be difficult to grasp,
nor obvious, or they will have no effect. The words, too,
ought to set the scene before our eyes; for events ought to
be seen in progress rather than in prospect. So we must
aim at these three points: Antithesis, Metaphor, and Actu- 35
ality.

Of the four kinds of Metaphor the most taking is the 1411ᵃ
proportional kind. Thus Pericles, for instance, said that
the vanishing from their country of the young men who
had fallen in the war was 'as if the spring were taken out
of the year'.[2] Leptines,[3] speaking of the Lacedaemonians,
said that he would not have the Athenians let Greece 'lose 5

[1] Isocrates, *Philippus*, 73.
[2] Cp. i, c. 7, 1365ᵃ32,33.
[3] [Probably the opponent of Demosthenes. The metaphor
may belong to the time of the Lacedaemonian embassy
to Athens after the Lacedaemonian defeat at Leuctra,
371 B.C.]

one of her two eyes'. When Chares[1] was pressing for
leave to be examined upon his share in the Olynthiac war,
Cephisodotus[2] was indignant, saying that he wanted his
examination to take place 'while he had his fingers upon
the people's throat'.[3] The same speaker once urged the
10 Athenians to march to Euboea, 'with Miltiades' decree as
their rations'.[4] Iphicrates,[5] indignant at the truce made by
the Athenians with Epidaurus and the neighbouring sea-
board, said that they had stripped themselves of their
travelling-money for the journey of war. Peitholaus[6] called
the state-galley 'the people's big stick', and Sestos 'the
15 corn-bin of the Peiraeus'. Pericles bade his countrymen
remove Aegina, 'that eyesore of the Peiraeus.' And Moer-
ocles[7] said he was no more a rascal than was a certain
respectable citizen he named, 'whose rascality was worth
over thirty per cent. per annum to him, instead of a mere
ten like his own'. There is also the iambic line of Anaxandrides about the way his daughters put off marrying—

20   My daughters' marriage-bonds are overdue.[8]

Polyeuctus[9] said of a paralytic man named Speusippus
that he could not keep quiet, 'though fortune had fastened
him in the pillory of disease'. Cephisodotus[10] called war-
ships 'painted millstones.' Diogenes[11] the Dog called tav-
25 erns 'the mess-rooms of Attica'. Aesion[12] said that the

---

[1] [Chares with his mercenaries took command in the Olyn-
thian war, 349 B.C.]
[2] [The orator, cp. 1407ª9.]
[3] i.e. while he was still in command of his mercenaries, and
so could coerce the people.
[4] ['With haste,' 'without provisioning and deliberation,' as
Miltiades had prescribed at the time of the first Persian
invasion.]
[5] [The Athenian general.]
[6] [The same as 1410ª17.]
[7] [A contemporary anti-Macedonian orator.]
[8] [Fragm. of Anaxandrides, writer of the Middle Comedy.]
[9] [A contemporary anti-Macedonian orator.]
[10] [Cp. 1411ª7.]
[11] [Diogenes of Sinope, founder of the Cynic school of
Philosophy.]
[12] [May have been a contemporary orator.]

Athenians had 'emptied' their town into Sicily: this is a graphic metaphor. 'Till all Hellas shouted aloud' may be regarded as a metaphor, and a graphic one again. Cephisodotus bade the Athenians take care not to hold too many 'parades'. Isocrates used the same word of those who [30] 'parade' at the national festivals.[1] Another example occurs in the Funeral Speech:[2] 'It is fitting that Greece should cut off her hair beside the tomb of those who fell at Salamis, since her freedom and their valour are buried in the same grave.' Even if the speaker here had only said that it was right to weep when valour was being buried in their grave, it would have been a metaphor, and a [35] graphic one; but the coupling of 'their valour' and 'her [1411ᵇ] freedom' presents a kind of antithesis as well. 'The course of my words', said Iphicrates,[3] 'lies straight through the middle of Chares' deeds': this is a proportional metaphor, and the phrase 'straight through the middle' makes it graphic. The expression 'to call in one danger to rescue [5] us from another' is a graphic metaphor. Lycoleon[4] said, defending Chabrias,[4] 'They did not respect even that bronze statue of his that intercedes for him yonder'. This was a metaphor for the moment, though it would not always apply; a vivid metaphor, however; Chabrias is in danger, and his statue intercedes for him—that lifeless yet living thing which records his services to his country.[5] [10] 'Practising in every way littleness of mind'[6] is metaphorical, for practising a quality implies increasing it. So is 'God kindled our reason to be a lamp within our souls',[7] for both reason and light reveal things. So is 'we are not

---

[1] Isocrates, *Philippus*, 12.
[2] [Uncertain which funeral speech and whether the Mss. are correct in having 'Salamis.']
[3] [For Chares cp. 1411ᵃ; for Iphicrates and the case cp. 1398ᵃ5.]
[4] [Of Lycoleon nothing is known but what can be gathered from this passage: that he was an orator who defended Chabrias the general, in his trial, 366 B.C. Cp. 1364ᵃ22.]
[5] Or, 'the great deeds of his country' (Chares' glory being regarded as the glory of Athens). . . .
[6] Isocrates, *Paneg.*, 151
[7] *Auct. Inc.*

15 putting an end to our wars, but only postponing them',[1] for both literal postponement and the making of such a peace as this apply to future action. So is such a saying as 'This treaty is a far nobler trophy than those we set up on fields of battle; *they* celebrate small gains and single successes; *it* celebrates our triumph in the war as a whole';[2] for both trophy and treaty are signs of victory. So is 'A country pays a heavy reckoning in being condemned by **20** the judgement of mankind',[3] for a reckoning is damage deservedly incurred.

It has already been mentioned that liveliness is got by **11** using the proportional type of metaphor and by being graphic (i.e. making your hearers *see* things). We have still to explain what we mean by their 'seeing things', and what must be done to effect this. By 'making them see **25** things' I mean using expressions that represent things as in a state of activity. Thus, to say that a good man is 'four-square'[4] is certainly a metaphor; both the good man and the square are perfect; but the metaphor does not suggest activity. On the other hand, in the expression 'with his vigor in full bloom'[5] there is a notion of activity; and so in 'But you must roam as free as a sacred victim';[6] and in

30   Thereat up sprang the Hellenes to their feet,[7]

where 'up sprang' gives us activity as well as metaphor, for it at once suggests swiftness. So with Homer's common practice of giving metaphorical life to lifeless things: all such passages are distinguished by the effect of activity they convey. Thus,

Downward anon to the valley rebounded the boulder *remorseless*;[8]

[1] Isocrates, *Paneg.*, 172.
[2] Ib., 180.
[3] *Auct. Inc.*; cp. Isocrates, *De Pace*, 120.
[4] [Fragm. of Simonides.]
[5] Isocrates, *Philippus*, 10.
[6] Ib., 127.
[7] Euripides, *Iph. Aul.*, 80. . . .
[8] *Odyssey*, xi. 598. . . .

and

> The ⟨bitter⟩ arrow *flew;*[1]

and

> Flying on *eagerly;*[2]   35

and

> Stuck in the earth, still *panting* to feed on the flesh *1412*[a]
> of the heroes;[3]

and

> And the point of the spear *in its fury* drove full through
> his breastbone.[4]

In all these examples the things have the effect of being
active because they are made into living beings; shameless
behaviour and fury and so on are all forms of activity. And
the poet has attached these ideas to the things by means
of proportional metaphors: as the stone is to Sisyphus, 5
so is the shameless man to his victim. In his famous
similes, too, he treats inanimate things in the same way:

> Curving and crested with white, host following host
> without ceasing.[5]

Here he represents everything as moving and living; and
activity is movement.

Metaphors must be drawn, as has been said already,[6]
from things that are related to the original thing, and yet 10
not obviously so related—just as in philosophy also an
acute mind will perceive resemblances even in things far
apart. Thus Archytas[7] said that an arbitrator and an altar
were the same, since the injured fly to both for refuge. Or
you might say that an anchor and an overhead hook were
the same, since both are in a way the same, only the one

---

[1] *Iliad*, xiii. 587. . . .
[2] *Iliad*, iv. 126. Here too an arrow is spoken of.
[3] *Iliad*, xi. 574. Spears are falling short of their mark.
[4] *Iliad*, xv. 542.
[5] *Iliad*, xiii. 799. Ocean waves rolling to the shore.
[6] iii, c. 10, 1410ᵇ32.
[7] [Pythagorean philosopher and mathematician, a friend of
Plato.]

15 secures things from below and the other from above. And
to speak of states as 'levelled'[1] is to identify two widely
different things, the equality of a physical surface and the
equality of political powers.

Liveliness is specially conveyed by metaphor, and by
the further power of surprising the hearer; because the
hearer expected something different, his acquisition of
20 the new idea impresses him all the more. His mind seems
to say, 'Yes, to be sure; I never thought of that'. The
liveliness of epigrammatic remarks is due to the meaning
not being just what the words say: as in the saying of
Stesichorus that 'the cicalas will chirp to themselves on
the ground'.[2] Well-constructed riddles are attractive for
the same reason; a new idea is conveyed, and there is
25 metaphorical expression. So with the 'novelties' of Theodorus.[3] In these the thought is startling, and, as Theodorus puts it, does not fit in with the ideas you already
have. They are like the burlesque words that one finds in
the comic writers. The effect is produced even by jokes
depending upon changes of the letters of a word;[4] this
too is a surprise. You find this in verse as well as in prose.
The word which comes is not what the hearer imagined:
thus

30   Onward he came, and his feet were shod with his—
        chilblains,[5]

where one imagined the word would be 'sandals'. But the
point should be clear the moment the words are uttered.
Jokes made by altering the letters of a word consist in
meaning, not just what you say, but something that gives
a twist to the word used; e.g. the remark of Theodorus
about Nicon the harpist Θρᾷττ' εἶ σύ ('you Thracian
35 slavey'), where he pretends to mean θράττεις σύ ('you
harp-player'), and surprises us when we find he means

---

[1] Cp. Isocrates, *Philippus*, 40.
[2] [Cp. 1395ª1.]
[3] [Cp. 1400ᵇ16.]
[4] Plays upon words are meant, here and eight lines lower down.
[5] *Auct. Inc.* Probably from some burlesque hexameter poem.

something else.[1] So you enjoy the point when you see it, *1412*^b
though the remark will fall flat unless you are aware that
Nicon is a Thracian. Or again: βούλει αὐτὸν πέρσαι.[2] In
both these cases the saying must fit the facts.[3] This is
also true of such lively remarks as the one to the effect
that to the Athenians their empire (ἀρχή) of the sea was
not the beginning (ἀρχή) of their troubles, since they 5
gained by it. Or the opposite one of Isocrates, that their
empire (ἀρχή) *was* the beginning (ἀρχή) of their troubles.[4] Either way, the speaker says something unexpected,
the soundness of which is thereupon recognized. There
would be nothing clever in saying 'empire is empire'.
Isocrates means more than that, and uses the word with
a new meaning. So too with the former saying, which
denies that ἀρχή in one sense was ἀρχή in another sense. 10
In all these jokes, whether a word is used in a second
sense or metaphorically, the joke is good if it fits the facts.
For instance, Ἀνάσχετος (proper name) οὐκ ἀνασχετός:[5]
where you say that what is so-and-so in one sense is not
so-and-so in another; well, if the man is unpleasant, the
joke fits the facts. Again, take—

> Thou must not be a stranger stranger than
> Thou should'st.[6]

Do not the words 'thou must not be', &c., amount to
saying that the stranger must not always be strange? Here 15
again is the use of one word in different senses. Of the
same kind also is the much-praised verse of Anaxandrides:

---

[1] [The above is an attractive conjectural explanation of a
difficult passage.]

[2] 'You wish (or, do you wish) to *persecute* him.' [Perhaps
a pun on 'Persians.']

[3] Or, 'there must be a proper enunciation,' i.e. a significant
stress must be laid on the ambiguous word. . . . But cp.
1412^b11 and 13.

[4] Cp. Isocrates, *Philippus*, 61; *Paneg.* 119; *De Pace* 101.

[5] 'Baring is past bearing.'

[6] [Fragm. of a comedy. There are serious textual difficulties
in the quotation and in the sentence which comments on
it.]

Death is most fit before you do
Deeds that would make death fit for you.[1]

This amounts to saying 'it is a fit thing to die when you
are not fit to die', or 'it is a fit thing to die when death is
20 not fit for you', i.e. when death is not the fit return for
what you are doing. The type of language employed is
the same in all these examples; but the more briefly and
antithetically such sayings can be expressed, the more
taking they are, for antithesis impresses the new idea more
firmly and brevity more quickly. They should always have
either some personal application or some merit of expres-
25 sion,[2] if they are to be true without being common-place—
two requirements not always satisfied simultaneously. Thus
'a man should die having done no wrong' is true but
dull: 'the right man should marry the right woman'[3] is
also true but dull. No, there must be both good qualities
together, as in 'it is fitting to die when you are not fit
for death'. The more a saying has these qualities, the
30 livelier it appears: if, for instance, its wording is metaphorical, metaphorical in the right way, antithetical, and
balanced, and at the same time it gives an idea of activity.

Successful similes also, as has been said above,[4] are in
a sense metaphors, since they always involve two relations
35 like the proportional metaphor. Thus: a shield, we say,
1413[a] is the 'drinking-bowl of Ares',[5] and a bow is the 'chordless
lyre'.[6] This way of putting a metaphor is not 'simple',
as it would be if we called the bow a lyre or the shield a
drinking-bowl. There are 'simple' similes also: we may say
that a flute-player is like a monkey, or that a short-sighted
man's eyes are like a lamp-flame with water dropping on
it, since both eyes and flame keep winking.[7] A simile

---

[1] [Fragm. of Anaxandrides.]
[2] . . . Implying the use of the *mot juste.*
[3] [Fragm. of an unidentified comedy.]
[4] iii, cc. 4 and 10.
[5] [Cp. 1407[a]15.]
[6] [Probably a phrase of Theognis the tragedian, a contemporary of Aristophanes, who mentions him with contempt.]
[7] Or, 'that a short-sighted man is like a sputtering lamp,
since both wink.' . . .

succeeds best when it is a converted metaphor, for it is
possible to say that a shield *is like* the drinking-bowl of 5
Ares, or that a ruin *is like* a house in rags, and to say
that Niceratus[1] *is like* a Philoctetes stung by Pratys—the
simile made by Thrasymachus[2] when he saw Niceratus,
who had been beaten by Pratys in a recitation competition, still going about unkempt and unwashed. It is in
these respects that poets fail worst when they fail, and 10
succeed best when they suceed, i.e. when they give the
resemblance pat, as in

> Those legs of his curl just like parsley leaves;[3]

and

> Just like Philammon struggling with his punch-ball.[4]

These are all similes; and that similes are metaphors has
been stated often already.

Proverbs, again, are metaphors from one species to another. Suppose, for instance, a man to start some under- 15
taking in hope of gain and then to lose by it later on,
'Here we have once more the man of Carpathus and his
hare',[5] says he. For both alike went through the said experience.

It has now been explained fairly completely how liveliness is secured and why it has the effect it has. Successful
hyperboles are also metaphors, e.g. the one about the
man with a black eye, 'you would have thought he was a 20
basket of mulberries'; here the 'black eye' is compared to
a mulberry because of its colour, the exaggeration lying

---

[1] [Niceratus, probably the son of a famous Athenian general of the Peloponnesian war, had risked a contest with
a professional rhapsodist, Pratys, and had been beaten.
The theme of the contest may have been the story of
Philoctetes, one of the heroes who sailed for Troy and
who was bitten by a snake. Cp. the tragedy *Philoctetes*
by Sophocles.]

[2] [The sophist.]

[3] [Fragm. from an unidentified comedy.]

[4] [Fragm. from an unidentified comedy.]

[5] Hares, introduced with good intention into the island, increased to a plague.

in the quantity of mulberries suggested. The phrase 'like so-and-so' may introduce a hyperbole under the form of a simile. Thus

> *Just like* Philammon struggling with his punch-ball

25 is equivalent to 'you would have thought he was Philammon struggling with his punch-ball'; and

> Those legs of his curl *just like* parsley leaves

is equivalent to 'his legs are so curly that *you would have thought* they were not legs but parsley leaves'. Hyperboles are for young men to use; they show vehemence of character; and this is why angry people use them more 30 than other people.

> Not though he gave me as much as the dust or the
>   sands of the sea . . .[1]
> But her, the daughter of Atreus' son, I never will marry,
> Nay, not though she were fairer than Aphrodite the
>   Golden,
> Defter of hand than Athene . . .[2]

1413[b] (The Attic orators are particularly fond of this method of speech.) Consequently it does not suit an elderly speaker.

It should be observed that each kind of rhetoric has its 12 own appropriate style. The style of written prose is not that of spoken oratory,[3] nor are those of political and 5 forensic speaking the same. Both written and spoken have to be known. To know the latter is to know how to speak good Greek. To know the former means that you are not obliged, as otherwise you are, to hold your tongue when you wish to communicate something to the general public.

The written style is the more finished: the spoken better 10 admits of dramatic delivery—alike the kind of oratory that reflects character and the kind that reflects emotion.

---

[1] *Iliad,* ix. 385.
[2] *Iliad,* ix. 388-90.
[3] . . . More strictly, the oratory of debate—of the actual 'struggles' of the law courts and the assembly; the 'combative,' 'controversial' style.

Hence actors look out for plays written in the latter style,
and poets for actors competent to act in such plays. Yet
poets whose plays are meant to be read *are* read and cir-
culated:[1] Chaeremon, for instance, who is as finished as
a professional speech-writer; and Licymnius among the
dithyrambic poets. Compared with those of others, the 15
speeches of professional writers sound thin in actual contests. Those of the orators, on the other hand, are good
to hear spoken, but look amateurish enough when they
pass into the hands of a reader. This is just because they
are so well suited for an actual tussle, and therefore con-
tain many dramatic touches, which, being robbed of all
dramatic rendering, fail to do their own proper work, and
consequently look silly. Thus strings of unconnected
words, and constant repetitions of words and phrases,
are very properly condemned in written speeches: but 20
not in spoken speeches—speakers use them freely, for
they have a dramatic effect. In this repetition there must
be variety of tone, paving the way, as it were, to dramatic
effect; e.g. 'This is the villain among you who deceived
you, who cheated you, who meant to betray you completely'. This is the sort of thing that Philemon the actor
used to do in the *Old Men's Madness*[2] of Anaxandrides,
whenever he spoke the words 'Rhadamanthus and Pala- 25
medes', and also in the prologue to the *Saints*[2] whenever
he pronounced the pronoun 'I'. If one does not deliver
such things cleverly, it becomes a case of 'the man who
swallowed a poker'.[3] So too with strings of unconnected
words, e.g. 'I came to him; I met him; I besought him'.
Such passages must be *acted,* not delivered with the same 30
quality and pitch of voice, as though they had only one
idea in them. They have the further peculiarity of suggest-
ing that a number of separate statements have been made
in the time usually occupied by one. Just as the use of
conjunctions makes many statements into a single one, so
the omission of conjunctions acts in the reverse way and
makes a single one into many. It thus makes everything

[1] [Perhaps] 'are carried about as pocket-companions.'
[2] [Comedies of Anaxandrides now lost.]
[3] Lit.. 'the man who carries the beam.'

more important: e.g. 'I came to him; I talked to him; I
1414^a entreated him'—what a lot of facts! the hearer thinks—
'he paid no attention to anything I said'.[1] This is the
effect which Homer seeks when he writes,

> Nireus likewise from Syme ⟨three well-fashioned ships
>   did bring⟩,
> Nireus, the son of Aglaia ⟨and Charopus, bright-faced
>   king⟩,
> Nireus, the comeliest man ⟨of all that to Ilium's
>   strand⟩.[2]

If many things are said about a man, his name must be
mentioned many times; and therefore people think that,
if his name is mentioned many times, many things have
been said about him. So that Homer, by means of this
5 illusion, has made a great deal of Nireus, though he has
mentioned him only in this one passage, and has preserved
his memory, though he nowhere says a word about him
afterwards.

Now the style of oratory addressed to public assemblies
is really just like scene-painting. The bigger the throng,
the more distant is the point of view: so that, in the one
and the other, high finish in detail is superfluous and
10 seems better away. The forensic style is more highly
finished; still more so is the style of language addressed to
a single judge, with whom there is very little room for
rhetorical artifices, since he can take the whole thing in
better, and judge of what is to the point and what is not;
the struggle is less intense and so the judgement is undis-
turbed. This is why the same speakers do not distinguish
themselves in all these branches at once; high finish is
15 wanted least where dramatic delivery is wanted most, and
here the speaker must have a good voice, and above all,
a strong one. It is ceremonial oratory that is most literary,
for it is meant to be read; and next to it forensic oratory.

To analyse style still further, and add that it must be
agreeable or magnificent, is useless; for why should it

---

[1] . . . 'The hearer seems to survey quite a number of things
that the speaker has said.' [The text is uncertain.]
[2] *Iliad,* ii. 671-3. . . -

have these traits any more than 'restraint', 'liberality', or **2** any other moral excellence? Obviously agreeableness will be produced by the qualities already mentioned, if our definition of excellence of style has been correct.[1] For what other reason should style be 'clear', and 'not mean' but 'appropriate'? If it is prolix, it is not clear; nor yet if it is curt. Plainly the middle way suits best. Again, style will **25** be made agreeable by the elements mentioned, namely by a good blending of ordinary and unusual words, by the rhythm, and by the persuasiveness that springs from appropriateness.

This concludes our discussion of style, both in its general aspects and in its special applications to the various branches of rhetoric. We have now to deal with Arrangement.

13   A speech has two parts. You must state your case, and **30** you must prove it. You cannot either state your case and omit to prove it, or prove it without having first stated it; since any proof must be a proof of something, and the only use of a preliminary statement is the proof that follows it. Of these two parts the first part is[2] called the Statement of the case, the second part the Argument, just as we distinguish[3] between Enunciation and Demon- **35** stration. The current division is absurd. For 'narration' surely is part of a forensic speech only: how in a political speech or a speech of display can there be 'narration' in the technical sense? or a reply to a forensic opponent? or **1414ᵇ** an epilogue[4] in closely-reasoned speeches? Again, introduction, comparison of conflicting arguments, and recapitulation are only found in political speeches when there is a struggle between two policies. They *may* occur then; so may even accusation and defence, often enough; but they form no essential part of a political speech. Even

---

[1] Cp. iii, c. 2 init.

[2] Sc. in rhetoric.

[3] Sc. in dialectic.

[4] Or 'peroration,' except that the ἐπίλογος, or conclusion of a speech, is usually a longer affair than what we now understand by 'peroration.'

5 forensic speeches do not always need epilogues; not, for instance, a short speech, nor one in which the facts are easy to remember, the effect of an epilogue being always a reduction in the apparent length. It follows, then, that the only necesary parts of a speech are the Statement and the Argument. These are the essential features of a speech; and it cannot in any case have more than Introduction, Statement, Argument, and Epilogue.[1] 'Refutation of the Opponent' is part of the arguments: so is 'Comparison'
10 of the opponent's case with your own, for that process is a magnifying of your own case and therefore a part of the arguments, since one who does this *proves* something. The Introduction does nothing like this; nor does the Epilogue—it merely reminds us of what has been said already. If we make such distinctions we shall end, like Theodorus and his followers, by distinguishing 'narration' proper from 'post-narration' and 'pre-narration', and 'refuta-
15 tion' from 'final refutation'.[2] But we ought only to bring in a new name if it indicates a real species with distinct specific qualities; otherwise the practice is pointless and silly, like the way Licymnius[3] invented names in his *Art of Rhetoric*—'Secundation',[4] Divagation', 'Ramification'.

The Introduction is the beginning of a speech, corre- 14
20 sponding to the prologue in poetry and the prelude in flute-music; they are all beginnings, paving the way, as it were, for what is to follow. The musical prelude resembles the introduction to speeches of display; as flute-players play first some brilliant passage they know well and then fit it on to the opening notes of the piece itself, so in speeches of display the writer should proceed in the same
25 way; he should begin with what best takes his fancy, and then strike up his theme and lead into it; which is indeed what *is* always done. (Take as an example the introduc-

---

[1] [For 'statement' we should probably read 'narration.' Aristotle here corrects what he said in 1414ª30.]
[2] [For a similar criticism of the excesses of earlier theories of rhetoric cp. Plato *Phaedrus*, 266, 267.]
[3] [A teacher of rhetoric and dithyrambic poet.]
[4] [A technical term of uncertain meaning.]

tion to the *Helen* of Isocrates—there is nothing in common between the 'eristics' and Helen.) And here, even if
you travel far from your subject, it is fitting, rather than
that there should be sameness in the entire speech.

The usual subject for the introductions to speeches of 30
display is some piece of praise or censure. Thus Gorgias
writes in his *Olympic Speech*, 'You deserve widespread admiration, men of Greece', praising thus those who started
the festival gatherings. Isocrates, on the other hand, censures them for awarding distinctions to fine athletes but
giving no prize for intellectual ability.[1] Or one may begin
with a piece of advice, thus: 'We ought to honour good 35
men and so I myself am praising Aristeides' or 'We ought
to honour those who are unpopular but not bad men, men
whose good qualities have never been noticed, like Alexander son of Priam.' Here the orator gives *advice*. Or we 1415ᵇ
may begin as speakers do in the law-courts; that is to say,
with appeals to the audience to excuse us if our speech is
about something paradoxical, difficult, or hackneyed; like
Choerilus in the lines—

But now when allotment of all has been made . . .[2]

Introductions to speeches of display, then, may be com- 5
posed of some piece of praise or censure, of advice to do
or not to do something, or of appeals to the audience; and
you must choose between making these preliminary passages connected or disconnected with the speech itself.

Introductions to forensic speeches, it must be observed,
have the same value as the prologues of dramas and the
introductions to epic poems; the dithyrambic prelude re-
sembling the introduction to a speech of display, as   10

For thee, and thy gifts, and thy battle-spoils . . .[3]

In prologues,[4] and in epic poetry, a foretaste of the

---

[1] Isocrates, *Paneg.* 1, 2.
[2] From the epic poem (*Perseis*) on the Persian war by
Choerilus of Samos. . . . The apology is for a theme as
hackneyed as the Persian war had become.
[3] [From an unidentified lyric poet.]
[4] Sc. dramatic prologues (cp. 1414ᵇ20 and 1415ᵃ9). . . .
[Reading is not quite certain.]

theme is given, intended to inform the hearers of it in advance instead of keeping their minds in suspense. Anything
vague puzzles them: so give them a grasp of the begin-
15 ning, and they can hold fast to it and follow the argument.
So we find—

> Sing, O goddess of song, of the Wrath . . .[1]

> Tell me, O Muse, of the hero . . .[2]

Lead me to tell a new tale, how there came great warfare
    to Europe
Out of the Asian land . . .[3]

The tragic poets, too, let us know the pivot of their
play; if not at the outset like Euripides, at least somewhere
20 in the preface to a speech[4] like Sopohocles—

> Polybus was my father . . . ;[5]

and so in Comedy. This, then, is the most essential function and distinctive property of the introduction, to show
what the aim of the speech is; and therefore no introduction ought to be employed where the subject is not long or
intricate.

25 The other kinds of introduction employed are remedial
in purpose, and may be used in any type of speech. They
are concerned with the speaker, the hearer, the subject, or
the speaker's opponent. Those concerned with the speaker
himself or with his opponent are directed to removing or
exciting prejudice. But whereas the defendant will begin
by dealing with this sort of thing, the prosecutor will take
quite another line and deal with such matters in the clos-
30 ing part of his speech. The reason for this is not far to
seek. The defendant, when he is going to bring himself
on the stage, must clear away any obstacles, and therefore
must begin by removing any prejudice felt against him.
But if you are to *excite* prejudice, you must do so at the

[1] *Iliad*, i. 1.
[2] *Odyssey*, i. 1.
[3] Choerilus? . . .
[4] [Text and meaning very uncertain.]
[5] Sophocles, *Oedipus Tyrannus*, 774.

close, so that the judges may more easily remember what
you have said.

The appeal to the hearer aims at securing his goodwill,
or at arousing his resentment, or sometimes at gaining his 35
serious attention to the case, or even at distracting it—for
gaining it is not always an advantage, and speakers will
often for that reason try to make him laugh.

You may use any means you choose to make your hearer
receptive; among others, giving him a good impression of
your character, which always helps to secure his attention.
He will be ready to attend to anything that touches him- 1415ᵇ
self, and to anything that is important, surprising, or agreeable; and you should accordingly convey to him the impression that what you have to say is of this nature. If
you wish to distract his attention, you should imply that
the subject does not affect him, or is trivial or disagreeable.
But observe, all this has nothing to do with the speech it- 5
self. It merely has to do with the weak-minded tendency
of the hearer to listen to what is beside the point. Where
this tendency is absent, no introduction is wanted beyond
a summary statement of your subject, to put a sort of head
on the main body of your speech. Moreover, calls for attention, when required, may come equally well in any part
of a speech; in fact, the beginning of it is just where there 10
is least slackness of interest; it is therefore ridiculous to
put this kind of thing at the beginning, when every one
is listening with most attention. Choose therefore any point
in the speech where such an appeal is needed, and then
say 'Now I beg you to note this point—it concerns you
quite as much as myself'; or

I will tell you that whose like you have never yet[1]

heard for terror, or for wonder. This is what Prodicus[2]
called 'slipping in a bit of the fifty-drachma show-lecture 15
for the audience whenever they began to nod'. It is plain
that such introductions are addressed not to ideal hearers,

[1] [Unidentified.]
[2] [Prodicus of Keos, famous sophist, contemporary of Socrates. On his 'fifty drachma show-lecture' cp. Plato *Cratylus* 384 B.]

but to hearers as we find them. The use of introductions
to excite prejudice or to dispel misgivings is universal—

> My lord, I will not say that eagerly . . .[1]

20 or

> Why all this preface?[2]

Introductions are popular with those whose case is weak,
or looks weak; it pays them to dwell on anything rather
than the actual facts of it. That is why slaves, instead of
answering the questions put to them, make indirect replies
with long preambles. The means of exciting in your hear-
25 ers goodwill and various other feelings of the same kind
have already been described.[3] The poet finely says

> May I find in Phaeacian hearts, at my coming, goodwill
>   and compassion;[4]

and these are the two things we should aim at. In speeches
of display we must make the hearer feel that the eulogy
includes either himself or his family or his way of life or
something or other of the kind. For it is true, as Socrates
30 says in the *Funeral Speech*,[5] that 'the difficulty is not to
praise the Athenians at Athens but at Sparta'.

The introductions of political oratory will be made out
of the same materials as those of the forensic kind, though
the nature of political oratory makes them very rare. The
subject is known already, and therefore the *facts* of the
case need no introduction; but you may have to say something on account of yourself or your opponents; or those
35 present may be inclined to treat the matter either more or
less seriously than you wish them to. You may accordingly
have to excite or dispel some prejudice, or to make the
matter under discussion seem more or less important than
before: for either of which purposes you will want an introduction. You may also want one to add elegance to
your remarks, feeling that otherwise they will have a cas-

---

[1] Sophocles, *Antigone*, 223.
[2] Cp. Euripides, *Iph. Taur.*, 1162.
[3] ii, cc. 1 ff.
[4] *Odyssey*, vi. 327.
[5] Cp. Plato, *Menexenus*, 235 D.

ual air, like Gorgias' eulogy of the Eleans, in which, with- *1416*
out any preliminary sparring or fencing, he begins straight
off with 'Happy city of Elis!'

15   In dealing with prejudice, one class of argument is that
whereby you can dispel objectionable suppositions about
yourself. It makes no practical difference whether such a 5
supposition has been put into words or not, so that this
distinction may be ignored. Another way is to meet any
of the issues directly: to deny the alleged fact; or to say
that you have done no harm, or none to *him*, or not as
much as he says; or that you have done him no injustice,
or not much; or that you have done nothing disgraceful,
or nothing disgraceful enough to matter: these are the sort
of questions on which the dispute hinges. Thus Iphicrates,[1]
replying to Nausicrates,[2] admitted that he had done the 10
deed alleged, and that he had done Nausicrates harm, but
not that he had done him wrong. Or you may admit the
wrong, but balance it with other facts, and say that, if the
deed harmed him, at any rate it was honourable; or that,
if it gave him pain, at least it did him good; or something
else like that. Another way is to allege that your action
was due to mistake, or bad luck, or necessity—as Sophocles[3] said he was not trembling, as his traducer maintained, 15
in order to make people think him an old man, but because he could not help it; he would rather *not* be eighty
years old. You may balance your motive against your actual deed; saying, for instance, that you did not mean to
injure him but to do so-and-so; that you did not do what
you are falsely charged with doing—the damage was accidental—'I should indeed be a detestable person if I had
deliberately intended this result.' Another way is open 20
when your calumniator, or any of his connexions, is or has
been subject to the same grounds for suspicion. Yet an-

---

[1] [The well-known general often cited by Aristotle in the
Rhetoric.]

[2] [A rhetorician.]

[3] [Not the tragedian but an Athenian statesman and orator
of the time of the Peloponnesian war. He was one of the
Thirty Tyrants. He is also mentioned in 1374[b]36 and
1419[a]27.]

other, when others are subject to the same grounds for
suspicion but are admitted to be in fact innocent of the
charge: e.g. 'Must I be a profligate because I am well-
groomed? Then so-and-so must be one too.' Another, if
other people have been calumniated by the same man or
25 some one else, or, without being calumniated, have been
suspected, like yourself now, and yet have been proved
innocent. Another way is to return calumny for calumny
and say, 'It is monstrous to trust the man's statements
when you cannot trust the man himself.' Another is when
the question has been already decided. So with Euripides'
reply to Hygiaenon, who, in the action for an exchange
30 of properties, accused him of impiety in having written a
line encouraging perjury—

My tongue hath sworn: no oath is on my soul.[1]

Euripides said that his opponent himself was guilty in
bringing into the law-courts cases whose decision belonged
to the Dionysiac contests. 'If I have not already answered
for my words there, I am ready to do so if you choose to
prosecute me there.'[2] Another method is to denounce calumny, showing what an enormity it is, and in particular
35 that it raises false issues,[3] and that it means a lack of confidence in the merits of his case. The argument from evi-
dential circumstances is available for both parties: thus in
1416b the Teucer[4] Odysseus says that Teucer is closely bound to
Priam, since his mother Hesione was Priam's sister. Teucer
replies that Telamon his father was Priam's enemy, and
that he himself did not betray the spies to Priam. Another
method, suitable for the calumniator, is to praise some trifling merit at great length, and then attack some impor-
5 tant failing concisely; or after mentioning a number of
good qualities to attack one bad one that really bears on
the question. This is the method of thoroughly skilful and

---

[1] Euripides, *Hippolytus*, 612.
[2] [The tragedian. Aristotle refers to another public speech
of Euripides in 1384b16.]
[3] Or, 'that it leads from one prosecution (trial) to another.'
[4] Sophocles, *Teucer*. . . .

unscrupulous prosecutors. By mixing up the man's merits with what is bad, they do their best to make use of them to damage him.

There is another method open to both calumniator and apologist. Since a given action can be done from many motives, the former must try to disparage it by selecting the worse motive of two, the latter to put the better construction on it. Thus one might argue that Diomedes chose Odysseus as his companion[1] because he supposed Odysseus to be the best man for the purpose; and you might reply to this that it was, on the contrary, because he was the only hero so worthless that Diomedes need not fear his rivalry.

16   We may now pass from the subject of calumny to that of Narration.

Narration in ceremonial oratory is not continuous but intermittent. There must, of course, be some survey of the actions that form the subject-matter of the speech. The speech is a composition containing two parts. One of these is not provided by the orator's art, viz. the actions themselves, of which the orator is in no sense author. The other part is provided by his art, namely, the proof (where proof is needed) that the actions were done, the description of their quality or of their extent, or even all these three things together. Now the reason why sometimes it is not desirable to make the whole narrative continuous is that the case thus expounded is hard to keep in mind. Show, therefore, from one set of facts that your hero is, e.g. brave, and from other sets of facts that he is able, just, &c. A speech thus arranged is comparatively simple, instead of being complicated and elaborate. You will have to recall well-known deeds among others; and because they are well-known, the hearer usually needs no narration of them; none, for instance, if your object is the praise of Achilles; we all know the facts of his life—what you have to do is to apply those facts. But if your object is the praise of

[1] Cp. *Iliad*, x. 242-7.

Critias, you *must* narrate his deeds, which not many people know of . . .[1]

Nowadays it is said, absurdly enough, that the narration
30 should be rapid. Remember what the man said to the baker who asked whether he was to make the cake hard or soft: 'What, can't you make it *right?*' Just so here. We are not to make long narrations, just as we are not to make long introductions or long arguments. Here, again,
35 rightness does not consist either in rapidity or in conciseness, but in the happy mean; that is, in saying just so much as will make the facts plain, or will lead the hearer to
1417[a] believe that the thing has happened, or that the man has caused injury or wrong to some one, or that the facts are really as important as you wish them to be thought: or the opposite facts to establish the opposite arguments.

You may also narrate as you go anything that does credit to yourself, e.g. 'I kept telling him to do his duty and not abandon his children'; or discredit to your adversary, e.g. 'But he answered me that, wherever he might
5 find himself, there he would find other children', the answer Herodotus[2] records of the Egyptian mutineers. Slip in anything else that the judges will enjoy.

The defendant will make less of the narration. He has to maintain that the thing has not happened, or did no harm, or was not unjust, or not so bad as is alleged. He
10 must therefore not waste time about what is admitted fact, unless this bears on his own contention; e.g. that the thing was done, but was not wrong. Further, we must speak of events as past and gone, except where they excite pity or indignation by being represented as present. The Story told to Alcinous[3] is an example of a brief chronicle, when it is repeated to Penelope in sixty lines.[4] Another instance
15 is the Epic Cycle as treated by Phayllus,[5] and the prologue to the *Oeneus*.[6]

[1] [Probably the Critias who was one of the Thirty Tyrants and was a famous man in his day.]
[2] Cp. Herodotus, ii. 30.
[3] *Odyssey*, ix-xii.
[4] *Odyssey*, xxiii. 264-84 and 310-43.
[5] [Completely unknown, mentioned only here.]
[6] Euripides, *Oeneus*, fragm. . . .

The narration should depict character; to which end you must know what makes it do so. One such thing is the indication of moral purpose; the quality of purpose indicated determines the quality of character depicted and is itself determined by the end pursued. Thus it is that mathematical discourses depict no character; they have nothing to do with moral purpose, for they represent nobody as pursuing any end. On the other hand, the Socratic dialogues do depict character, being concerned with moral 20 questions. This end will also be gained by describing the manifestations of various types of character, e.g. 'he kept walking along as he talked', which shows the man's recklessness and rough manners. Do not let your words seem inspired so much by intelligence, in the manner now current, as by moral purpose: e.g. 'I willed this; aye, it was my moral purpose; true, I gained nothing by it, still it is 25 better thus.' For the other way shows good sense, but this shows good character; good sense making us go after what is useful, and good character after what is noble. Where any detail may appear incredible, then add the cause of it; of this Sophocles provides an example in the *Antigone*, where Antigone says she had cared more for her brother than for husband or children, since if the latter perished they might be replaced, 30

> But since my father and mother in their graves
> Lie dead, no brother can be born to me.[1]

If you have no such cause to suggest, just say that you are aware that no one will believe your words, but the fact remains that such is your nature, however hard the world may find it to believe that a man deliberately does any- 35 thing except what pays him.

Again, you must make use of the emotions. Relate the familiar manifestations of them, and those that distinguish yourself and your opponent; for instance, 'he went away scowling at me'. So Aeschines[2] described Cratylus as 'hiss- *1417*[b]

[1] Sophocles, *Antigone*, 911, 912.
[2] [Aeschines may be the friend of Socrates and Cratylus (who was Plato's instructor in Heraclitean philosophy), but this is uncertain.]

ing with fury and shaking his fists'. These details carry
conviction: the audience take the truth of what they know
as so much evidence for the truth of what they do not.
Plenty of such details may be found in Homer:

5   Thus did she say: but the old woman buried her face in
       her hands:[1]

a true touch—people beginning to cry do put their hands
over their eyes.

Bring yourself on the stage from the first in the right
character, that people may regard you in that light; and
the same with your adversary; but do not let them see
what you are about. How easily such impressions may be
conveyed we can see from the way in which we get some
10 inkling of things we know nothing of by the mere look of
the messenger bringing news of them. Have some narrative in many different parts of your speech; and sometimes
let there be none at the beginning of it.

In political oratory there is very little opening for narration; nobody can 'narrate' what has not yet happened.
If there is narration at all, it will be of past events, the
recollection of which is to help the hearers to make better
15 plans for the future. Or it may be employed to attack some
one's character, or to eulogize him—only then you will not
be doing what the political speaker, as such, has to do.

If any statement you make is hard to believe, you must
guarantee its truth, and at once offer an explanation, and
then furnish it with such particulars as will be expected.[2]
Thus Carcinus'[3] Jocasta, in his *Oedipus*, keeps guarantee-
ing the truth of her answers to the inquiries of the man
20 who is seeking her son; and so with Haemon in Sophocles.[4]

The duty of the Arguments is to attempt demonstrative 17
proofs. These proofs must bear directly upon the question

---

[1] *Odyssey*, xix. 361.
[2] Or possibly, 'and then arrange your reasons systematically
    for those who demand them.' . . .
[3] [A tragic poet of the 5th cent.]
[4] Cp. Sophocles, *Antigone*. 635-8, 701-4.

in dispute, which must fall under one of four heads. (1)
If you maintain that the act *was not committed,* your main
task in court is to prove this. (2) If you maintain that the
act *did no harm,* prove this. If you maintain that (3) the
act was *less* than is alleged, or (4) *justified,* prove these
facts, just as you would prove the act not to have been
committed if you were maintaining that.

It should be noted that only where the question in dispute falls under the first of these heads can it be true that
one of the two parties is necessarily a rogue. Here ignorance cannot be pleaded, as it might if the dispute were
whether the act was justified or not. This argument must
therefore be used [1] in this case only, not in the others.

In ceremonial speeches you will develop your case
mainly by arguing that what has been done is, e.g., noble
and useful. The facts themselves are to be taken on trust;
proof of them is only submitted on those rare occasions
when they are not easily credible or when they have been
set down to some one else.

In political speeches you may maintain that a proposal
is impracticable; or that, though practicable, it is unjust,
or will do no good, or is not so important as its proposer
thinks. Note any falsehoods about irrelevant matters—they
will look like proof that his other statements also are false. *1418ᵃ*
Argument by 'example' is highly suitable for political oratory, argument by 'enthymeme' better suits forensic. Political oratory deals with future events, of which it can do
no more than quote past events as examples. Forensic oratory deals with what is or is not *now* true, which can better be demonstrated, because not contingent—there is no
contingency in what has now already happened. Do not
use a continuous succession of enthymemes: intersperse
them with other matter, or they will spoil one another's
effect. There are limits to their number—

Friend, you have spoken *as much* as a sensible man would
     have spoken.[2]—

---

[1] [An alternative reading is 'must be dwelt upon,' 'time
   must be given to.']
[2] *Odyssey,* iv. 204.

'as *much*' says Homer, not 'as *well*'. Nor should you try to make enthymemes on every point; if you do, you will be
10 acting just like some students of philosophy, whose conclusions are more familiar and believable than the premisses from which they draw them. And avoid the enthymeme form when you are trying to rouse feeling; for it will either kill the feeling or will itself fall flat: all simultaneous motions tend to cancel each other either completely or partially. Nor should you go after the enthy-
15 meme form in a passage where you are depicting character—the process of demonstration can express neither moral character nor moral purpose. Maxims should be employed in the Arguments—and in the Narration too—since these do express character: 'I have given him this, though I am quite aware that one should "Trust no man".' Or if you are appealing to the emotions: 'I do not regret it, though
20 I have been wronged; if he has the profit on his side, I have justice on mine.'

Political oratory is a more difficult task than forensic; and naturally so, since it deals with the future, whereas the pleader deals with the past, which, as Epimenides of Crete[1] said, even the diviners already know. (Epimenides did not practise divination about the future; only about
25 the obscurities of the past.) Besides, in forensic oratory you have a basis in the law; and once you have a starting-point, you can prove anything with comparative ease. Then again, political oratory affords few chances for those leisurely digressions in which you may attack your adversary, talk about yourself, or work on your hearers' emotions; fewer chances, indeed, than any other affords, unless your set purpose is to divert your hearers' attention.[2] Accordingly, if you find yourself in difficulties, follow the lead of
30 the Athenian speakers, and that of Isocrates, who makes regular attacks upon people in the course of a political speech, e.g. upon the Lacedaemonians in the *Panegyricus*

[1] [A saintlike figure known for a variety of religious practices.]
[2] . . . Or, 'without quitting your proper ground.' . . .
[3] Isocrates, *Paneg.*, 110-14.

and upon Chares in the speech about the allies.[1] In ceremonial oratory, intersperse your speech with bits of episodic eulogy, like Isocrates, who is always bringing some
one forward for this purpose.[2] And this is what Gorgias
meant by saying that he always found something to talk
about. For if he speaks of Achilles, he praises Peleus, then 35
Aeacus, then Zeus; and in like manner the virtue of valour,
describing its good results, and saying what it is like.[3]

Now if you have proofs to bring forward, bring them
forward, and your moral discourse as well; if you have no
enthymemes, then fall back upon moral discourse: after all, 1418ᵇ
it is more fitting for a good man to display himself as an
honest fellow than as a subtle reasoner. Refutative enthymemes are more popular than demonstrative ones: their
logical cogency is more striking: the facts about two opposites always stand out clearly when the two are put side
by side.

The 'Reply to the Opponent' is not a separate division 5
of the speech; it is part of the Arguments to break down
the opponent's case, whether by objection or by counter-
syllogism. Both in political speaking and when pleading
in court, if you are the first speaker you should put your
own arguments forward first, and then meet the arguments
on the other side by refuting them and pulling them to
pieces before hand. If, however, the case for the other side
contains a great variety of arguments, begin with these,
like Callistratus[4] in the Messenian assembly, when he de- 10
molished the arguments likely to be used against him
before giving his own. If you speak later, you must first,
by means of refutation and counter-syllogism, attempt

---

[1] Cp. Isocrates, *De Pace*, 27.
[2] Isocrates has episodic passages on Theseus (*Helena*
23-28), on Paris (*Helena* 41-8), on Pythagoras and the
Egyptian priests (*Busiris* 21-9), on the poets (*Busiris*
38-40), and on Agamemnon (*Panathenaicus*, 72-84).
[3] More briefly: 'and in like manner the value and goodness
of that great virtue Courage.'
[4] [A distinguished Athenian orator and politician, cp. 1364ᵃ
19. He was sent on an embassy into the Peloponnesus in
362 B.C.]

some answer to your opponent's speech, especially if his arguments have been well received. For just as our minds refuse a favourable reception to a *person* against whom 15 they are prejudiced, so they refuse it to a speech when they have been favourably impressed by the speech on the other side. You should, therefore, make room in the minds of the audience for your coming speech; and this will be done by getting your opponent's speech out of the way. So attack that first—either the whole of it, or the most important, successful, or vulnerable points in it, and thus 20 inspire confidence in what you have to say yourself—

> First, champion will I be of Goddesses . . .
> Never, I ween, would Hera . . . :[1]

where the speaker has attacked the silliest argument first. So much for the Arguments.

With regard to the element of moral character: there are assertions which, if made about yourself, may excite 25 dislike, appear tedious, or expose you to the risk of contradiction; and other things which you cannot say about your opponent without seeming abusive or ill-bred. Put such remarks, therefore, into the mouth of some third person. This is what Isocrates does in the *Philippus*[2] and in the *Antidosis*,[3] and Archilochus in his satires. The latter represents the father himself as attacking his daughter in the lampoon

> Think nought impossible at all,
> Nor swear that it shall not befall . . .[4]

30 and puts into the mouth of Charon the carpenter the lampoon which begins

> Not for the wealth of Gyges. . . .[4]

So too Sophocles makes Haemon appeal to his father on behalf of Antigone as if it were others who were speaking.[5]

---

[1] Euripides, *Troades*, 969 and 971.
[2] Isocrates, *Philippus*, 4-7.
[3] Ib., *Antidosis*, 132-9, 141-9.
[4] [Two fragments of Archilochus.]
[5] Sophocles, *Antigone*, 688-700.

Again, sometimes you should restate your enthymemes in the form of maxims; e.g. 'Wise men will come to terms in the hour of success; for they will gain most if they 35 do'.[1] Expressed as an enthymeme, this would run, '*If* we ought to come to terms when doing so will enable us to gain the greatest advantage, *then* we ought to come tr terms in the hour of success.'

28   Next as to Interrogation. The best moment to employ this is when your opponent has so answered one question **1419ᵃ** that the putting of just one more lands him in absurdity. Thus Pericles questioned Lampon about the way of celebrating the rites of the Saviour Goddess.[2] Lampon declared that no uninitiated person could be told of them. Pericles then asked, 'Do you know them yourself?' 'Yes', answered Lampon. 'Why', said Pericles, 'how can that be, when you are uninitiatcd?'   5

Another good moment is when one premiss of an argument is obviously true, and you can see that your opponent must say 'yes' if you ask him whether the other is true. Having first got this answer about the other, do not go on to ask him about the obviously true one, but just state the conclusion yourself. Thus, when Meletus denied that Socrates believed in the existence of gods but admitted[3] that he talked about a supernatural power, Soc- 10 rates proceeded to ask whether 'supernatural beings were not either children of the gods or in some way divine?' 'Yes', said Meletus. 'Then', replied Socrates, 'is there any one who believes in the existence of children of the gods and yet not in the existence of the gods themselves?'[4] Another good occasion is when you expect to show that your opponent is contradicting either his own words or what every one believes. A fourth is when it is impossible for him to meet your question except by an evasive answer. If he answers 'True, and yet not true', or 'Partly true and 15 partly not true', or 'True in one sense but not in another',

---

[1] Cp. Isocrates, *Archidamus*, 50.
[2] Sc. Demeter.
[3] [The translation is based on conjectures.]
[4] Cp. Plato, *Apology*, 27 C.

the audience thinks he is in difficulties, and applauds his discomfiture. In other cases do not attempt interrogation; for if your opponent gets in an objection, you are felt to have been worsted. You cannot ask a series of questions owing to the incapacity of the audience to follow them; and for this reason you should also make your enthymemes as compact as possible.

20 In replying, you must meet ambiguous questions by drawing reasonable distinctions, not by a curt answer. In meeting questions that seem to involve you in a contradiction, offer the explanation at the outset of your answer, before your opponent asks the next question or draws his conclusion. For it is not difficult to see the drift of his argument in advance. This point, however, as well as the various means of refutation, may be regarded as known to us from the *Topics*.[1]

25 When your opponent in drawing his conclusion puts it in the form of a question, you must justify your answer. Thus when Sophocles[2] was asked by Peisander whether he had, like the other members of the Board of Safety, voted for setting up the Four Hundred, he said 'Yes.' 'Why, did you not think it wicked?'—'Yes.'—'So *you* committed this 30 wickedness?'—'Yes', said Sophocles, 'for there was nothing better to do.' Again, the Lacedaemonian, when he was being examined on his conduct as ephor, was asked whether he thought that the other ephors had been justly put to death. 'Yes', he said. 'Well then', asked his opponent, 'did not *you* propose the same measures as they?'—'Yes.'— 'Well then, would not *you* too be justly put to death?'— 35 'Not at all', said he; '*they* were bribed to do it, and I did it from conviction'. Hence you should not ask any further 1419[b] questions after drawing the conclusion, nor put the conclusion itself in the form of a further question, unless there is a large balance of truth on your side.

As to jests. These are supposed to be of some service in controversy. Gorgias said that you should kill your opponents' earnestness with jesting and their jesting with earnestness; in which he was right. Jests have been classified

---

[1] *Topics*, vii.
[2] [The statesman and orator, cp. 1416ᵃ14.]

in the *Poetics*.[1] Some are becoming to a gentleman, others
are not; see that you choose such as become *you*. Irony
better befits a gentleman than buffoonery; the ironical man
jokes to amuse himself, the buffoon to amuse other people.

19   The Epilogue has four parts. You must (1) make the
audience well-disposed towards yourself and ill-disposed
towards your opponent, (2) magnify or minimize the leading facts, (3) excite the required state of emotion in your
hearers, and (4) refresh their memories.

(1) Having shown your own truthfulness and the un-
truthfulness of your opponent, the natural thing is to com-
mend yourself, censure him, and hammer in your points.
You must aim at one of two objects—you must make yourself out a good man and him a bad one either in yourselves
or in relation to your hearers. How this is to be managed
—by what lines of argument you are to represent people
as good or bad—this has been already explained.[2]

(2) The facts having been proved, the natural thing to
do next is to magnify or minimize their importance. The
facts must be admitted before you can discuss how important they are; just as the body cannot grow except from
something already present. The proper lines of argument
to be used for this purpose of amplification and depreciation have already been set forth.[3]

(3) Next, when the facts and their importance are
clearly understood, you must excite your hearers' emotions.
These emotions are pity, indignation, anger, hatred, envy,
emulation, pugnacity. The lines of argument to be used
for these purposes also have been previously mentioned.[4]

(4) Finally you have to review what you have already
said. Here you may properly do what some wrongly recommend doing in the introduction—repeat your points
frequently so as to make them easily understood. What
you *should* do in your introduction is to state your subject,
in order that the point to be judged may be quite plain;
in the epilogue you should summarize the arguments by
which your case has been proved. The first step in this re-

---

[1] [Probably in the lost second book which dealt with
comedy.]

[2] i, c. 9.   [3] ii, c. 19.   [4] ii, cc. 1-11.

viewing process is to observe that you have done what
you undertook to do. You must, then, state what you have
said and why you have said it. Your method may be a
comparison of your own case with that of your opponent;
35 and you may compare either the ways you have both handled the same point or make your comparison less direct:
'My opponent said so-and-so on this point; I said so-and-so,
1420ᵃ and this is why I said it'. Or with modest irony, e.g. 'He
certainly said so-and-so, but I said so-and-so'. Or 'How
vain he would have been if he had proved all this instead
of *that!*' Or put it in the form of a question, 'What has *not*
been proved by me?' or 'What *has* my opponent proved?'
You may proceed, then, either in this way by setting point
against point, or by following the natural order of the ar-
1420ᵇ guments as spoken, first giving your own, and then separately, if you wish, those of your opponent.

For the conclusion, the disconnected style of language
is appropriate, and will mark the difference between the
oration and the peroration. 'I have done. You have heard
me. The facts are before you. I ask for your judgement.'[1]

[1] Cp. Lysias, *Eratosthenes*, fin.

POETICS

TRANSLATED BY INGRAM BYWATER

CONTENTS

POETICS

1   Our subject being Poetry, I propose to speak not only of 1447^a
the art in general but also of its species and their respective capacities; of the structure of plot required for a good
poem; of the number and nature of the constituent parts 10
of a poem; and likewise of any other matters in the same
line of inquiry. Let us follow the natural order and begin
with the primary facts.

Epic poetry and Tragedy, as also Comedy, Dithyrambic
poetry, and most flute-playing and lyre-playing, are all, 15
viewed as a whole, modes of imitation. But at the same
time they differ from one another in three ways, either by
a difference of kind in their means, or by differences in the
objects, or in the manner of their imitations.

I. Just as colour and form are used as means by some,
who (whether by art or constant practice) imitate and
portray many things by their aid, and the voice is used by 20
others; so also in the above-mentioned group of arts, the
means with them as a whole are rhythm, language, and
harmony—used, however, either singly or in certain combinations. A combination of harmony and rhythm alone is
the means in flute-playing and lyre-playing, and any other
arts there may be of the same description, e.g. imitative 25
piping. Rhythm alone, without harmony, is the means in
the dancer's imitations; for even he, by the rhythms of
his attitudes, may represent men's characters, as well as
what they do and suffer. There is further an art which
imitates by language alone, without harmony, in prose or
in verse, and if in verse, either in some one or in a plural- 1447^b
ity of metres. This form of imitation is to this day without a name. We have no common name for a mime of 10

Sophron[1] or Xenarchus and a Socratic Conversation;[1] and
we should still be without one even if the imitation in the
two instances were in trimeters or elegiacs or some other
kind of verse—though it is the way with people to tack on
'poet' to the name of a metre, and talk of elegiac-poets and
epic-poets, thinking that they call them poets not by reason
25 of the imitative nature of their work, but indiscriminately
by reason of the metre they write in. Even if a theory of
medicine or physical philosophy be put forth in a metrical
form, it is usual to describe the writer in this way; Homer
and Empedocles, however, have really nothing in common
apart from their metre;[2] so that, if the one is to be called
20 a poet, the other should be termed a physicist rather than
a poet. We should be in the same position also, if the imitation in these instances were in all the metres, like the
Centaur (a rhapsody in a medley of all metres) of Chaeremon;[3] and Chaeremon one has to recognize as a poet. So
much, then, as to these arts. There are, lastly, certain
other arts, which combine all the means enumerated,
25 rhythm, melody, and verse, e.g. Dithyrambic and Nomic
poetry, Tragedy and Comedy; with this difference, however, that the three kinds of means are in some of them
all employed together, and in others brought in separately,
one after the other. These elements of difference in the
above arts I term the means of their imitation.

1448ᵃ   II. The objects the imitator represents are actions, with 2
agents who are necessarily either good men or bad—the
diversities of human character being nearly always deriva-
tive from this primary distinction, since the line between
virtue and vice is one dividing the whole of mankind. It
follows, therefore, that the agents represented must be

[1] [Sophron and his son Xenarchus wrote brief prose dialogues on rural and city life, called 'mimes.' Sophron was
much admired by Plato, who, in writing his 'Socratic Con-
versations,' the dialogues, was thought to have been influenced by Sophron's technique.]
[2] [Empedocles of Agrigentum, the physical philosopher
used hexameters, the metre of the epics, for his philosophical poems.]
[3] [Tragedian of the 4th cent.]

either above our own level of goodness, or beneath it, or just such as we are; in the same way as, with the painters, the personages of Polygnotus[1] are better than we are, those of Pauson[2] worse, and those of Dionysius[3] just like ourselves. It is clear that each of the above-mentioned arts will admit of these differences, and that it will become a separate art by representing objects with this point of difference. Even in dancing, flute-playing, and lyre-playing such diversities are possible; and they are also possible in the nameless art that uses language, prose or verse without harmony, as its means; Homer's personages, for instance, are better than we are; Cleophon's[4] are on our own level; and those of Hegemon[5] of Thasos, the first writer of parodies, and Nicochares,[6] the author of the *Diliad*, are beneath it. The same is true of the Dithyramb and the Nome: the personages may be presented in them with the difference exemplified in the . . . of . . . and Argas,[7] and in the Cyclopses of Timotheus and Philoxenus.[8] This difference it is that distinguishes Tragedy and Comedy also; the one would make its personages worse, and the other better, than the men of the present day.

3   III. A third difference in these arts is in the manner in which each kind of object is represented. Given both the

---

[1] [Polygnotus of Thasus, the great painter, active between 475-445 B.C.]

[2] [A painter of the time of Aristophanes, who makes fun of him.]

[3] [Dionysius of Colophon, a contemporary of Polygnotus, was admired for his realistic portraits.]

[4] [Cleophon may be the tragedian, more likely an epic poet of the same name, cp. *Rhet.* 1408ª15.]

[5] [Hegemon of Thasus, active in late 5th cent.; the passage must mean that he invented the genre.]

[6] [It is not likely that the comedian is meant here; the poem is lost.]

[7] [Argas is a tempting conjecture. If it is correct Aristotle here is speaking of the well-known cytharoede and poet of the 4th cent.]

[1] [Timotheus of Milet and Philoxenus of Citera, poets of the 5th and 4th centuries. Of their poems 'Cyclops' fragments are left.]

same means and the same kind of object for imitation, one
may either (1) speak at one moment in narrative and at
another in an assumed character, as Homer does; or (2)
one may remain the same throughout, without any such
change; or (3) the imitators may represent the whole
story dramatically, as though they were actually doing the
things described.

As we said at the beginning, therefore, the differences
in the imitation of these arts come under three heads, their
means, their objects, and their manner.

25 So that as an imitator Sophocles will be on one side akin
to Homer, both portraying good men; and on another to
Aristophanes, since both present their personages as acting
and doing. This in fact, according to some, is the reason
for plays being termed dramas, because in a play the per-
30 sonages act the story. Hence too both Tragedy and Comedy are claimed by the Dorians as their discoveries; Comedy by the Megarians—by those in Greece as having arisen
when Megara became a democracy, and by the Sicilian
Megarians on the ground that the poet Epicharmus[1] was
of their country, and a good deal earlier than Chion-
ides[2] and Magnes; even Tragedy also is claimed by certain of the Peloponnesian Dorians. In support of this claim
35 they point to the words 'comedy' and 'drama'. Their word
for the outlying hamlets, they say, is *comae,* whereas Athenians call them *demes*—thus assuming that comedians got
the name not from their *comoe* or revels, but from their
strolling from hamlet to hamlet, lack of appreciation keep-
1448ᵇ ing them out of the city. Their word also for 'to act', they
say, is *dran,* whereas Athenians use *prattein.*

So much, then, as to the number and nature of the
points of difference in the imitation of these arts.

It is clear that the general origin of poetry was due to 4
5 two causes, each of them part of human nature. Imitation
is natural to man from childhood, one of his advantages
over the lower animals being this, that he is the most imi-

---

[1] [Sicilian writer of comedies of the 6th or 5th cent.]
[2] [Chionides and Magnes, Attic writers of comedy of the
5th cent.]

tative creature in the world, and learns at first by imitation. And it is also natural for all to delight in works of
imitation. The truth of this second point is shown by experience: though the objects themselves may be painful to
see, we delight to view the most realistic representations
of them in art, the forms for example of the lowest animals
and of dead bodies. The explanation is to be found in a
further fact: to be learning something is the greatest of
pleasures not only to the philosopher but also to the rest
of mankind, however small their capacity for it; the reason
of the delight in seeing the picture is that one is at the
same time learning—gathering the meaning of things, e.g.
that the man there is so-and-so; for if one has not seen the
thing before, one's pleasure will not be in the picture as
an imitation of it, but will be due to the execution or col-
ouring or some similar cause. Imitation, then, being natural to us—as also the sense of harmony and rhythm, the
metres being obviously species of rhythms—it was through
their original aptitude, and by a series of improvements
for the most part gradual on their first efforts, that they
created poetry out of their improvisations.

Poetry, however, soon broke up into two kinds according to the differences of character in the individual poets;
for the graver among them would represent noble actions,
and those of noble personages; and the meaner sort the
actions of the ignoble. The latter class produced invectives
at first, just as others did hymns and panegyrics. We know
of no such poem by any of the pre-Homeric poets, though
there were probably many such writers among them; instances, however, may be found from Homer downwards,
e.g. his *Margites*,[1] and the similar poems of others. In this
poetry of invective its natural fitness brought an iambic
metre into use; hence our present term 'iambic', because
it was the metre of their 'iambs' or invectives against one
another. The result was that the old poets became some
of them writers of heroic and others of iambic verse.
Homer's position, however, is peculiar: just as he was in
the serious style the poet of poets, standing alone not

[1] [This burlesque poem was generally attributed to Homer
until long after Aristotle's time.]

only through the literary excellence, but also through the
dramatic character of his imitations, so too he was the first
to outline for us the general forms of Comedy by producing not a dramatic invective, but a dramatic picture of the
Ridiculous; his *Margites* in fact stands in the same relation
1449ᵃ to our comedies as the *Iliad* and *Odyssey* to our tragedies.
As soon, however, as Tragedy and Comedy appeared in
the field, those naturally drawn to the one line of poetry
5 became writers of comedies instead of iambs, and those
naturally drawn to the other, writers of tragedies instead
of epics, because these new modes of art were grander
and of more esteem than the old.

If it be asked whether Tragedy is now all that it need
be in its formative elements, to consider that, and decide
it theoretically and in relation to the theatres, is a matter
for another inquiry.

10 It certainly began in improvisations—as did also Comedy; the one originating with the authors of the Dithyramb, the other with those of the phallic songs, which still
survive as institutions in many of our cities. And its advance after that was little by little, through their improv-
ing on whatever they had before them at each stage. It
was in fact only after a long series of changes that the
15 movement of Tragedy stopped on its attaining to its natural form. (1) The number of actors was first increased
to two by Aeschylus, who curtailed the business of the
Chorus, and made the dialogue, or spoken portion, take
the leading part in the play. (2) A third actor and scen-
ery were due to Sophocles. (3) Tragedy acquired also its
20 magnitude. Discarding short stories and a ludicrous diction, through its passing out of its satyric stage, it assumed,
though only at a late point in its progress, a tone of dignity; and its metre changed then from trochaic to iambic
The reason for their original use of the trochaic tetrameter was that their poetry was satyric and more connected
with dancing than it now is. As soon, however, as a spoken
part came in, nature herself found the appropriate metre.
25 The iambic, we know, is the most speakable of metres, as
is shown by the fact that we very often fall into it in
conversation, whereas we rarely talk hexameters, and only

when we depart from the speaking tone of voice. (4) Another change was a plurality of episodes or acts. As for the remaining matters, the superadded embellishments and the account of their introduction, these must be taken as said, as it would probably be a long piece of work to go 30 through the details.

5   As for Comedy, it is (as has been observed [1]) an imitation of men worse than the average; worse, however, not as regards any and every sort of fault, but only as regards one particular kind, the Ridiculous, which is a species of the Ugly. The Ridiculous may be defined as a mistake or deformity not productive of pain or harm to others; the 35 mask, for instance, that excites laughter, is something ugly and distorted without causing pain.

Though the successive changes in Tragedy and their authors are not unknown, we cannot say the same of Comedy; its early stages passed unnoticed, because it was not as yet taken up in a serious way. It was only at a late 1449ᵇ point in its progress that a chorus of comedians was officially granted by the archon;[2] they used to be mere volunteers. It had also already certain definite forms at the time when the record of those termed comic poets begins. Who it was who supplied it with masks, or prologues, or a plurality of actors and the like, has remained unknown. The invented Fable, or Plot, however, originated in Sicily, 5 with Epicharmus and Phormis;[3] of Athenian poets Crates[4] was the first to drop the Comedy of invective and frame stories of a general and non-personal nature, in other words, Fables or Plots.

Epic poetry, then, has been seen to agree with Tragedy to this extent, that of being an imitation of serious sub- 10 jects in a grand kind of verse. It differs from it, however, (1) in that it is in one kind of verse and in narrative form; and (2) in its length—which is due to its action having

---

[1] 1448ᵃ17; 1448ᵇ37.
[2] [A competition of comedies was admitted to the Great Dionysians in 486 B.C., to the Lenaeans in 440 B.C.]
[3] [Sicilian writer of comedies, younger contemporary of Epicharmus.]
[4] [Athenian writer of comedies of the middle 5th cent.]

no fixed limit of time, whereas Tragedy endeavours to keep as far as possible within a single circuit of the sun, or something near that. This, I say, is another point of
15 difference between them, though at first the practice in this respect was just the same in tragedies as in epic poems. They differ also (3) in their constituents, some being common to both and others peculiar to Tragedy—hence a judge of good and bad in Tragedy is a judge of that in epic poetry also. All the parts of an epic are included in Tragedy; but those of Tragedy are not all of them to be found in the Epic.

20   Reserving hexameter poetry and Comedy for considera-6 tion hereafter,[1] let us proceed now to the discussion of Tragedy; before doing so, however, we must gather up the definition resulting from what has been said. A tragedy, then, is the imitation of an action that is serious and also,
25 as having magnitude, complete in itself; in language with pleasurable accessories, each kind brought in separately in the parts of the work; in a dramatic, not in a narrative form; with incidents arousing pity and fear, wherewith to accomplish its catharsis of such emotions. Here by 'language with pleasurable accessories' I mean that with rhythm and harmony or song superadded; and by 'the
30 kinds separately' I mean that some portions are worked out with verse only, and others in turn with song.

I. As they act the stories, it follows that in the first place the Spectacle (or stage-appearance of the actors) must be some part of the whole; and in the second Melody and Diction, these two being the means of their imitation. Here by 'Diction' I mean merely this, the composition of the
35 verses; and by 'Melody', what is too completely understood to require explanation. But further: the subject represented also is an action; and the action involves agents, who must necessarily have their distinctive qualities both of character and thought, since it is from these that we
1450ᵃ ascribe certain qualities to their actions. There are in the natural order of things, therefore, two causes, Thought and

[1] For hexameter poetry cf. chap. 23 f.; comedy was treated of in the lost Second book.

Character, of their actions, and consequently of their success or failure in their lives. Now the action (that which
was done) is represented in the play by the Fable or Plot.
The Fable, in our present sense of the term, is simply this,
the combination of the incidents, or things done in the
story; whereas Character is what makes us ascribe certain 5
moral qualities to the agents; and Thought is shown in all
they say when proving a particular point or, it may be,
enunciating a general truth. There are six parts consequently of every tragedy, as a whole (that is) of such or
such quality, viz. a Fable or Plot, Characters, Diction,
Thought, Spectacle, and Melody; two of them arising from 10
the means, one from the manner, and three from the objects of the dramatic imitation; and there is nothing else
besides these six. Of these, its formative elements, then,
not a few of the dramatists have made due use, as every
play, one may say, admits of Spectacle, Character, Fable,
Diction, Melody, and Thought.

II. The most important of the six is the combination 15
of the incidents of the story. Tragedy is essentially an
imitation not of persons but of action and life, of happiness and misery. All human happiness or misery takes the
form of action; the end for which we live is a certain kind
of activity, not a quality. Character gives us qualities, but
it is in our actions—what we do—that we are happy or
the reverse. In a play accordingly they do not act in order 20
to portray the Characters; they include the Characters for
the sake of the action. So that it is the action in it, i.e. its
Fable or Plot, that is the end and purpose of the tragedy;
and the end is everywhere the chief thing. Besides this,
a tragedy is impossible without action, but there may be
one without Character. The tragedies of most of the mod- 25
erns are characterless—a defect common among poets of
all kinds, and with its counterpart in painting in Zeuxis[1]
as compared with Polygnotus; for whereas the latter *i*
strong in character, the work of Zeuxis is devoid of it.
And again: one may string together a series of characteristic speeches of the utmost finish as regards Diction and

[1] [Zeuxis of Heraclea, distinguished painter of late 5th and
early 4th cent. For Polygnotus cp. 1448ᵃ6.]

30 Thought, and yet fail to produce the true tragic effect; but
one will have much better success with a tragedy which,
however inferior in these respects, has a Plot, a combination of incidents, in it. And again: the most powerful elements of attraction in Tragedy, the Peripeties and Discov-
35 eries, are parts of the Plot. A further proof is in the fact
that beginners succeed earlier with the Diction and Characters than with the construction of a story; and the same
may be said of nearly all the early dramatists. We maintain, therefore, that the first essential, the life and soul, so
to speak, of Tragedy is the Plot; and that the Characters
1450ᵇ come second—compare the parallel in painting, where the
most beautiful colours laid on without order will not give
one the same pleasure as a simple black-and-white sketch
of a portrait. We maintain that Tragedy is primarily an
imitation of action, and that it is mainly for the sake of the
action that it imitates the personal agents. Third comes
5 the element of Thought, i.e. the power of saying whatever
can be said, or what is appropriate to the occasion. This
is what, in the speeches in Tragedy, falls under the arts
of Politics and Rhetoric; for the older poets make their
personages discourse like statesmen, and the moderns like
rhetoricians. One must not confuse it with Character. Character in a play is that which reveals the moral purpose of
the agents, i.e. the sort of thing they seek or avoid, where
that is not obvious—hence there is no room for Character
10 in a speech on a purely indifferent subject. Thought, on
the other hand, is shown in all they say when proving or
disproving some particular point, or enunciating some
universal proposition. Fourth among the literary elements
is the Diction of the personages, i.e., as before explained,[1]
the expression of their thoughts in words, which is practi-
15 cally the same thing with verse as with prose. As for the
two remaining parts, the Melody is the greatest of the
pleasurable accessories of Tragedy. The Spectacle, though
an attraction, is the least artistic of all the parts, and has
least to do with the art of poetry. The tragic effect is quite
possible without a public performance and actors; and

[1] 1449ᵇ34.

besides, the getting-up of the Spectacle is more a matter
for the costumier than the poet.   20

7   Having thus distinguished the parts, let us now consider
the proper construction of the Fable or Plot, as that is at
once the first and the most important thing in Tragedy.
We have laid it down that a tragedy is an imitation of an
action that is complete in itself, as a whole of some magnitude; for a whole may be of no magnitude to speak of. 25
Now a whole is that which has beginning, middle, and
end. A beginning is that which is not itself necessarily
after anything else, and which has naturally something
else after it; an end is that which is naturally after something itself, either as its necessary or usual consequent, and 30
with nothing else after it; and a middle, that which is by
nature after one thing and has also another after it. A well-
constructed Plot, therefore, cannot either begin or end at
any point one likes; beginning and end in it must be of
the forms just described. Again: to be beautiful, a living
creature, and every whole made up of parts, must not only 35
present a certain order in its arrangement of parts, but also
be of a certain definite magnitude. Beauty is a matter of
size and order, and therefore impossible either (1) in a
very minute creature, since our perception becomes indis-
tinct as it approaches instantaneity; or (2) in a creature
of vast size—one, say, 1,000 miles long—as in that case,
instead of the object being seen all at once, the unity and 1451ᵃ
wholeness of it is lost to the beholder. Just in the same
way, then, as a beautiful whole made up of parts, or a
beautiful living creature, must be of some size, but a size
to be taken in by the eye, so a story or Plot must be of 5
some length, but of a length to be taken in by the memory. As for the limit of its length, so far as that is relative
to public performances and spectators, it does not fall
within the theory of poetry. If they had to perform a hundred tragedies, they would be timed by water-clocks, as
they are said to have been at one period. The limit, however, set by the actual nature of the thing is this: the
longer the story, consistently with its being comprehensi- 10
ble as a whole, the finer it is by reason of its magnitude.

As a rough general formula, 'a length which allows of the
hero passing by a series of probable or necessary stages
from misfortune to happiness, or from happiness to mis-
15 fortune', may suffice as a limit for the magnitude of the
story.

The Unity of a Plot does not consist, as some suppose, 8
in its having one man as its subject. An infinity of things
befall that one man, some of which it is impossible to reduce to unity; and in like manner there are many actions
of one man which cannot be made to form one action.
20 One sees, therefore, the mistake of all the poets who have
written a *Heracleid*, a *Theseid*, or similar poems; they
suppose that, because Heracles was one man, the story also
of Heracles must be one story. Homer, however, evidently
understood this point quite well, whether by art or instinct,
just in the same way as he excels the rest in every other
respect. In writing an *Odyssey*, he did not make the poem
25 cover all that ever befell his hero—it befell him, for instance, to get wounded on Parnassus and also to feign
madness at the time of the call to arms, but the two incidents had no necessary or probable connexion with one
another—instead of doing that, he took as the subject of
the *Odyssey*, as also of the *Iliad*, an action with a Unity of
30 the kind we are describing. The truth is that, just as in the
other imitative arts one imitation is always of one thing,
so in poetry the story, as an imitation of action, must represent one action, a complete whole, with its several incidents so closely connected that the transposal or withdrawal of any one of them will disjoin and dislocate the
whole. For that which makes no perceptible difference by
35 its presence or absence is no real part of the whole.

From what we have said it will be seen that the poet's 9
function is to describe, not the thing that has happened,
but a kind of thing that might happen, i.e. what is possible as being probable or necessary. The distinction be-
1451^b tween historian and poet is not in the one writing prose
and the other verse—you might put the work of Herodotus
into verse, and it would still be a species of history; it consists really in this, that the one describes the thing that has

been, and the other a kind of thing that might be. Hence 5
poetry is something more philosophic and of graver import
than history, since its statements are of the nature rather
of universals, whereas those of history are singulars. By a
universal statement I mean one as to what such or such
a kind of man will probably or necessarily say or do—
which is the aim of poetry, though it affixes proper names
to the characters; by a singular statement, one as to what, 10
say, Alcibiades did or had done to him. In Comedy this
has become clear by this time; it is only when their plot
is already made up of probable incidents that they give it
a basis of proper names, choosing for the purpose any
names that may occur to them, instead of writing like the
old iambic poets about particular persons. In Tragedy, 15
however, they still adhere to the historic names; and for
this reason: what convinces is the possible; now whereas
we are not yet sure as to the possibility of that which has
not happened, that which has happened is manifestly possible, else it would not have come to pass. Nevertheless
even in Tragedy there are some plays with but one or two
known names in them, the rest being inventions; and there 20
are some without a single known name, e.g. Agathon's
Antheus,[1] in which both incidents and names are of the
poet's invention; and it is no less delightful on that account. So that one must not aim at a rigid adherence to
the traditional stories on which tragedies are based. It 25
would be absurd, in fact, to do so, as even the known stories are only known to a few, though they are a delight
none the less to all.

It is evident from the above that the poet must be more
the poet of his stories or Plots than of his verses, inasmuch
as he is a poet by virtue of the imitative element in his
work, and it is actions that he imitates. And if he should
come to take a subject from actual history, he is none the
less a poet for that; since some historic occurrences may 30
very well be in the probable and possible order of things;
and it is in that aspect of them that he is their poet.

Of simple Plots and actions the episodic are the worst.

[1] [Agathon, tragedian of late 5th—early 4th cent. The name
of this lost tragedy has given rise to many speculations.]

I call a Plot episodic when there is neither probability nor
35 necessity in the sequence of its episodes. Actions of this
sort bad poets construct through their own fault, and good
ones on account of the players. His work being for public
performance, a good poet often stretches out a Plot beyond its capabilities, and is thus obliged to twist the
sequence of incident.

1452ᵃ   Tragedy, however, is an imitation not only of a complete action, but also of incidents arousing pity and fear.
Such incidents have the very greatest effect on the mind
when they occur unexpectedly and at the same time in
consequence of one another; there is more of the marvel-
5 lous in them then than if they happened of themselves or
by mere chance. Even matters of chance seem most marvellous if there is an appearance of design as it were in
them; as for instance the statue of Mitys at Argos[1] killed
the author of Mity's death by falling down on him when
a looker-on at a public spectacle; for incidents like that we
10 think to be not without a meaning. A Plot, therefore, of
this sort is necessarily finer than others.

Plots are either simple or complex, since the actions 10
they represent are naturally of this twofold description.
15 The action, proceeding in the way defined, as one continuous whole, I call simple, when the change in the hero's
fortunes takes place without Peripety or Discovery; and
complex, when it involves one or the other, or both. These
should each of them arise out of the structure of the Plot
itself, so as to be the consequence, necessary or probable,
20 of the antecedents. There is a great difference between a
thing happening *propter hoc* and *post hoc*.

A Peripety is the change of the kind described from one 11
state of things within the play to its opposite, and that
too in the way we are saying, in the probable or necessary
25 sequence of events; as it is for instance in *Oedipus:* here
the opposite state of things is produced by the Messenger,
who, coming to gladden Oedipus and to remove his fears

---

[1] [Nothing definite known of the man or the event.]

as to his mother, reveals the secret of his birth.[1] And in
Lynceus:[2] just as he is being led off for execution, with
Danaus at his side to put him to death, the incidents preceding this bring it about that he is saved and Danaus put
to death. A Discovery is, as the very word implies, a 30
change from ignorance to knowledge, and thus to either
love or hate, in the personages marked for good or evil
fortune. The finest form of Discovery is one attended by
Peripeties, like that which goes with the Discovery in
Oedipus. There are no doubt other forms of it; what we
have said may happen in a way in reference to inanimate
things, even things of a very casual kind; and it is also 35
possible to discover whether some one has done or not
done something. But the form most directly connected with
the Plot and the action of the piece is the first-mentioned.
This, with a Peripety, will arouse either pity or fear—ac- *1452b*
tions of that nature being what Tragedy is assumed to represent; and it will also serve to bring about the happy or
unhappy ending. The Discovery, then, being of persons, it
may be that of one party only to the other, the latter being
already known; or both the parties may have to discover 5
themselves. Iphigenia, for instance, was discovered to Orestes by sending the letter;[3] and another Discovery was required to reveal him to Iphigenia.

Two parts of the Plot, then, Peripety and Discovery, are
on matters of this sort. A third part is Suffering; which we 10
may define as an action of a destructive or painful nature,
such as murders on the stage, tortures, woundings, and the
like. The other two have been already explained.

12   The parts of Tragedy to be treated as formative elements in the whole were mentioned in a previous Chap- 15
ter.[4] From the point of view, however, of its quantity, i.e.
the separate sections into which it is divided, a tragedy
has the following parts: Prologue, Episode, Exode, and a
choral portion, distinguished into Parode and Stasimon;
these two are common to all tragedies, whereas songs from

---

[1] *O.T.* 911-1085.   [2] By Theodectes.
[3] Eurip. *Iph. Taur.* 727 ff.   [4] Ch. 6

20 the stage and *Commoe* are only found in some. The Prologue is all that precedes the Parode of the chorus; an Episode all that comes in between two whole choral songs; the Exode all that follows after the last choral song. In the choral portion the Parode is the whole first statement of the chorus; a Stasimon, a song of the chorus without anapaests or trochees; a *Commos*, a lamentation sung by chorus and actor in concert. The parts of Tragedy to be used as formative elements in the whole we have already mentioned; the above are its parts from the point of view of its quantity, or the separate sections into which it is divided.

The next points after what we have said above will be 13 these: (1) What is the poet to aim at, and what is he to avoid, in constructing his Plots? and (2) What are the conditions on which the tragic effect depends?

30 We assume that, for the finest form of Tragedy, the Plot must be not simple but complex; and further, that it must imitate actions arousing fear and pity, since that is the distinctive function of this kind of imitation. It follows, therefore, that there are three forms of Plot to be avoided. (1) A good man must not be seen passing from happiness to misery, or (2) a bad man from misery to happiness. The 35 first situation is not fear-inspiring or piteous, but simply odious to us. The second is the most untragic that can be; it has no one of the requisites of Tragedy; it does not appeal either to the human feeling in us, or to our pity, or 1453ᵃ to our fears. Nor, on the other hand, should (3) an extremely bad man be seen falling from happiness into misery. Such a story may arouse the human feeling in us, but 5 it will not move us to either pity or fear; pity is occasioned by undeserved misfortune, and fear by that of one like ourselves; so that there will be nothing either piteous or fear-inspiring in the situation. There remains, then, the intermediate kind of personage, a man not preeminently virtuous and just, whose misfortune, however, is brought upon him not by vice and depravity but by some error of 10 judgement, of the number of those in the enjoyment of

great reputation and prosperity; e.g. Oedipus, Thyestes, and the men of note of similar families. The perfect Plot, accordingly, must have a single, and not (as some tell us) a double issue; the change in the hero's fortunes must be not from misery to happiness, but on the contrary from happiness to misery; and the cause of it must lie not in 15 any depravity, but in some great error in his part; the man himself being either such as we have described, or better, not worse, than that. Fact also confirms our theory. Though the poets began by accepting any tragic story that came to hand, in these days the finest tragedies are always on the story of some few houses, on that of Alcmeon, Oedipus, 20 Orestes, Meleager, Thyestes, Telephus, or any others that may have been involved, as either agents or sufferers, in some deed of horror. The theoretically best tragedy, then, has a Plot of this description. The critics, therefore, are wrong who blame Euripides for taking this line in his trag-edies, and giving many of them an unhappy ending. It is, 25 as we have said, the right line to take. The best proof is this: on the stage, and in the public performances, such plays, properly worked out, are seen to be the most truly tragic; and Euripides, even if his execution be faulty in every other point, is seen to be nevertheless the most tragic certainly of the dramatists. After this comes the construc- 30 tion of Plot which some rank first, one with a double story (like the *Odyssey*) and an opposite issue for the good and the bad personages. It is ranked as first only through the weakness of the audiences; the poets merely follow their public, writing as its wishes dictate. But the pleasure here 35 is not that of Tragedy. It belongs rather to Comedy, where the bitterest enemies in the piece (e.g. Orestes and Aegis-thus) walk off good friends at the end, with no slaying of any one by any one.

14   The tragic fear and pity may be aroused by the Spec- *1453*ᵇ
tacle; but they may also be aroused by the very structure and incidents of the play—which is the better way and shows the better poet. The Plot in fact should be so framed that even without seeing the things take place,

5 he who simply hears the account of them shall be filled
with horror and pity at the incidents; which is just the
effect that the mere recital of the story in *Oedipus* would
have on one. To produce this same effect by means of the
Spectacle is less artistic, and requires extraneous aid.
Those, however, who make use of the Spectacle to put
before us that which is merely monstrous and not produc-
10 tive of fear, are wholly out of touch with Tragedy; not
every kind of pleasure should be required of a tragedy,
but only its own proper pleasure.

The tragic pleasure is that of pity and fear, and the poet
has to produce it by a work of imitation; it is clear, therefore, that the causes should be included in the incidents
of his story. Let us see, then, what kinds of incident strike
15 one as horrible, or rather as piteous. In a deed of this description the parties must necessarily be either friends, or
enemies, or indifferent to one another. Now when enemy
does it on enemy, there is nothing to move us to pity either
in his doing or in his meditating the deed, except so far as
the actual pain of the sufferer is concerned; and the same
is true when the parties are indifferent to one another.
Whenever the tragic deed, however, is done within the
20 family—when murder or the like is done or meditated by
brother on brother, by son on father, by mother on son, or
son on mother—these are the situations the poet should
seek after. The traditional stories, accordingly, must be kept
as they are, e.g. the murder of Clytaemnestra by Orestes
and of Eriphyle by Alcmeon. At the same time even with
25 these there is something left to the poet himself; it is for
him to devise the right way of treating them. Let us explain more clearly what we mean by 'the right way'. The
deed of horror may be done by the doer knowingly and
consciously, as in the old poets, and in Medea's murder
of her children in Euripides.[1] Or he may do it, but in
30 ignorance of his relationship, and discover that afterwards,
as does the Oedipus in Sophocles. Here the deed is outside the play; but it may be within it, like the act of the

[1] *Med.* 1236.

Alcmeon in Astydamas,[1] or that of the Telegonus[2] in
Ulysses Wounded. A third possibility is for one meditating
some deadly injury to another, in ignorance of his relation- 35
ship, to make the discovery in time to draw back. These
exhaust the possibilities, since the deed must necessarily
be either done or not done, and either knowingly or un-
knowingly.

The worst situation is when the personage is with full
knowledge on the point of doing the deed, and leaves it
undone. It is odious and also (through the absence of
suffering) untragic; hence it is that no one is made to act
thus except in some few instances, e.g. Haemon and 1454[a]
Creon in *Antigone*.[3] Next after this comes the actual per-
petration of the deed meditated. A better situation than
that, however, is for the deed to be done in ignorance,
and the relationship discovered afterwards, since there is
nothing odious in it, and the Discovery will serve to
astound us. But the best of all is the last; what we have 5
in *Cresphontes*,[4] for example, where Merope, on the point
of slaying her son, recognizes him in time; in *Iphigenia*,
where sister and brother are in a like position; and in
Helle,[5] where the son recognizes his mother, when on the
point of giving her up to her enemy.

This will explain why our tragedies are restricted (as we
said just now)[6] to such a small number of families. It was 10
accident rather than art that led the poets in quest of
subjects to embody this kind of incident in their Plots.
They are still obliged, accordingly, to have recourse to the
families in which such horrors have occurred.

On the construction of the Plot, and the kind of Plot
required for Tragedy, enough has now been said.   15

---

[1] [A much produced tragedian, contemporary of Aristotle.]
[2] [Telegonus, the son of Odysseus and Circe, sets out to find
his father and without recognizing him wounds him
fatally. This post-Homeric theme was the subject of a
tragedy of Sophocles, which may be the play Aristotle here
has in mind.]
[3] l. 1231.   [4] By Euripides.
[5] Authorship unknown.   [6] 1453[a]19.

In the Characters there are four points to aim at. First 15 and foremost, that they shall be good. There will be an element of character in the play, if (as has been observed)[1] what a personage says or does reveals a certain moral purpose; and a good element of character, if the purpose so revealed is good. Such goodness is possible in 20 every type of personage, even in a woman or a slave, though the one is perhaps an inferior, and the other a wholly worthless being. The second point is to make them appropriate. The Character before us may be, say, manly; but it is not appropriate in a female Character to be manly, or clever. The third is to make them like the real-25 ity, which is not the same as their being good and appropriate, in our sense of the term. The fourth is to make them consistent and the same throughout; even if inconsistency be part of the man before one for imitation as presenting that form of character, he should still be consistently inconsistent. We have an instance of baseness of character, not required for the story, in the Menelaus in 30 *Orestes;*[2] of the incongruous and unbefitting in the lamentation of Ulysses in *Scylla,*[3] and in the (clever) speech of Melanippe;[4] and of inconsistency in *Iphigenia at Aulis,*[5] where Iphigenia the suppliant is utterly unlike the later Iphigenia. The right thing, however, is in the Characters just as in the incidents of the play to endeavour always 35 after the necessary or the probable; so that whenever such-and-such a personage says or does such-and-such a thing, it shall be the necessary or probable outcome of his character; and whenever this incident follows on that, it shall be either the necessary or the probable consequence of it. From this one sees (to digress for a moment) that the 1454[b] Dénouement also should arise out of the plot itself, and not depend on a stage-artifice, as in *Medea,*[6] or in the story of the (arrested) departure of the Greeks in the *Iliad.*[7] The artifice must be reserved for matters outside the play—for past events beyond human knowledge, or

[1] 1450[b]8.   [2] [Euripides.]
[3] A dithyramb by Timotheus.   [4] Euripides.
[5] ll. 1211 ff., 1368 ff.   [6] l. 1317.
[7] ii. 155.

events yet to come, which require to be foretold or an-5
nounced; since it is the privilege of the gods to know
everything. There should be nothing improbable among
the actual incidents. If it be unavoidable, however, it
should be outside the tragedy, like the improbability in
the *Oedipus* of Sophocles. But to return to the Characters.
As Tragedy is an imitation of personages better than the
ordinary man, we in our way should follow the example of
good portrait-painters, who reproduce the distinctive fea-10
tures of a man, and at the same time, without losing the
likeness, make him handsomer than he is. The poet in like
manner, in portraying men quick or slow to anger, or with
similar infirmities of character, must know how to represent them as such, and at the same time as good men, as
Agathon and Homer have represented Achilles.

All these rules one must keep in mind throughout, and, 15
further, those also for such points of stage-effect as directly
depend on the art of the poet, since in these too one may
often make mistakes. Enough, however, has been said on
the subject in one of our published writings.[1]

16 Discovery in general has been explained already.[2] As
for the species of Discovery, the first to be noted is (1) 20
the least artistic form of it, of which the poets make most
use through mere lack of invention, Discovery by signs or
marks. Of these signs some are congenital, like the 'lance-
head which the Earth-born have on them',[3] or 'stars', such
as Carcinus[4] brings in his *Thyestes;* others acquired after
birth—these latter being either marks on the body, e.g.
scars, or external tokens, like necklaces, or (to take another
sort of instance) the ark in the Discovery in *Tyro*.[5] Even 25
these, however, admit of two uses, a better and a worse;
the scar of Ulysses is an instance; the Discovery of him
through it is made in one way by the nurse[6] and in an-

---

[1] In the lost dialogue *On Poets*.
[2] 1452^{a}29.
[3] Authorship unknown.
[4] [Tragedian of the 5th century.]
[5] [By Sophocles.]
[6] *Od*. xix. 386-475.

other by the swineherds.[1] A Discovery using signs as a means of assurance is less artistic, as indeed are all such as imply reflection; whereas one bringing them in all of a 30 sudden, as in the *Bath-story*,[2] is of a better order. Next after these are (2) Discoveries made directly by the poet; which are inartistic for that very reason; e.g. Orestes' Discovery of himself in *Iphigenia:* whereas his sister reveals who she is by the letter,[3] Orestes is made to say himself 35 what the poet rather than the story demands.[4] This, therefore, is not far removed from the first-mentioned fault, since he might have presented certain tokens as well. Another instance is the 'shuttle's voice' in the *Tereus* of Sophocles.

(3) A third species is Discovery through memory, from a 1455[a] man's consciousness being awakened by something seen. Thus in *The Cyprioe* of Dicaeogenes,[5] the sight of the picture makes the man burst into tears; and in the *Tale of Alcinous*,[6] hearing the harper Ulysses is reminded of the past and weeps; the Discovery of them being the result.

(4) A fourth kind is Discovery through reasoning; e.g. in 5 *The Choephoroe;*[7] 'One like me is here; there is no one like me but Orestes; he, therefore, must be here.' Or that which Polyidus the Sophist[8] suggested for *Iphigenia;* since it was natural for Orestes to reflect: 'My sister was sacrificed and I am to be sacrificed like her.' Or that in the *Tydeus* of Theodectes:[9] 'I came to find a son, and am to 10 die myself.' Or that in *The Phinidae:*[10] on seeing the place the women inferred their fate, that they were to die there, since they had also been exposed there. (5) There is, too, a composite Discovery arising from bad reasoning on the side of the other party. An instance of it is in *Ulysses the false Messenger:* he said he should know the bow—which

---

[1] *Od.* xxi. 205-25.　　[2] *Od.* xix. 392.
[3] Eurip. *Iph. Taur.* 727 ff.　　[4] Ib., 800 ff.
[5] [Writer of dithyrambs and tragedies, late 5th and early 4th cent.]
[6] *Od.* viii. 521 ff. (cf. viii. 83 ff.)
[7] ll. 168-234.
[8] [Noted writer of dithyrambs of late 5th and early 4th cent.]
[9] [The tragedian and rhetorician, a friend of Aristotle.]
[10] [Timotheus composed a dithyrambus 'The Phinidae.']

he had not seen; but to suppose from that that he would 15
know it again (as though he had once seen it) was bad
reasoning. (6) The best of all Discoveries, however, is
that arising from the incidents themselves, when the great
surprise comes about through a probable incident, like
that in the *Oedipus* of Sophocles; and also in *Iphigenia;*[1]
for it was not improbable that she should wish to have a
letter taken home. These last are the only Discoveries independent of the artifice of signs and necklaces. Next after 20
them come Discoveries through reasoning.

17   At the time when he is constructing his Plots, and engaged on the Diction in which they are worked out, the
poet should remember (1) to put the actual scenes as far
as possible before his eyes. In this way, seeing everything
with the vividness of an eye-witness as it were, he will 25
devise what is appropriate, and be least likely to overlook
incongruities. This is shown by what was censured in
Carcinus, the return of Amphiaraus from the sanctuary; it
would have passed unnoticed, if it had not been actually
seen by the audience; but on the stage his play failed, the
incongruity of the incident offending the spectators. (2)
As far as may be, too, the poet should even act his story
with the very gestures of his personages. Given the same 30
natural qualifications, he who feels the emotions to be described will be the most convincing; distress and anger,
for instance, are portrayed most truthfully by one who is
feeling them at the moment. Hence it is that poetry demands a man with a special gift for it, or else one with a
touch of madness in him; the former can easily assume
the required mood, and the latter may be actually beside
himself with emotion. (3) His story, again, whether already made or of his own making, he should first simplify
and reduce to a universal form, before proceeding to 1455[b]
lengthen it out by the insertion of episodes. The following
will show how the universal element in *Iphigenia,* for instance, may be viewed: A certain maiden having been
offered in sacrifice, and spirited away from her sacrificers

---

[1] Eurip. *Iph. Taur.* 582.

5 into another land, where the custom was to sacrifice all
strangers to the Goddess, she was made there the priestess
of this rite. Long after that the brother of the priestess
happened to come; the fact, however, of the oracle having
for a certain reason bidden him go thither, and his object
in going, are outside the Plot of the play. On his coming
he was arrested, and about to be sacrificed, when he revealed who he was—either as Euripides puts it, or (as
10 suggested by Polyidus) by the not improbable exclama-
tion, 'So I too am doomed to be sacrificed, as my sister
was'; and the disclosure led to his salvation. This done,
the next thing, after the proper names have been fixed as
a basis for the story, is to work in episodes or accessory
incidents. One must mind, however, that the episodes are
appropriate, like the fit of madness[1] in Orestes, which led
15 to his arrest, and the purifying,[2] which brought about his
salvation. In plays, then, the episodes are short; in epic
poetry they serve to lengthen out the poem. The argument
of the *Odyssey* is not a long one. A certain man has been
abroad many years; Poseidon is ever on the watch for him,
and he is all alone. Matters at home too have come to this,
20 that his substance is being wasted and his son's death
plotted by suitors to his wife. Then he arrives there himself after his grievous sufferings; reveals himself, and falls
on his enemies; and the end is his salvation and their
death. This being all that is proper to the *Odyssey,* everything else in it is episode.

(4) There is a further point to be borne in mind. Every 18
tragedy is in part Complication and in part Dénouement;
the incidents before the opening scene, and often certain
also of those within the play, forming the Complication;
25 and the rest the Dénouement. By Complication I mean
all from the beginning of the story to the point just before
the change in the hero's fortunes; by Dénouement, all from
the beginning of the change to the end. In the *Lynceus* of
30 Theodectes, for instance, the Complication includes, together with the presupposed incidents, the seizure of the

---

[1] *Iph. Taur.* 281 ff.   [2] Ib., 1163 ff.

child and that in turn of the parents; and the Dénouement
all from the indictment for the murder to the end. Now it $1456^a 7$
is right, when one speaks of a tragedy as the same or not
the same as another, to do so on the ground before all else
of their Plot, i.e. as having the same or not the same Complication and Dénouement. Yet there are many dramatists
who, after a good Complication, fail in the Dénouement.
But it is necessary for both points of construction to be
always duly mastered.[1] (5) There are four distinct species 1455^b
of Tragedy—that being the number of the constituents   32
also that have been mentioned:[2] first, the complex Tragedy, which is all Peripety and Discovery; second, the
Tragedy of suffering, e.g. the *Ajaxes* and *Ixions;*[3] third,
the Tragedy of character, e.g. *The Phthiotides* and *Pe-* 1456^a
leus.[4] The fourth constituent is that of 'Spectacle', exemplified in *The Phorcides,*[5] in *Prometheus,*[5] and in all plays
with the scene laid in the nether world. The poet's aim,
then, should be to combine every element of interest, if
possible, or else the more important and the major part
of them. This is now especially necessary owing to the un-
fair criticism to which the poet is subjected in these days.
Just because there have been poets before him strong in 5
the several species of tragedy, the critics now expect the
one man to surpass that which was the strong point of
each one of his predecessors. (6) One should also remem- 10
ber what has been said more than once,[6] and not write a
tragedy of an epic body of incident (i.e. one with a plurality of stories in it), by attempting to dramatize, for instance, the entire story of the *Iliad*. In the epic owing to
its scale every part is treated at proper length; with a
drama, however, on the same story the result is very dis- 15
appointing. This is shown by the fact that all who have

[1] [Not everybody would accept the transposition in the text
which the translator makes here.]
[2] This does not agree with anything actually said before.
[3] [Tragedies of the type of the *Ajax* of Sophocles and of the
Ixion of Euripides.]
[4] [Tragedies of the type of these plays of Sophocles.]
[5] [Both are plays of Aeschylus.]
[6] A loose reference to $1449^b 12$, $1466^b 15$.

dramatized the fall of Ilium in its entirety, and not part by
part, like Euripides, or the whole of the Niobe story, instead of a portion, like Aeschylus, either fail utterly or
have but ill success on the stage; for that and that alone
was enough to ruin even a play by Agathon. Yet in their
20 Peripeties, as also in their simple plots, the poets I mean
show wonderful skill in aiming at the kind of effect they
desire—a tragic situation that arouses the human feeling
in one, like the clever villain (e.g. Sisyphus) deceived, or
the brave wrongdoer worsted. This is probable, however,
only in Agathon's[1] sense, when he speaks of the probability of even improbabilities coming to pass. (7) The Chorus
25 too should be regarded as one of the actors; it should be
an integral part of the whole, and take a share in the action—that which it has in Sophocles, rather than in Euripides. With the later poets, however, the songs in a play of
theirs have no more to do with the Plot of that than of any
other tragedy. Hence it is that they are now singing inter-
calary pieces, a practice first introduced by Agathon. And
30 yet what real difference is there between singing such in-
tercalary pieces, and attempting to fit in a speech, or even
a whole act, from one play into another?

The Plot and Characters having been discussed, it re- 19
mains to consider the Diction and Thought. As for the
Thought, we may assume what is said of it in our Art of
35 Rhetoric,[2] as it belongs more properly to that department
of inquiry. The Thought of the personages is shown in
everything to be effected by their language—in every
effort to prove or disprove, to arouse emotion (pity, fear,
1456ᵇ anger, and the like), or to maximize or minimize things.
It is clear, also, that their mental procedure must be on
the same lines in their actions likewise, whenever they
wish them to arouse pity or horror, or to have a look of
5 importance or probability. The only difference is that with
the act the impression has to be made without explana-

---

[1] [Tragedian of the late 5th cent.]
[2] Cf. especially *Rhet.* 1356ᵃ1. [However, Aristotle probably
is thinking of his doctrine of proofs and emotions as set
forth in the greater part of Books I and II of the *Rhetoric*.]

tion; whereas with the spoken word it has to be produced
by the speaker, and result from his language. What, indeed, would be the good of the speaker, if things appeared
in the required light even apart from anything he says?

As regards the Diction, one subject for inquiry under
this head is the turns given to the language when spoken;
e.g. the difference between command and prayer, simple
statement and threat, question and answer, and so forth.
The theory of such matters, however, belongs to Elocution
and the professors of that art. Whether the poet knows
these things or not, his art as a poet is never seriously
criticized on that account. What fault can one see in
Homer's 'Sing of the wrath, Goddess'?—which Protagoras[1]
has criticized as being a command where a prayer was
meant, since to bid one do or not do, he tells us, is a command. Let us pass over this, then, as appertaining to another art, and not to that of poetry.

20   The Diction viewed as a whole is made up of the following parts: the Letter (or ultimate element), the Syllable,
the Conjunction, the Article, the Noun, the Verb, the Case,
and the Speech. (1) The Letter is an indivisible sound of
a particular kind, one that may become a factor in an
intelligible sound. Indivisible sounds are uttered by the
brutes also, but no one of these is a Letter in our sense of
the term. These elementary sounds are either vowels, semi-
vowels, or mutes. A vowel is a Letter having an audible
sound without the addition of another Letter. A semivowel, one having an audible sound by the addition of
another Letter; e.g. S and R. A mute, one having no
sound at all by itself, but becoming audible by an addition, that of one of the Letters which have a sound of some
sort of their own; e.g. G and D. The Letters differ in various ways: as produced by different conformations or in
different regions of the mouth; as aspirated, not aspirated,
or sometimes one and sometimes the other; as long, short,
or of variable quantity; and further as having an acute,
grave, or intermediate accent. The details of these matters

[1] [Famous sophist of 5th cent.]

we must leave to the metricians. (2) A Syllable is a non-
35 significant composite sound, made up of a mute and a Letter having a sound (a vowel or semivowel); for GR, without an A, is just as much a Syllable as GRA, with an A.
The various forms of the Syllable also belong to the theory
of metre. (3) A Conjunction is (a) a non-significant sound
1457ᵃ which, when one significant sound is formable out of several, neither hinders nor aids the union, and which, if the
Speech thus formed stands by itself (apart from other
Speeches), must not be inserted at the beginning of it;
e.g. μέν, δή, τοι, δέ. Or (b) a non-significant sound capable of combining two or more significant sounds into one;
5 e.g. ἀμφί, περί, &c. (4) An Article is a non-significant
sound marking the beginning, end, or dividing-point of a
10 Speech, its natural place being either at the extremities or
in the middle. (5) A Noun or name is a composite significant sound not involving the idea of time, with parts
which have no significance by themselves in it. It is to be
remembered that in a compound we do not think of the
parts as having a significance also by themselves; in the
name 'Theodorus', for instance, the δῶρον means nothing
to us. (6) A Verb is a composite significant sound involving the idea of time, with parts which (just as in the
15 Noun) have no significance by themselves in it. Whereas
the word 'man' or 'white' does not imply *when,* 'walks' and
'has walked' involve in addition to the idea of walking that
of time present or time past. (7) A Case of a Noun or
Verb is when the word means 'of' or 'to' a thing, and so
20 forth, or for one or many (e.g. 'man' and 'men'); or it
may consist merely in the mode of utterance, e.g. in question, command, &c. 'Walked?' and 'Walk!' are Cases of the
verb 'to walk' of this last kind. (8) A Speech is a composite
significant sound, some of the parts of which have a certain significance by themselves. It may be observed that a
Speech is not always made up of Noun and Verb; it may
25 be without a Verb, like the definition of man; but it will
always have some part with a certain significance by itself.
In the Speech 'Cleon walks', 'Cleon' is an instance of such
a part. A Speech is said to be one in two ways, either as
signifying one thing, or as a union of several Speeches

made into one by conjunction. Thus the *Iliad* is one Speech
by conjunction of several; and the definition of man is one 30
through its signifying one thing.

21   Nouns are of two kinds, either (1) simple, i.e. made up
of non-significant parts, like the word γῆ, or (2) double;
in the latter case the word may be made up either of a
significant and a non-significant part (a distinction which
disappears in the compound), or of two significant parts.
It is possible also to have triple, quadruple, or higher com- 35
pounds, like most of our amplified names; e.g. 'Hermocaï-
coxanthus' and the like.

Whatever its structure, a Noun must always be either 1457ᵇ
(1) the ordinary word for the thing, or (2) a strange
word, or (3) a metaphor, or (4) an ornamental word, or
(5) a coined word, or (6) a word lengthened out, or (7)
curtailed, or (8) altered in form. By the ordinary word I
mean that in general use in a country; and by a strange
word, one in use elsewhere. So that the same word may
obviously be at once strange and ordinary, though not in 5
reference to the same people; σίγυνον, for instance, is an
ordinary word in Cyprus, and a strange word with us.
Metaphor consists in giving the thing a name that belongs
to something else; the transference being either from genus
to species, or from species to genus, or from species to species, or on grounds of analogy. That from genus to species
is exemplified in 'Here stands my ship';[1] for lying at an- 10
chor is the 'standing' of a particular kind of thing. That
from species to genus in 'Truly ten thousand good deeds
has Ulysses wrought',[2] where 'ten thousand', which is a
particular large number, is put in place of the generic 'a
large number'. That from species to species in 'Drawing
the life with the bronze',[3] and in 'Severing with the en-
during bronze';[3] where the poet uses 'draw' in the sense
of 'sever' and 'sever' in that of 'draw', both words mean- 15
ing to 'take away' something. That from analogy is possible whenever there are four terms so related that the sec-

[1] *Od.* i. 185, xxiv. 308.
[2] *Il.* ii. 272.
[3] [Fragm. of Empedocles' *Purifications.*]

ond (B) is to the first (A), as the fourth (D) to the third
(C); for one may then metaphorically put D in lieu of B,
and B in lieu of D. Now and then, too, they qualify the
20 metaphor by adding on to it that to which the word it sup
plants is relative. Thus a cup (B) is in relation to Dionysus (A) what a shield (D) is to Ares (C). The cup accordingly will be metaphorically described as the 'shield
of Dionysus' (D + A), and the shield as the 'cup *of Ares*' [1]
(B + C). Or to take another instance: As old age (D) is
to life (C), so is evening (B) to day (A). One will accordingly describe evening (B) as the 'old age *of the day*'
(D + A)—or by the Empedoclean equivalent; and old age
(D) as the 'evening' or 'sunset *of life*' (B + C). It may be
25 that some of the terms thus related have no special name
of their own, but for all that they will be metaphorically
described in just the same way. Thus to cast forth seed-
corn is called 'sowing'; but to cast forth its flame, as said
of the sun, has no special name. This nameless act (B),
however, stands in just the same relation to its object, sun-
light (A), as sowing (D) to the seed-corn (C). Hence
the expression in the poet, 'sowing around a god-created
30 *flame*' [2] (D + A). There is also another form of qualified
metaphor. Having given the thing the alien name, one may
by a negative addition deny of it one of the attributes naturally associated with its new name. An instance of this
would be to call the shield not the 'cup *of Ares*', as in the
former case, but a 'cup *that holds no ·*ine'. . . . A coined
word is a name which, being quite unknown among a people, is given by the poet himself; e.g. (for there are some
words that seem to be of this origin) ἔρνυγες for horns, and
35 ἀρητήρ for priest. A word is said to be lengthened out,
1458ᵃ when it has a short vowel made long, or an extra syllable inserted; e.g. πόληος for πόλεως, Πηληιάδεω for Πηλείδου.
It is said to be curtailed, when it has lost a part; e.g.
5 κρῖ, δῶ, and ὄψ in μία γίνεται ἀμφοτέρων ὄψ.[3] It is an altered
word, when part is left as it was and part is of the poet's
making; e.g. δεξιτερόν for δεξιόν, in δεξιτερὸν κατὰ μαζόν.[4]

---

[1] [Fragm. of Timotheus.]   [2] Authorship unknown.
[3] [Fragm. of Empedocles.]   [4] *Il.* v. 393.

The Nouns themselves (to whatever class they may belong) are either masculines, feminines, or intermediates
(neuter). All ending in N, P, Σ, or in the two compounds
if this last, Ψ and Ξ, are masculines. All ending in the 10
invariable long vowels, H and Ω, and in A among the
vowels that may be long, are feminines. So that there is
an equal number of masculine and feminine terminations,
as Ψ and Ξ are the same as Σ, and need not be counted.
There is no Noun, however, ending in a mute or in either
of the two short vowels, E and O. Only three (μέλι, κόμμι, 15
πέπερι) end in I, and five in Υ. The intermediates, or neu-
ters, end in the variable vowels or in N, P, Σ.

22   The perfection of Diction is for it to be at once clear
and not mean. The clearest indeed is that made up of the
ordinary words for things, but it is mean, as is shown by 20
the poetry of Cleophon[1] and Sthenelus.[2] On the other
hand the Diction becomes distinguished and non-prosaic
by the use of unfamiliar terms, i.e. strange words, metaphors, lengthened forms, and everything that deviates from
the ordinary modes of speech.—But a whole statement in
such terms will be either a riddle or a barbarism, a riddle, 25
if made up of metaphors, a barbarism, if made up of
strange words. The very nature indeed of a riddle is this,
to describe a fact in an impossible combination of words
(which cannot be done with the real names for things, but
can be with their metaphorical substitutes); e.g. 'I saw a
man glue brass on another with fire',[3] and the like. The 30
corresponding use of strange words results in a barbarism.
—A certain admixture, accordingly, of unfamiliar terms is
necessary. These, the strange word, the metaphor, the ornamental equivalent, &c., will save the language from
seeming mean and prosaic, while the ordinary words in it
will secure the requisite clearness. What helps most, how- *1458ᵇ*
ever, to render the Diction at once clear and non-prosaic
is the use of the lengthened, curtailed, and altered forms

---

[1] [An Athenian writer of tragedies, cp. *Rhet.* 1408ª15.]
[2] [Probably the tragic poet of the late 5th cent.]
[3] [A riddle famous already at the time of Aristotle and often
quoted later.]

of words. Their deviation from the ordinary words will, by making the language unlike that in general use, give it a non-prosaic appearance; and their having much in common
5 with the words in general use will give it the quality of clearness. It is not right, then, to condemn these modes of speech, and ridicule the poet for using them, as some have done; e.g. the elder Euclid,[1] who said it was easy to make poetry if one were to be allowed to lengthen the words in the statement itself as much as one likes—a procedure he
10 caricatured by reading Ἐπιχάρην εἶδον Μαραθῶνάδε βαδί-ζοντα,[2] and οὐκ ἄν γ' ἐράμενος τὸν ἐκείνου ἐλλέβορον[3] as verses. A too apparent use of these licences has certainly a ludicrous effect, but they are not alone in that; the rule of moderation applies to all the constituents of the poetic vocabulary; even with metaphors, strange words, and the rest, the effect will be the same, if one uses them improperly and with a view to provoking laughter. The proper
15 use of them is a very different thing. To realize the difference one should take an epic verse and see how it reads when the normal words are introduced. The same should be done too with the strange word, the metaphor, and the rest; for one has only to put the ordinary words in their place to see the truth of what we are saying. The same iambic, for instance, is found in Aeschylus and Euripides, and as it stands in the former it is a poor line; whereas
20 Euripides, by the change of a single word, the substitution of a strange for what is by usage the ordinary word, has made it seem a fine one. Aeschylus having said in his *Philoctetes*:

φαγέδαινα ἥ μου σάρκας ἐσθίει ποδός.[4]

Euripides has merely altered the ἐσθίει here into θοινᾶται.[5] Or suppose

[1] [Athenian wit and collector of books, famous for his brilliant remarks.]
[2] ['I saw Epichares a-walking Marathon-wards'.]
[3] [The text is corrupt.]
[4] ['The cancer that is eating the flesh of my foot', the play is lost and so is the play of Euripides mentioned next.]
[5] [Euripides replaces 'is eating' by 'feasts on'.]

νῦν δέ μ' ἐὼν ὀλίγος τε καὶ οὐτιδανὸς καὶ ἀεικής[1]   25

to be altered, by the substitution of the ordinary words, into

νῦν δέ μ' ἐὼν μικρός τε καὶ ἀσθενικὸς καὶ ἀειδής.[2]

Or the line

δίφρον ἀεικέλιον καταθεὶς ὀλίγην τε τράπεζαν[3]

into

δίφρον μοχθηρὸν καταθεὶς μικράν τε τράπεζαν.[4]   30

Or ἠιόνες βοόωσιν into ἠιόνες κράζουσιν.[5] Add to this that Ariphrades[6] used to ridicule the tragedians for introducing expressions unknown in the language of common life, δωμάτων ἄπο (for ἀπὸ δωμάτων), σέθεν, ἐγὼ δέ νιν, Ἀχιλλέως πέρι (for περὶ Ἀχιλλέως),[7] and the like. The mere fact *1459ᵃ* of their not being in ordinary speech gives the Diction a non-prosaic character; but Ariphrades was unaware of that. It is a great thing, indeed, to make a proper use of the poetical forms, as also of compounds and strange words. But the greatest thing by far is to be a master of metaphor. 5 It is the one thing that cannot be learnt from others; and it is also a sign of genius, since a good metaphor implies an intuitive perception of the similarity in dissimilars.

Of the kinds of words we have enumerated it may be observed that compounds are most in place in the dithyramb, strange words in heroic, and metaphors in iambic poetry. Heroic poetry, indeed, may avail itself of them all. 10 But in iambic verse, which models itself as far as possible

[1] ['Lo, now a dwarf, a man of no worth and a weakling' *Od.* ix. 515.]
[2] ['See, now, a small man, feeble, and unprepossessing'.]
[3] ['And placed for him an unseemly settle and a meagre table' *Od.* xx. 259.]
[4] ['And brought him a sorry chair and a small table'.]
[5] [Or 'the sea-beach bellows' (*Il.* xvii. 265) into 'the beach is roaring'.]
[6] [His identity is not known to us.]
[7] ['From the house away' (for 'away from the house'), 'of thee' (for 'yours'), 'Achilles about' (for 'about Achilles').]

on the spoken language, only those kinds of words are in place which are allowable also in an oration, i.e. the ordinary word, the metaphor, and the ornamental equivalent.

15 Let this, then, suffice as an account of Tragedy, the art imitating by means of action on the stage.

As for the poetry which merely narrates, or imitates by 23 means of versified language (without action), it is evident that it has several points in common with Tragedy.

I. The construction of its stories should clearly be like that in a drama; they should be based on a single action, one that is a complete whole in itself, with a beginning, 20 middle, and end, so as to enable the work to produce its own proper pleasure with all the organic unity of a living creature. Nor should one suppose that there is anything like them in our usual histories. A history has to deal not with one action, but with one period and all that happened in that to one or more persons, however disconnected the several events may have been. Just as two 25 events may take place at the same time, e.g. the sea-fight off Salamis and the battle with the Carthaginians in Sicily, without converging to the same end, so too of two consecutive events one may sometimes come after the other with no one end as their common issue. Nevertheless most of our epic poets, one may say, ignore the distinction.

30 Herein, then, to repeat what we have said before,[1] we have a further proof of Homer's marvellous superiority to the rest. He did not attempt to deal even with the Trojan war in its entirety, though it was a whole with a definite beginning and end—through a feeling apparently that it was too long a story to be taken in in one view, or if not 35 that, too complicated from the variety of incident in it. As it is, he has singled out one section of the whole; many of the other incidents, however, he brings in as episodes, using the Catalogue of the Ships, for instance, and other episodes to relieve the uniformity of his narrative. As for the other epic poets, they treat of one man, or one period; or else of an action which, although one, has a multiplic-
1459ᵇ ity of parts in it. This last is what the authors of the

[1] 1451ᵃ23 ff.

Cypria[1] and *Little Iliad*[1] have done. And the result is that whereas the *Iliad* or *Odyssey* supplies materials for only one, or at most two tragedies, the *Cypria* does that for several and the *Little Iliad* for more than eight: for an [5] *Adjudgment of Arms,* a *Philoctetes,* a *Neoptolemus,* a *Eurypylus,* a *Ulysses as Beggar,* a *Laconian Women,* a *Fall of Ilium,* and a *Departure of the Fleet;* as also a *Simon,* and a *Women of Troy.*

24   II. Besides this, Epic poetry must divide into the same species as Tragedy; it must be either simple or complex, a story of character or one of suffering. Its parts, too, with the exception of Song and Spectacle, must be the same, as [10] it requires Peripeties, Discoveries, and scenes of suffering just like Tragedy. Lastly, the Thought and Diction in it must be good in their way. All these elements appear in Homer first; and he has made due use of them. His two poems are each examples of construction, the *Iliad* simple and a story of suffering, the *Odyssey* complex (there is [15] Discovery throughout it) and a story of character. And they are more than this, since in Diction and Thought too they surpass all other poems.

There is, however, a difference in the Epic as compared with Tragedy, (1) in its length, and (2) in its metre. (1) As to its length, the limit already suggested[2] will suffice: it must be possible for the beginning and end of the work to be taken in in one view—a condition which will be ful-[20] filled if the poem be shorter than the old epics, and about as long as the series of tragedies offered for one hearing. For the extension of its length epic poetry has a special advantage, of which it makes large use. In a play one cannot represent an action with a number of parts going on simultaneously; one is limited to the part on the stage and [25] connected with the actors. Whereas in epic poetry the narrative form makes it possible for one to describe a number of simultaneous incidents; and these, if germane to the

[1] Authorship unknown. [Epics belonging to the early epic cycle and dealing with events before and after those included in Homer's *Iliad*.]

[2] 1451[a]3.

subject, increase the body of the poem. This then is a gain
to the Epic, tending to give it grandeur, and also variety
30 of interest and room for episodes of diverse kinds. Uniformity of incident by the satiety it soon creates is apt to
ruin tragedies on the stage. (2) As for its metre, the heroic
has been assigned it from experience; were any one to attempt a narrative poem in some one, or in several, of the
other metres, the incongruity of the thing would be apparent. The heroic in fact is the gravest and weightiest of
35 metres—which is what makes it more tolerant than the
rest of strange words and metaphors, that also being a
point in which the narrative form of poetry goes beyond
all others. The iambic and trochaic, on the other hand, are
metres of movement, the one representing that of life and
1460ᵃaction, the other that of the dance. Still more unnatural
would it appear, if one were to write an epic in a medley
of metres, as Chaeremon did.[1] Hence it is that no one has
ever written a long story in any but heroic verse; nature
herself, as we have said,[2] teaches us to select the metre
appropriate to such a story.

5   Homer, admirable as he is in every other respect, is
especially so in this, that he alone among epic poets is not
unaware of the part to be played by the poet himself in
the poem. The poet should say very little *in propria per-
sona,* as he is no imitator when doing that. Whereas the
other poets are perpetually coming forward in person, and
say but little, and that only here and there, as imitators,
10 Homer after a brief preface brings in forthwith a man, a
woman, or some other Character—no one of them characterless, but each with distinctive characteristics.

The marvellous is certainly required in Tragedy. The
Epic, however, affords more opening for the improbable,
the chief factor in the marvellous, because in it the agents
are not visibly before one. The scene of the pursuit of
15 Hector would be ridiculous on the stage—the Greeks halt-
ing instead of pursuing him, and Achilles shaking his head
to stop them;[3] but in the poem the absurdity is overlooked.
The marvellous, however, is a cause of pleasure, as is

[1] *Centaur,* cf. 1447ᵇ21.   [2] 1449ᵃ24.
[3] *Il.* xxii. 205.

shown by the fact that we all tell a story with additions, in the belief that we are doing our hearers a pleasure.

Homer more than any other has taught the rest of us the art of framing lies in the right way. I mean the use of paralogism. Whenever, if A is or happens, a consequent, B, is or happens, men's notion is that, if the B is, the A also is—but that is a false conclusion. Accordingly, if A is untrue, but there is something else, B, that on the assumption of its truth follows as its consequent, the right thing then is to add on the B. Just because we know the truth of the consequent, we are in our own minds led on to the erroneous inference of the truth of the antecedent. Here is an instance, from the *Bath-story* in the *Odyssey*.[1]

A likely impossibility is always preferable to an unconvincing possibility. The story should never be made up of improbable incidents; there should be nothing of the sort in it. If, however, such incidents are unavoidable, they should be outside the piece, like the hero's ignorance in *Oedipus* of the circumstances of Laius' death; not within it, like the report of the Pythian games in *Electra*,[2] or the man's having come to Mysia from Tegea without uttering a word on the way in *The Mysians*.[3] So that it is ridiculous to say that one's Plot would have been spoilt without them, since it is fundamentally wrong to make up such Plots. If the poet has taken such a Plot, however, and one sees that he might have put it in a more probable form, he is guilty of absurdity as well as a fault of art. Even in the *Odyssey* the improbabilities in the setting-ashore of Ulysses[4] would be clearly intolerable in the hands of an inferior poet. As it is, the poet conceals them, his other excellences veiling their absurdity. Elaborate Diction, however, is required only in places where there is no action, and no Character or Thought to be revealed. Where there is Character or Thought, on the other hand, an over-ornate Diction tends to obscure them.

25   As regards Problems and their Solutions, one may see the number and nature of the assumptions on which they

---

[1] xix. 164-260.   [2] Soph. *El.* 660 ff.
[3] Probably by Aeschylus.   [4] xiii. 116 ff.

proceed by viewing the matter in the following way. (1)
The poet being an imitator just like the painter or other
maker of likenesses, he must necessarily in all instances
10 represent things in one or other of three aspects, either as
they were or are, or as they are said or thought to be or to
have been, or as they ought to be. (2) All this he does in
language, with an admixture, it may be, of strange words
and metaphors, as also of the various modified forms of
words, since the use of these is conceded in poetry. (3) It
is to be remembered, too, that there is not the same kind
of correctness in poetry as in politics, or indeed any other
15 art. There is, however, within the limits of poetry itself a
possibility of two kinds of error, the one directly, the other
only accidentally connected with the art. If the poet meant
to describe the thing correctly, and failed through lack of
power of expression, his art itself is at fault. But if it was
through his having meant to describe it in some incorrect
way (e.g. to make the horse in movement have both right
legs thrown forward) that the technical error (one in a
20 matter of, say, medicine or some other special science), or
impossibilities of whatever kind they may be, have got into
his description, his error in that case is not in the essentials
of the poetic art. These, therefore, must be the premisses
of the Solutions in answer to the criticisms involved in the
Problems.

I. As to the criticisms relating to the poet's art itself.
Any impossibilities there may be in his descriptions of
things are faults. But from another point of view they are
justifiable, if they serve the end of poetry itself—if (to
25 assume what we have said of that end)[1] they make the
effect of either that very portion of the work or some other
portion more astounding. The Pursuit of Hector is an instance in point. If, however, the poetic end might have
been as well or better attained without sacrifice of technical correctness in such matters, the impossibility is not
to be justified, since the description should be, if it can,
30 entirely free from error. One may ask, too, whether the
error is in a matter directly or only accidentally connected
with the poetic art; since it is a lesser error in an artist not

[1] 1452ª4, 1454ª4, 1455ª17, 1460ª11.

to know, for instance, that the hind has no horns, than to
produce an unrecognizable picture of one.

II. If the poet's description be criticized as not true to
fact, one may urge perhaps that the object ought to be as
described—an answer like that of Sophocles, who said that
he drew men as they ought to be, and Euripides as they
were. If the description, however, be neither true nor of 35
the thing as it ought to be, the answer must be then, that
it is in accordance with opinion. The tales about gods, for
instance, may be as wrong as Xenophanes thinks,[1] neither
true nor the better thing to say; but they are certainly in
accordance with opinion. Of other statements in poetry 1461ᵃ
one may perhaps say, not that they are better than the
truth, but that the fact was so at the time; e.g. the description of the arms: 'their spears stood upright, butt-end upon
the ground';[2] for that was the usual way of fixing them
then, as it is still with the Illyrians. As for the question
whether something said or done in a poem is morally right
or not, in dealing with that one should consider not only 5
the intrinsic quality of the actual word or deed, but also
the person who says or does it, the person to whom he
says or does it, the time, the means, and the motive of the
agent—whether he does it to attain a greater good, or to
avoid a greater evil.

III. Other criticisms one must meet by considering the
language of the poet: (1) by the assumption of a strange 10
word in a passage like οὐρῆας μὲν πρῶτον,[3] where by οὐρῆας
Homer may perhaps mean not mules but sentinels. And in
saying of Dolon, ὅς ῥ' ἦ τοι εἶδος μὲν ἔην κακός,[4] his meaning may perhaps be, not that Dolon's body was deformed,
but that his face was ugly, as εὐειδής is the Cretan word for
handsome-faced. So, too, ζωρότερον δὲ κέραιε[5] may mean
not 'mix the wine stronger', as though for topers, but 'mix 15
it quicker'. (2) Other expressions in Homer may be ex-

---

[1] [Xenophanes of Colophon, traditionally associated with the
Eleatic school of philosophy.]
[2] *Il.* x. 152.
[3] *Il.* i. 50.
[4] ['He was ill-favored of figure.' *Il.* x. 11-13.]
['Mix the drink livelier.' *Il.* ix. 202.]

plained as metaphorical; e.g. in ἄλλοι μὲν ῥα θεοί τε καὶ
ἀνέρες εὖδον ⟨ἅπαντες⟩ παννύχιοι,[1] as compared with what he
tells us at the same time, ἦ τιο ὅτ᾽ ἐς πεδίον τὸ Τρωικὸν ἀθρή-
σειεν, αὐλῶν συρίγγων †τε ὁμαδόν†,[2] the word ἅπαντες, 'all',
is metaphorically put for 'many', since 'all' is a species of
20 'many'. So also his οἴη δ᾽ ἄμμορος[3] is metaphorical, the
best known standing 'alone'. (3) A change, as Hippias of
Thasos[4] suggested, in the mode of reading a word will
solve the difficulty in δίδομεν δέ οἱ,[5] and in τὸ μὲν οὗ καταπύ-
θεται ὄμβρῳ.[6] (4) Other difficulties may be solved by another punctuation; e.g. in Empedocles, αἶψα δὲ θνήτ᾽
25 ἐφύοντο, τὰ πρὶν μάθον ἀθάνατα ζωρά τε πρὶν κέκρητο.[7] Or
(5) by the assumption of an equivocal term, as in παρώ-
χηκεν δὲ πλέω νύξ,[8] where πλέω is equivocal. Or (6) by an
appeal to the custom of language. Wine-and-water we call
'wine'; and it is on the same principle that Homer speaks
of a κνημὶς νεοτεύκτου κασσιτέροιο,[9] a 'greave of new-wrought
tin'. A worker in iron we call a 'brazier'; and it is on the
same principle that Ganymede is described as the '*wine-*
30 server' of Zeus,[10] though the gods do not drink wine. This
latter, however, may be an instance of metaphor. But

---

[1] ['Now *all* gods and men were sleeping through the night.'
Il. ii. 1, x. 1.]

[2] ['And whenever he looked at the Trojan plain he mar-
velled at the sound of flutes and pipes.' *Il.* x. 11-13.]

[3] ['and she alone hath no part' (sc. the Bear alone has no
part in the bath of the Ocean) *Il.* xviii. 489, *Od.* v. 275.]

[4] [A grammarian mentioned only here.]

[5] [The Greek for 'we grant him to obtain his prayer' may
also be construed as meaning 'grant him . . .' (The
reference is to *Il.* ii. 15 where however our manuscripts
have an entirely different text.)]

[6] ['The wood of which is rotted with rain' *Il.* xxiii. 327 (the
alternative interpretation would be 'the wood is not
rotted.').]

[7] ['Suddenly things became mortal that before had learnt
to be immortal and things unmixed before mixed' (Fragm.
of Empedocles; the ambiguity lies in the construction of
the last four words).]

[8] ['Of the night full two watches are spent' *Il.* x. 251 (πλέω
corresponds to 'full').]

[9] *Il.* xxi. 592.

[10] *Il.* xx. 234.

whenever also a word seems to imply some contradiction, it is necessary to reflect how many ways there may be of understanding it in the passage in question; e.g. in Homer's τῇ ῥ᾽ ἔσχετο χάλκεον ἔγχος[1] one should consider the possible senses of 'was stopped there'—whether by taking it in this sense or in that one will best avoid the fault of which Glaucon[2] speaks: "They start with some improbable presumption; and having so decreed it themselves, proceed to draw inferences, and censure the poet as though he had actually said whatever they happen to believe, if his statement conflicts with their own notion of things.' This is how Homer's silence about Icarius has been treated. Starting with the notion of his having been a Lacedaemonian, the critics think it strange for Telemachus not to have met him when he went to Lacedaemon. Whereas the fact may have been as the Cephallenians say, that the wife of Ulysses was of a Cephallenian family, and that her father's name was Icadius, not Icarius. So that it is probably a mistake of the critics that has given rise to the Problem.

Speaking generally, one has to justify (1) the Impossible by reference to the requirements of poetry, or to the better, or to opinion. For the purposes of poetry a convincing impossibility is preferable to an unconvincing possibility; and if men such as Zeuxis depicted the impossible, the answer is that it is better they should be like that, as the artist ought to improve on his model. (2) The Improbable one has to justify either by showing it to be in accordance with opinion, or by urging that at times it is not improbable; for there is a probability of things happening also against probability. (3) The contradictions found in the poet's language one should first test as one does an opponent's confutation in a dialectical argument, so as to see whether he means the same thing, in the same relation, and in the same sense, before admitting that he has contradicted either something he has said himself or what a man of sound sense assumes as true. But there is no possible apology for improbability of Plot or depravity of

---

[1] ['There stuck the spear of bronze' *Il.* xx. 267.]

[2] [Probably the same Glaucon whom Plato (*Ion* 530 D) mentions as an authority on the explanation of Homer.]

20 character, when they are not necessary and no use is made of them, like the improbability in the appearance of Aegeus in *Medea* and the baseness of Menelaus in *Orestes*.

The objections, then, of critics start with faults of five kinds: the allegation is always that something is either (1) impossible, (2) improbable, (3) corrupting, (4) contradictory, or (5) against technical correctness. The answers to these objections must be sought under one or other of 25 the above-mentioned heads, which are twelve in number.

The question may be raised whether the epic or the 26 tragic is the higher form of imitation. It may be argued that, if the less vulgar is the higher, and the less vulgar is always that which addresses the better public, an art addressing any and every one is of a very vulgar order. It is a belief that their public cannot see the meaning, unless 30 they add something themselves, that causes the perpetual movements of the performers—bad flute-players, for instance, rolling about, if quoit-throwing is to be represented, and pulling at the conductor, if Scylla is the subject of the piece. Tragedy, then, is said to be an art of this order—to be in fact just what the later actors were in the eyes of their predecessors; for Mynniscus used to call Callippides[1] 35 'the ape', because he thought he so overacted his parts; 1462ᵃ and a similar view was taken of Pindarus also. All Tragedy, however, is said to stand to the Epic as the newer to the older school of actors. The one, accordingly, is said to address a cultivated audience, which does not need the accompaniment of gesture; the other, an uncultivated one. 5 If, therefore, Tragedy is a vulgar art, it must clearly be lower than the Epic.

The answer to this is twofold. In the first place, one may urge (1) that the censure does not touch the art of the dramatic poet, but only that of his interpreter; for it is quite possible to overdo the gesturing even in an epic recital, as did Sosistratus, and in a singing contest, as did

---

[1] [Mynniscus of Chalcis, an actor; Callippides, a much admired writer of tragedies of the late 5th cent.]

Mnasitheus of Opus.[1] (2) That one should not condemn all
movement, unless one means to condemn even the dance,
but only that of ignoble people—which is the point of the
criticism passed on Callippides and in the present day on
others, that their women are not like gentlewomen. (3) 10
That Tragedy may produce its effect even without movement or action in just the same way as Epic poetry; for
from the mere reading of a play its quality may be seen.
So that, if it be superior in all other respects, this element
of inferiority is no necessary part of it.

In the second place, one must remember (1) that Tragedy has everything that the Epic has (even the epic metre
being admissible), together with a not inconsiderable addi- 15
tion in the shape of the Music (a very real factor in the
pleasure of the drama) and the Spectacle. (2) That its
reality of presentation is felt in the play as read, as well
as in the play as acted. (3) That the tragic imitation requires less space for the attainment of its end; which is a *1462*[b]
great advantage, since the more concentrated effect is more
pleasurable than one with a large admixture of time to
dilute it—consider the *Oedipus* of Sophocles, for instance,
and the effect of expanding it into the number of lines of
the *Iliad*. (4) That there is less unity in the imitation of
the epic poets, as is proved by the fact that any one work
of theirs supplies matter for several tragedies; the result 5
being that, if they take what is really a single story, it
seems curt when briefly told, and thin and waterish when
on the scale of length usual with their verse. In saying that
there is less unity in an epic, I mean an epic made up of
a plurality of actions, in the same way as the *Iliad* and
Odyssey have many such parts, each one of them in itself
of some magnitude; yet the structure of the two Homeric 10
poems is as perfect as can be, and the action in them is
as nearly as possible one action. If, then, Tragedy is superior in these respects, and also, besides these, in its poetic
effect (since the two forms of poetry should give us, not
any or every pleasure, but the very special kind we have

[1] [Both rhapsodes are mentioned only here.]

mentioned, it is clear that, as attaining the poetic effect better than the Epic, it will be the higher form of art.

So much for Tragedy and Epic poetry—for these two arts in general and their species; the number and nature of their constituent parts; the causes of success and failure in them; the Objections of the critics, and the Solutions in answer to them.

INDEX TO *RHETORIC*

References are to the chapter and line numbers shown in the outer margin of the text.

Index

Index   273

Evagoras, 1399ᵃ 4, 6.

Evenus quoted, 1370ᵃ 10.

'example,' 1356ᵇ 5, 12; 1368ᵃ 29; 1393ᵃ 24 ff.

exceptional men: the stocks of genius continue their yield for a while and then decline, 1390ᵇ 26 ff.

exhortation, 1358ᵇ 8 ff.

expediency: see 'interest.'

eye as the seat of shame, 1384ᵃ 36; the two eyes of Greece, Athens and Sparta, 1411ᵃ 6; setting things before the eyes of hearers and readers, 1411ᵇ 23 ff.

fables, 1393ᵃ 30; 1393ᵇ 9 ff.

fact past and future, topic of, 1392ᵇ 15 ff.

fallacious arguments, some causes of: (1) language, 1401ᵃ 1, 10; (2) confusion of parts and whole, 1401ᵃ 24; (3) passionate exaggeration, 1401ᵇ 3; (4) a 'sign,' or single instance, 1401ᵇ 9; (5) an accident, 1401ᵇ 15; (6) the consequence, 1401ᵇ 20; (7) *post hoc ergo propter hoc*, 1401ᵇ 30; (8) omission of time and circumstance, 1401ᵇ 35; (9) confusion of the absolute with the particular, 1402ᵃ 4.

farmers, small: 1373ᵃ 8; 1381ᵃ 24.

favour: see 'kindness.'

fear, 1382ᵃ 21 ff.

feeling: see 'passion.'

fever, 1357ᵇ 15; 1370ᵇ 17.

fickleness of youth, 1389ᵃ 6.

figure (form, fashion) of wording or sentence, 1401ᵃ 7; 1408ᵇ 21.

food-supply, 1360ᵃ 12 (cp. 1359ᵇ 22).

foreign (distinguished) air of style, 1404ᵇ 36; 1405ᵃ 8; 1406ᵃ 15.

forensic (legal, judicial) oratory: bk. i, c. 3 and cc. 10-15.

Also: 1354ᵇ 29; 1355ᵃ 20; 1414ᵃ 11, 38; 1414ᵇ 5; 1415ᵃ 2, 8.

foretaste of a theme in poetry 1415ᵃ 12.

fortune, good, 1361ᵇ 39 ff.; 1369ᵗ 32; 1389ᵃ 1; 1391ᵃ 30 ff.

foul language, 1405ᵇ 9 ff.

fox and the hedgehog, fable of the, 1393ᵇ 23 ff.

free-running style, 1409ᵃ 24 ff.

friendship, 1361ᵇ 36 (friend defined); 1380ᵇ 35 ff. (ii, c. 4); 1381ᵇ 34 (forms of friendship) —Friendlessness, 1386ᵃ 10; possession of few friends, many friends, good friends, 1360ᵇ 20; 1361ᵇ 35; 1386ᵃ 10; 1388ᵇ 5.

frigidities of style (viz. things in bad taste that fall flat and are 'a frost'), 1405ᵇ 34 ff.

funeral speech, anonymous, 1411ᵃ 31.

Gelon, 1373ᵃ 23.

genders, 1407ᵇ 7.

generalization, spurious, 1395ᵃ 8.

geometry, 1355ᵇ 29; 1404ᵃ 12.

Glaucon of Teos, 1403ᵇ 26.

good, its general principles and its varieties, 1362ᵃ 21 ff.—relative goodness, 1363ᵇ 5 ff.

Gorgias: 1404ᵃ 26 (his poetical prose-style); 1405ᵇ 37 (compound words); 1406ᵇ 9 (extravagant metaphors); 1406ᵇ 15 (irony); 1408ᵇ 20 (irony); 1414ᵇ 31 (Olympic Speech); 1416ᵃ 1 (encomium on the men of Elis); 1418ᵃ 35 (his unfailing fund of talk); 1419ᵇ 4 (earnestness to meet jest, jest to meet earnestness).

government, forms of, 1360ᵃ 21 ff.; 1365ᵇ 29 ff.

gratitude: see 'kindness.'

greatness and smallness, 1359ᵃ 23; 1393ᵃ 9 ff.

INDEX TO *POETICS*

MODERN LIBRARY
COLLEGE EDITIONS